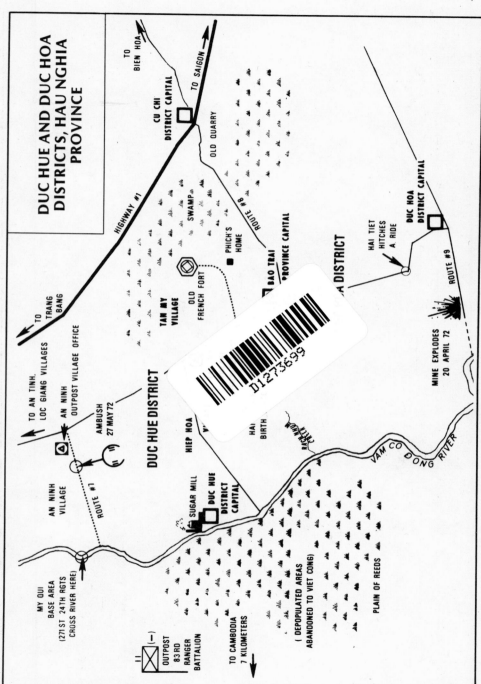

DUC HUE AND DUC HOA DISTRICTS, HAU NGHIA PROVINCE

TO BIEN HOA

TO SAIGON

HIGHWAY #1

CU CHI
DISTRICT CAPITAL

OLD QUARRY

ROUTE #8

SWAMP

PHICH'S HOME

BAO TRAI
PROVINCE CAPITAL

TAN MY VILLAGE

OLD FRENCH FORT

DUC HOA DISTRICT

HAI TIET HITCHES A RIDE

DUC HOA
DISTRICT CAPITAL

ROUTE #9

MINE EXPLODES
20 APRIL 72

TO TRANG BANG

TO AN TINH,
LOC GIANG VILLAGES

AN NINH
OUTPOST VILLAGE OFFICE

AMBUSH
27 MAY 72

ROUTE #7

AN NINH VILLAGE

DUC HUE DISTRICT

HIEP HOA VILLAGE

HAI BIRTH

ROCKETS

VAM CO DONG RIVER

SUGAR MILL

DUC HUE
DISTRICT CAPITAL

MY QUI
BASE AREA
(271ST 24TH RGTS
CROSS RIVER HERE)

(—)
OUTPOST
83RD
RANGER
BATTALION

TO CAMBODIA
7 KILOMETERS

(DEPOPULATED AREAS
ABANDONED TO VIET CONG)

PLAIN OF REEDS

Silence Was a Weapon

THE VIETNAM WAR IN THE VILLAGES

HAU NGHIA PROVINCE

1971 Population: 229,000
Province Capital: Bao Trai

DISTRICTS

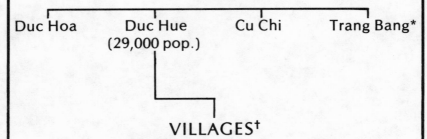

Duc Hoa   Duc Hue   Cu Chi   Trang Bang*
               (29,000 pop.)

VILLAGES†

Tan My Hiep Hoa An Ninh My Thanh Dong

*An Tinh Village (see chapter seven) was a part of Trang Bang District.

†Each village was subdivided into hamlets, usually from four to seven per village. A typical hamlet consisted of some 1,000 residents.

Silence Was a Weapon

THE VIETNAM WAR IN THE VILLAGES

A Personal Perspective

Stuart A. Herrington

PRESIDIO

Published by Presidio Press, 31 Pamaron Way, Novato, CA 94947

Library of Congress Cataloging in Publication Data

Herrington, Stuart A., 1941-
  Silence was a weapon.

  Includes index.
    1. Vietnamese Conflict, 1961-1975—Underground move-
ments. 2. Counterinsurgency—Vietnam. 3. Vietnamese
Conflict, 1961-1975—Personal narratives, American.
4. Herrington, Stuart A., 1941-   . I. Title.
DS558.92.H47   959.704'3   81-17901
ISBN 0-89141-140-2   AAC R2

Jacket design by Bill Yenne Studio
Typesetting by Helen Epperson

Printed in the United States of America

092511

To Lee and Pluma Herrington
of Venice, Florida
who have given me everything
that a son could expect of his parents.

CONTENTS

PREFACE

Americans tend to approach problems with a confidence and self-assurance that one might expect of a people whose ancestors turned the untamed wilderness of North America into a global power in the brief span of two hundred years. By the time President John F. Kennedy entered our lives, many of us had come to believe that our nation was virtually omnipotent. And so, when the new president announced that the United States would put a man on the moon within the decade, we thrilled to his challenge and knew that American drive and ingenuity would somehow make good his pledge. And when Kennedy eloquently put the world on notice that the United States would ". . . bear any burden, meet any hardship, support any friend, oppose any foe to assure the survival and the success of liberty,"* few young people doubted that we would do just that. Swept along on a wave of idealism, Americans of all ages joined the Peace Corps. Others volunteered for the elite U.S. Army Special Forces—the Green Berets—whose motto, *De Oppresso Liber*, "To Free from Oppression," symbolized the challenge of the sixties. Before the young president's assassination, he committed the Army and the Green Berets to an increased role in the defense of beleaguered South Vietnam. The United States would protect the freedom of the Vietnamese people and disprove Chairman Mao's oft-quoted maxim that "political power flows from the barrel of a gun."

Ten years later, the final contingent of a 543,000-man American expeditionary force withdrew from Vietnam, having lost more than 50,000 men killed in vain pursuit of an elusive victory over the Vietcong

*Inaugural address, January 20, 1961.

insurgents and their North Vietnamese sponsors. Americans breathed a
collective sigh of relief at the terms of the Paris Agreement. Our troops
and our prisoners of war were finally coming home, and the Vietnamese
adversaries would resolve their differences peacefully under the aegis of
a long-awaited cease-fire. Asians would henceforth be the actors in what
should have been an Asian drama all along.

But it was not to be. Two years later, sixteen North Vietnamese divisions overran Saigon, and the South Vietnamese president called on the
shattered remnants of his army to lay down their arms. Saigon became
"Ho Chi Minh City" overnight. Having first failed to win the war, we
had lost the peace. The United States had been dealt a defeat unparal-
leled in its history.

During the six years since the fall of Saigon, Americans have vacil-
lated between a desire to erase the ugly memories of Vietnam and an
inner compulsion to comprehend why our country could not master
events in that faraway corner of the globe and prevail over "a ragged
peasant army." Our involvement in Vietnam was a complex drama that
defies oversimplification, but one aspect of the whole affair can be stated
with relative assurance. The United States lost in a contest of wills with
the Communists, who simply outlasted us on the battlefield until the
frustrated and disillusioned American people wearied of the war and
pressured their elected representatives to bring the troops back home.
Like the French before us, we lacked the staying power to engage in a
protracted conflict in that remote theater. The American people had
demanded a quick, American-style victory and the military had failed
to deliver.

Why? Why did the war drag on, stubbornly defying the best efforts of
the nation that went to the moon to defuse it? The question is a deeply
complex one—one for which there is no simple answer. But perhaps the
best place to begin the quest for an answer is in the Vietnamese village,
for it was here that the Vietcong insurgency took hold. The dynamics of
this peasant movement, and how it changed as American and North
Vietnamese forces intervened in the conflict, is the theme of the following
pages. They represent one participant's experiences and reflections, and
are offered with the sincere hope that they will assist in clarifying why
the well-intentioned efforts of our country to win the "hearts and minds"
of the South Vietnamese people ended with the ignominious departure of
our ambassador from the roof of his embassy in an evacuation helicopter.

ACKNOWLEDGMENTS

I am grateful to the students and faculty of the University of South Florida, Tampa, Florida, whose demanding and penetrating questions on the Vietnam War moved me to write this book. Both Gen. Ted Conway, U.S. Army (Ret.) and Col. Tom Jones, U.S. Army (Ret.) provided invaluable guidance and encouragement once I had taken pen in hand. Without Tom Jones's persistent monitoring of my progress and his stubborn loyalty to the project, it would have died in 1978. I am also indebted to Col. Thomas Fabyanic of the Air War College, who read the manuscript and offered sound advice on its content and on how an unpublished novice locates a publisher. Likewise, Col. Harry G. Summers, Jr. of the U.S. Army War College provided me with timely advice and support. I also benefited greatly from a close personal and professional relationship with Mr. J. C. Smith of Air University, whose techniques of imparting impact to English prose have indelibly altered my writing habits. Ambassador Charles S. Whitehouse struggled through a draft of the manuscript and suggested refinements of its scope and perspective. Maj. Gen. John E. Murray, U.S. Army (Ret.), former Defense Attaché, Saigon, was equally generous with his time and volunteered numerous thoughtful comments that substantially improved the final product. Lt. Gen. Jack Flynn, U.S. Air Force (Ret.), who was the ranking American POW in Hanoi, read the work and proffered advice based upon his unique understanding of the North Vietnamese mind-set. Maj. Gen. Edward G. Lansdale, U.S. Air Force (Ret.), whose grasp of the subtleties of the Asian environment is unequaled, gave generously of his support and counsel when I needed it the most. I am also indebted to Brig. Gen. Dave Palmer, author of *The Summons of the Trumpet*, for his candid and perceptive critique of the manuscript. During the long and arduous process of preparing draft manuscripts, I benefited from the gracious assistance of Harriett Steinbraker, Becky Davis, Nate Conne, Pete Varisano, Bill O'Malley, and Mary Ann Grobler. Finally, I owe a special thanks to my wife, a girl of the Mekong Delta, whose patience, understanding, and guidance over the years helped lead me to at least a partial understanding of her people.

Heidelberg, Germany

SAH
January 1982

Introduction

A WORD ON PERSPECTIVE

Long before I took pen in hand, I had considered writing a book about Vietnam. After all, the luck (or unluck) of the draw had made me an eyewitness and participant in our first lost war—first as an intelligence advisor to the South Vietnamese military, and then as a member of the U.S. Mission in Saigon during the stillborn cease-fire from 1973 to 1975. During the war, I had lived and fought for almost two years in one of Vietnam's most notorious provinces. During the "peace," I had served as a negotiator in a vain attempt to pry information on our missing-in-action personnel from the stubborn Vietnamese Communists. This quest for information on our missing servicemen had led me to Hanoi on numerous occasions, an experience that had enhanced my perspective of the great struggle that had engulfed me, my countrymen, and the Vietnamese people.

Nonetheless, each time the impulse to write hit me, I suppressed it. Initially, it was simply too difficult to be objective—too soon after the fall of Saigon, when I had fled the roof of the U.S. Embassy in a marine helicopter scant hours before North Vietnamese tanks had triumphantly entered the city. The traumatic, emotion-charged atmosphere of those final days in Saigon made any objective recounting of what had befallen us difficult, if not impossible.

I was also inhibited by the fact that I was a low-level actor in the overall sweep of events that unfolded around me in Vietnam. Captains don't write the histories of wars—generals inherit that task. The whole world awaited General Westmoreland's memoirs, but who would be interested in the thoughts of one of the thousands of junior officers who served in Vietnam? Each time I was tempted to write, I reminded myself of this,

and of the fact that career officers customarily wait until their retire-
ment (or at least until they have served twenty years) before speaking out.

Military men often quote a self-deprecating joke among themselves—
that fairy tales and war stories differ only in the first line. Fairy tales
begin with "Once upon a time . . ."; war stories, with "There I was . . . ."
I didn't want to bore anyone with my story, regardless of how it might
begin.

But time slowly eased the pain of Saigon's final agony. In spite of my
reservations, I succumbed to the temptation to commit my thoughts to
writing—influenced by friends (who argued persuasively that the American people had not yet grasped the reasons for our failure in Vietnam),
and by my own gradual realization that my perspective as a low-level
actor was an asset rather than a liability.

Not that the contributions of high-ranking policymakers and imple-
menters are unimportant. On the contrary, the chronicles of our military
and political leaders are essential to an understanding of history. Their
positions as ambassadors, generals, or influential members of their
governments allow them to share with their readership a feel for the
atmosphere in the conference rooms and operations centers. In this
sense, it becomes almost an obligation of citizenship that they commit
their experiences to writing—as many of the principal actors in Vietnam
have already done. Their collective reflections on the war provide a
fascinating—though far from comprehensive—treatment of the subject.

But the advantages afforded by the view from the top are sometimes
offset by the danger of insulation from the actual events that are set in
motion by our government's policy decisions. These events invariably
impinge on people's lives, attitudes, and motivations. All too often, they
create new problems to confront the decision-makers. High-ranking
diplomats and military officers in a foreign country tend to come into
contact with their equally high-ranking opposite numbers—who may or
may not choose to convey accurate feedback about ongoing events. Such
men may themselves be isolated; or they may have what they perceive to
be compelling reasons to misrepresent reality to their American friends.

Hence there is something to be said for the perspective of the low-level
actor—who is a participant in the events that are triggered by policy
decisions reached half a world away. If he is curious, has not fallen
victim to culture shock, and can conquer the language barrier, he will
often learn things that are virtually unknowable for others. Thus, the
Vietnam that I came to know from 1971 to 1975 differed in many ways
from the Vietnam of other Americans.

Like so many others, I didn't want to go to Vietnam. Not that I was

afraid—though I guess I really was. I was, in my own way, a member of
the increasingly large number of Americans who had come to be known
as "doves" in the rhetoric of the day. What set me apart from many of
my fellow skeptics was that I had opposed the war from its origins in the
early nineteen-sixties, and I was a career Army officer.

As an undergraduate in political science at Duquesne University, and
later as a graduate student in international relations in the idyllic surroundings of the University of Florida, I had studied the undoing of the
French at Dien Bien Phu and convinced myself that an American war in
Indochina would surpass even the frustrations of our Korean experience.
My knowledge of the situation faced by the French and the reasons for
their defeat was superficial, but this belief remained with me when I
entered the Army in 1967 to begin a two-year service obligation as a
military intelligence officer.

As a student officer at the Infantry School, Fort Benning, Georgia, I
took the "Combat Platoon Leader" course. Most of the officers in my
company were infantry lieutenants who had been commissioned through
ROTC one month earlier. For nine weeks, we studied the tactics of the
Vietcong—"Ol' Charlie," as our combat veteran instructors respectfully
called the enemy, or simply "Charles." I remember that the infantry
officers in my company seemed young and strangely unconcerned about
their impending assignments to Vietnam. I was twenty-six at the time
and had even been promoted to first lieutenant in graduate school. I was
almost certain that I would be Vietnam-bound after additional intelligence training, so I paid close attention to my infantry instructors. They
seemed to have a universal respect for the Vietcong, who were uniformly
depicted as cunning and brave. On several occasions, I met infantry officers at the officers' club who shared with me the war stories of their Vietnam tours. These tales invariably contained overtones of frustration over
the difficulties of fighting a war against a nearly invisible enemy. One
captain told me that he had spent an entire year in Vietnam and never
seen a single live Vietcong. Most of what I heard at Fort Benning reinforced what I had always felt about Vietnam, and I became more
strongly convinced than ever that it was the wrong place to attempt to
halt Communism's "salami tactic" of world conquest.

Fort Holabird, Maryland, was the home of the U.S. Army Intelligence
School. Located in the decaying Dundalk area of Baltimore, Holabird
would have been sufficiently depressing by itself, without the heavy
knowledge that we were all Vietnam-bound at the end of our six months
of training. To make matters worse, in the middle of our schooling the
Tet Offensive of 1968 burst into our living rooms in living color. We all

heard of the fate of the intelligence operatives in the doomed city of Hue. Their villas had been pointed out to the enemy troops by Communist students from the ancient university. Tet of '68 ruined our spring. A brief spark of hope was ignited by North Korea's seizure of the U.S.S. *Pueblo*. The Pentagon diverted at least one class of enlisted students to Korea, and the rumor spread quickly that our class might be equally fortunate. Ultimately though, almost my entire class went to Vietnam in time to share in the Tet mopping up operations. As for me, with only two weeks to go until graduation, I received an unexpected alert for assignment to West Berlin, Germany. I can still recall the lieutenant in personnel as he handed me my priceless orders with a knowing smile and asked, "Do you know someone, Herrington?"

I served almost two years in Berlin, including a six-month extension beyond the expiration of my two-year hitch. I had been promoted to captain a few months after my arrival in Berlin, exactly one year from the day I entered active duty. Promotions were quick during the war, even if one was sitting it out in Germany.

I liked army life and loved Germany, but I separated from active duty in December, 1969. There were other considerations, of course, but the Vietnam War was the main reason I became a civilian. To have remained on active duty would have been to volunteer for Vietnam. The guy who said every young man wants to be a war hero never asked me.

I lasted seven months as a civilian. Selling detergent only leads to the exalted responsibility of supervising other salesmen, and this just wasn't for me. When my company's district office launched its "Make W.A.R. (We Are Relentless), not Love" campaign to boost sales, I called Washington and requested immediate recall to active duty.

I reentered active duty in June, 1970, with the understanding that I was due for a "utilization tour" in Vietnam. I didn't even flinch when the assignments officer mentioned it, since this time around I was career-oriented. If a trip to Southeast Asia was the price of admission, then so be it. My orders called for me to report to the U.S. Army Intelligence School at Fort Holabird for the "Tactical Intelligence Officer" course.

At Holabird, we grappled with the intricacies of combat intelligence ("To provide the commander with information on the enemy, the weather, and the terrain to enable him to plan and conduct tactical operations"). After Holabird, I spent six weeks at Fort Bragg, North Carolina, as a student officer in the MATA course ("Military Assistance Training Advisor"). The course was good training and consisted of a brief introduction to Vietnam and the ways of the Vietnamese most likely to frustrate new advisors. Little did I know.

Finally, to complete my reorientation to the Southeast Asian theater, I traveled to Fort Bliss, Texas, for eight weeks of Vietnamese language training. I tackled Vietnamese enthusiastically, remembering how crucial my German language training had been to my ability to get along in West Berlin. Our Vietnamese instructors were mostly pretty young, and they quickly won the hearts of all but the most insensitive students. Fort Bliss was fun, and the course had modest learning objectives. A graduate was supposed to be able to make "elemental needs" known. ("I am an American. Can you please take me to the nearest government outpost? Did the Vietcong come through your village last night?") I worked hard to surpass these goals and voluntarily attended three additional weeks of classes during my leave time. I had already learned that I would serve as a district intelligence advisor to the Vietnamese, with responsibility for "neutralizing" the Vietcong's so-called shadow government. This work was what we called in intelligence jargon counterespionage/countersubversion work, and I knew from my German experience that it required more than a passing acquaintance with the language. Before I left Fort Bliss, I had become moderately conversational in the musical Vietnamese language. I was apprehensive about my impending tour of duty, but kept reassuring myself that I had indeed been well trained to meet the challenge. During this training, I had developed an intense curiosity about Vietnam and was anxious to get on with whatever lay ahead. Nonetheless, I remained privately skeptical about our chances of accomplishing our objectives there. Had history repeated itself and I suddenly received a last minute diversion to Germany, I would have gone with a will.

1

"A MODEL REVOLUTIONARY VILLAGE"

The closer the World Airways charter jet got to Vietnam, the quieter the two hundred GIs on board became. We approached Saigon's Tan Son Nhut Air Base at 5:00 A.M. Flares lit up the horizon sporadically as we glided down our approach, and we could see that the entire base was blacked out as we taxied to the reception area. The glow from the exhausts of the F-4 Phantoms in the concrete revetments reminded me of something I didn't need to be reminded of—we were in a war zone. My stomach knew it before I did, and I felt lousy as we disembarked into the tropical heat and followed the MPs' directions to the in-processing hangar.

Three days in Saigon convinced me that I didn't want to draw an assignment there. The city was filthy, overcrowded, hectic, and overrun with hustlers of all types. You name the negative modifier, it fit Saigon in early 1971. Not even the graffiti on the latrine walls at the reception center could dampen my enthusiasm for getting out of Saigon—the sooner the better.

The Vietnamese flag is well-designed.
Where they're not red, they're yellow.

If the good lord had wanted me to come to this stinking land and walk through the swamps for a year, he would have given me baggy green skin.
[Penned in immediately below:]
Don't worry. After one year, you'll have baggy green skin!

I had a game plan to get a good assignment, if indeed there was such a thing in Vietnam. A friend of mine had just returned from a tour in

1

Phuoc Tuy, a coastal province southeast of Saigon best known for its resort town of Vung Tau. He had described duty in Phuoc Tuy in glowing terms—silver beaches, giant lobsters, and not too many Vietcong. There was even a contingent of fun-loving Australians stationed in the province, and my friend told incredible tales of their nonmilitary exploits. The plan was for me to go to the officer assignment folks at headquarters, rattle off a few words of Vietnamese, and Vung Tau, here I come.

It didn't work. The sergeant in the assignments branch merely laughed as he explained that Phuoc Tuy province would not hold all of the men who had volunteered to go there in the defense of democracy. The best I was able to do was to wrangle orders to Military Region III, the area around Saigon. I was to report the following morning to Bien Hoa city, a few miles north of Saigon, for an interview with a colonel who would decide where I would actually be assigned.

The colonel turned out to be the officer who was responsible for the "Phoenix" program in Military Region III. Phoenix was the code name for the attack on the Vietcong shadow government. The interview lasted only a few minutes. The colonel told me that since I had done so well at language school, Hau Nghia province would be the perfect assignment for me. Province Senior Advisor Colonel Jack Weissinger was a "hard-charger" who had already served almost two years in Hau Nghia. The colonel explained that Weissinger "needed good people," and I was to fly the following morning to Hau Nghia on the daily courier flight.

I went to the club that last night in Bien Hoa and sat at the bar downing Budweisers in a futile attempt to conceal my concern for what lay ahead. I had already figured out what "Weissinger needs good men" meant. Hau Nghia was not Phuoc Tuy. I was scared, and the Vietnamese and Americans at the club didn't offer much solace. The Americans nodded knowingly when I told them I was going to Hau Nghia. It seemed that Hau Nghia province was famous for two things—Colonel Jack Weissinger and the Vietcong. The issue was in doubt whether it was Colonel Weissinger or the Vietcong that was the most feared thing about the province.

I tried out my school Vietnamese on the girls who tended bar. It was interesting to watch their surprised reaction when an American spoke their language. Their initial response was always the same; they asked a series of questions that to an American seemed nosey:

How old are you, captain?
Do you have a wife, captain?
How many children do you have, captain?

How much do you weigh, captain?
Where are you going, captain?

And when I answered "Hau Nghia" to this last question, the response was ominous. "Oh God, Dai Uy!* Hau Nghia! Beaucoup VC, Dai Uy!"

I spent that last night in the transient billets, watching the occasional flares and the streams of tracers that erupted on the horizon around the perimeter of the base. I could hear the "thud" of outgoing artillery, and found myself wondering if the perimeter were under attack. Later I learned that the artillerymen were firing routine "H and I" (harassment and interdiction) missions at suspected enemy locations. The flares and tracers I had seen were also routine—the troops periodically opened fire to test their weapons and to let the enemy know that they were awake. Unfortunately, no one told me all of this in Bien Hoa, so I slept with my M-16 rifle uncomfortably draped over one arm.

I flew to Hau Nghia in a Swiss-built Porter aircraft that was known for its short takeoff and landing capabilities. During the short flight, I had the first of many looks at Vietnam from the air. I can still recall my pure astonishment at the lush beauty of the countryside. Conditioned as I was by the images of Vietnam drawn by others for the American people, I was unprepared for the tropical beauty that was spread out below. What about the infamous defoliation operations? Where were the wasted "free fire zones" that I had read about? Hadn't our artillery laid waste to vast stretches of the rural countryside? Finally, around a triangular mud fort somewhere west of Bien Hoa, I spotted a sea of craters. Still, what I saw (and what I didn't see) during that flight activated a tiny caution lamp in my head, and I warned myself to be careful of preconceived notions and generalizations.

My thoughts on the rural beauty of Vietnam came to an abrupt halt as the pilot demonstrated his aircraft's tricks. From five thousand feet directly above the Hau Nghia airstrip, he corkscrewed his way down and landed in a stomach-turner that made a believer out of me. The aircraft halted almost instantly. The pilot yelled at me to get out, and the enlisted mail clerk threw the cargo out on the runway. The entire operation took less than a minute. Just when I thought I was going to be left alone on the tiny airstrip, a jeep charged around the tail of the aircraft, and within seconds I was on my way to the headquarters of Advisory Team 43. The silver aircraft was airborne within thirty seconds. First Sergeant Willie Tate, the jeep driver, introduced himself and made an unflattering reference to skittish civilian pilots.

*Dai Uy: Pronounced "Die Wee." Vietnamese for "Captain."

The province capital of Bao Trai consisted of a single asphalt main street which was crowded with peasants on their way to and from the bustling central market. Both sides of the street were lined with small shops, and the town's citizens walked in the middle of the street, oblivious to the intrusions of the motorbikes and three-wheeled Lambrettas that plied their way back and forth. Chickens, ducks, dogs, and even pigs roamed the streets freely, and Tate maneuvered around the plodding ox carts of the farmers. The sergeant pushed the jeep through the chaos, blowing his horn impatiently. Bao Trai was dirty, crowded, and small. If this was the province capital, what would a district town look like?*

The ride through Bao Trai took only a couple of minutes with Tate driving. It would have taken me three times as long. We pulled into the walled compound that housed the advisory team, and the sergeant informed me that I would stay there for one or two nights before going one step farther—to one of Hau Nghia province's four districts.

At the team's orderly room, I learned the worst. There had been a memorial service that morning for two men who had been killed in an ambush earlier in the week. The unfortunate men had been stationed in Cu Chi, one of the four districts. When a government outpost in their district came under a Vietcong attack, the two advisors jumped in their jeep and followed their Vietnamese counterparts to the scene of the action. They never made it. The Vietcong ambushed their hastily formed (and poorly thought-out) reaction force, and both were killed when an antitank rocket hit their jeep.

Later in the day, I met Maj. Dick Culp, the intelligence officer who ran the American side of the Hau Nghia Phoenix effort. The major explained the peculiarities of the program in Hau Nghia. The mission, he explained, was quite easy to define—kill or capture Vietcong agents—but it was seemingly impossible to get the Vietnamese to accomplish it. Our job as Phoenix advisors was to assist the Vietnamese intelligence services (our counterparts) in identifying the members of the "Vietcong infrastructure" (VCI) and in planning the operations to "neutralize" them. Neutralize was a euphemism that actually meant kill, capture, or convince to surrender.

Culp was obviously a frustrated man, discouraged because he believed in the rationale of the Phoenix concept, but had been unable to get the Vietnamese to cooperate in its execution. I sensed from his remarks that

---

*Vietnam was organized into forty-four provinces, each approximately the size of a large county. Provinces usually contained 4–6 districts. There were 247 districts in South Vietnam. The district was the lowest level to which American advisors were assigned.

Colonel Weissinger was a problem, though he discreetly avoided discussing the details of his relationship with the colonel. Other members of the team cautioned me that being a Phoenix advisor on Team 43 was risky business and that the risks had more to do with Colonel Weissinger than they did with the Vietcong.

Two days later, I was still in Bao Trai, and I had not yet met the elusive Colonel Weissinger. The team's personnel officer confided in me that I would be going either to Duc Hue or to Duc Hoa district, but that the boss had not yet decided. A captain who was on his way back to the States warned me that Weissinger was stubborn, merciless with his subordinates, and not fond of military intelligence officers. He told me that I would probably be "granted an audience" with the colonel soon. If I were smart, I would keep my mouth shut and my ears open during that first meeting.

By now I had convinced myself that I didn't like Bao Trai any more than I had liked Saigon, and I was beginning to conclude that the problem was Vietnam itself. Morale among the Americans on Team 43 was low, partly because of Colonel Weissinger's style, and partly because most of the men seemed to hate being advisors to the Vietnamese. My bunkmate confided to me that Colonel Weissinger had only recently chewed out one of his staff officers during the morning briefing. The dressing down had taken place in front of most of the staff and was still being talked about several days later. The chief topic of speculation among the team's men seemed to be whether or not the colonel would again extend his tour or depart in May as scheduled. Even though I had not yet met the colonel, I found myself hoping that he would not extend.

My big moment finally arrived after lunch on that second day. Colonel Weissinger was sitting on a stone bench under a banana tree as I left the mess hall, and he called out my name when he spotted me. I reported in, saluting him as I approached the bench. I can remember that interview as if it were yesterday.

The colonel invited me to sit down beside him on the bench. The tall, sandy-haired officer wore the insignia of the field artillery, and his piercing eyes inspected me as he began to talk. Colonel Weissinger was extremely articulate and, I quickly learned, equally blunt. After we talked briefly about my background, he asked me if I thought I was qualified to take on the task of tracking down Vietcong agents, saboteurs, and guerrillas.

I replied that I had given that same question much thought ever since learning that I was to be a district Phoenix officer. On the positive side, my experience in West Berlin and my recent stateside training would enable me to learn quickly what I needed to know to function effectively. I added my belief that my knowledge of Vietnamese would help, but that I was not certain that I could credibly advise the Vietnamese how to fight a war that they had been fighting for years.

The colonel's reaction told me that I had said the wrong thing. "Let me stop you right there," he interrupted. "Don't make the mistake of being negative." For the next ten minutes, in words that left no doubt about his dedication, Colonel Weissinger gave me my marching orders. I was to go to Duc Hue district, where there was an urgent need for someone to tackle an important job. The district was infested with Vietcong, although the Vietnamese wouldn't admit it. The problem was the Duc Hue district chief, an army major named Nghiem. Colonel Weissinger explained that Nghiem was "not fighting the war aggressively," and as a consequence, the Vietcong were "thriving" in Duc Hue. I was to waste no time worrying about my qualifications. "Just get involved, the sooner the better." My predecessor, a Japanese-American lieutenant, had "wasted his tour" in Duc Hue trying to get the Vietnamese Phoenix office to keep correct files. The colonel said the word "Phoenix" as if it were a swear word. I should not make the same mistake of wasting my time with paperwork. I was, the colonel repeated, to "become totally involved" with the enemy situation in Duc Hue. The Vietcong in the district had been allowed to operate unmolested for too long. Now it was time to expose and destroy their apparatus. Colonel Weissinger terminated the interview with this ominous observation: "Frankly, Herrington, I haven't been too impressed with the military intelligence officers who've worked for me until now. You seem to be different. For your sake, I hope so."

It had only taken the colonel a few minutes to place the Duc Hue monkey squarely on my back. He had left no doubt that he was personally concerned about the Duc Hue situation and that he expected results. Later that day, I learned from Major Culp that the South Vietnamese had recently captured a Vietcong document in which the Communists had praised one of Duc Hue's villages, Tan My, as a "model revolutionary village." This document had incensed Colonel Weissinger, and he had informed Maj. Cliff Eby, Duc Hue district senior advisor, that he would tolerate no such thing. There would be no "model revolutionary villages" in Col. Jack Weissinger's province.

The more I thought about Colonel Weissinger's insistence that I not worry about my qualifications to advise the Vietnamese, the more it bothered me. Between the lines of his guidance had been a clear message: If you can't get the Vietnamese in Duc Hue to root out the insurgency, then do it yourself. There's no time to waste.

During the remainder of that final day in Bao Trai, I sought out the various men at team headquarters with whom I would be working. I soon learned that they envied the Duc Hue team for its old French villa that overlooked the Vam Co Dong (Oriental) River; the view there was serene and beautiful, and the location was safely out of range of the colonel. In spite of Colonel Weissinger's comments about Lieutenant Furumoto, my predecessor, several officers told me that he was "worshipped by the Vietnamese," whose language he had learned. Furumoto was "just like one of them," which gave him a marked advantage as an advisor.

I traveled to Duc Hue with Major Eby, who had come to Bao Trai to pick up the mail. Curiously enough, the major was armed only with a .45 caliber pistol, and he had driven his jeep to Bao Trai accompanied only by a small German shepherd dog. The road to Duc Hue took us through paddy lands, past a long canal, and through several villages clustered by the main intersections. Major Eby pointed out the sights to me as he drove, while I nervously fingered my M-16 rifle. I had heard that the major's predecessor had been evacuated to the States after being wounded in an ambush in Tan My village. As we drove through the "model revolutionary village," I was on the lookout for trouble.

But the farther we went, the more frequent were the waves and smiles of the villagers. Their animated reactions at the sight of two Americans and their dog in a jeep were hardly what I had expected. As we drove slowly through the last hamlet before the district headquarters, the cheerful Major Eby even halted the jeep to pick up several grinning South Vietnamese for a free ride. Excited children ran along beside us, calling out *My! My!* ("Americans! Americans!"). By the time we arrived in Duc Hue, I had all but forgotten about my M-16 and the Vietcong.

The district headquarters and our advisory team house were colocated with a large sugar mill. Our team of some ten Americans lived in a small compound adjacent to the district chief's house on the east bank of the river. I could see why the men in Bao Trai envied us. The Vam Co Dong was about two hundred yards wide, and clustered on the far bank was a picturesque hamlet of thatched huts in a coconut grove. But also across the river, a short march away, was the infamous "Parrot's Beak," a salient of Cambodian territory that had long been used by the Communists as a sanctuary in the war. Prior to the 1968 Tet Offensive, many large Vietcong units had staged in the Parrot's Beak and moved undetected through Duc Hue on their way to attack Saigon.

Duc Hue district was the home of twenty-nine thousand people, all but a handful of whom lived on our side of the river. The lands across the

river were a depopulated no-man's-land that had long since been abandoned to the Vietcong. In the middle of this empty territory sat the outpost of the 83d Border Ranger Battalion. The ranger outpost was one of
the many remote border posts left over from the days when American
helicopters were plentiful and resupply by air possible. The Duc Hue
advisory team knew little about the rangers' operations because they
were not under the control of our district.

During an introductory briefing on our role as advisors, Major Eby
painted a complex picture of American involvement in virtually all matters in Duc Hue. Our small team even included a civil affairs officer, a
young lieutenant who coordinated the American role in the Vietnamese
Village Self-Development program. There were also three MAT (Military
Assistance and Training) teams in the district, whose men worked with
the Regional Forces and Popular Forces militia units. Major Eby was
also directly responsible for advising the district chief in all matters,
military, economic, and social welfare. Finally, the major had to keep up
with the enemy military and political situation within the district—
including South Vietnamese efforts to cope with communist subversion.
Needless to say, his reporting requirements were voluminous.

It was this final task that had the major worried. The immediate
problem was Tan My—Duc Hue's "model revolutionary village." Tan
My had become Colonel Weissinger's personal barometer for measuring
Major Eby's performance as a district senior advisor. The major confided in me that Colonel Weissinger had recently visited Duc Hue. Behind
the closed doors of the major's office, he had put my new boss on notice.
Eby would do something to reverse the situation in Tan My village—or
else. Weissinger had then directed the major to begin sleeping in a government outpost in the middle of Tan My to show his counterpart our
deep concern over the Vietcong presence in the village. The colonel
apparently envisioned that Major Nghiem would note Major Eby's new
sleeping arrangements and join him in Tan My. This, in turn, would
force the commander of the ineffective government militia unit in the
village to step up his unit's operations against the Vietcong.

Major Eby was personally skeptical about the value of sleeping in
Tan My, but he had dutifully taken an army cot to the Bao Cong outpost
in the heart of the village and bunked there for several nights, waiting in
vain for Major Nghiem to take the hint and join him. By the time I
arrived in Duc Hue, the major had retrieved his sleeping gear in disgust.
The ploy had accomplished nothing, and the man who gave me my welcome briefing to Duc Hue was one frustrated officer.

As an advisor, Major Eby could personally do little to correct the poor
showing of the Duc Hue forces against the Vietcong. The district chief

was all-powerful within his district, and only he could take whatever steps were required to remedy the situation. Unfortunately for Major Eby, his counterpart was apparently unwilling or unable to tackle the problem at hand. Even worse, it was becoming increasingly clear that the good district chief didn't even admit to the existence of the problem. Major Eby told me that there were many pressing problems in Duc Hue that required his attention, but that he could do nothing with them as long as Colonel Weissinger remained obsessed with Tan My village alone. The only way out of this dilemma was to achieve some sort of dramatic success in Tan My. This would convince Colonel Weissinger that the Duc Hue team was doing its job and relieve the pressure on Major Eby. The major made no secret of the fact that he was counting on me to help bail him out of his Tan My dilemma.

That evening I attended a farewell dinner for Lieutenant Furumoto. Held in the home of the police chief, the meal was an exotic adventure into the world of Vietnamese cuisine. Curried eel, barbecued duck, and shrimp egg rolls highlighted the feast, all washed down with tall glasses of French cognac and soda—or bottles of Vietnam's famous "33" beer for those who preferred it. I was at first taken aback by the three dogs under the table, but soon adjusted to the local custom of discarding my bones and other garbage on the floor at my feet, where they became the prize of the quickest canine. Our hosts proposed polite toasts to thank the departing lieutenant for all he had done for Duc Hue during his tour. Maybe they didn't "worship" Furumoto, but it certainly seemed that the Vietnamese liked him well enough. It would be difficult to follow in his footsteps.

Before the lieutenant departed later that week, he took me on a tour of Duc Hue's villages. We met the four village chiefs and received a village-by-village rundown on the enemy situation. Duc Hue's most dangerous village, according to Furumoto, was An Ninh, and he advised me not to travel on Route 7 into the village—day or night.

I was more interested in Tan My and surprised to learn that Furumoto considered the Vietcong there to be weaker than I had heard from Colonel Weissinger. The lieutenant explained that there were only a handful of die-hard Vietcong insurgents in the village's revolutionary committee, who were protected by a squad of guerrillas—about ten men in all. He believed that the Vietcong routinely exaggerated their reports to their superiors, and that this inflated reporting of revolutionary activities in Tan My had resulted in the awarding of the "model revolutionary village" appellation.

At the Tan My village office, I met the village chief and his senior national police officer. The two men were all smiles as they delivered a neatly packaged briefing on the village's insurgent organization. Their depiction of the Vietcong threat in Tan My was identical to Lieutenant Furumoto's. They insisted that the Vietcong were weaker than ever and spent most of their time hiding in the swamps. This was the real reason why so few of them had been killed during the last year, and why the government troops in the village rarely encountered any Vietcong. Both men scoffed at the "model revolutionary village" story.

Later that week I met with Lieutenant Bong, the district intelligence officer (S-2). Bong was responsible for keeping track of both the Vietcong military forces and the network of agents that we called the shadow government. In this latter capacity, he shared responsibility with the policeman who supervised the Phoenix office. Lieutenant Bong agreed with the view that the Vietcong in Duc Hue were a weak and disorganized force. He explained that this condition stemmed from the joint American–South Vietnamese raids into Communist sanctuaries in nearby Cambodia in mid-1970. These raids had crippled the Vietcong who operated in Hau Nghia, for the Cambodian bases were the source of much of their support. Bong also believed that the operations of Duc Hue's militia soldiers now forced the Vietcong to spend much of their time hiding in Cambodia. These militia troops had been fully armed with the M-16 rifle and the M-79 grenade launcher, and they were thus too strong for the Vietcong to engage.

Major Nghiem seconded Lieutenant Bong's optimistic assessment. A personable man who spoke fluent French and passable English, Nghiem told me that he believed there were "about a platoon" (thirty to forty men) of Vietcong in Duc Hue district. The enemy was thus capable of conducting small-scale ambushes and harassing operations, but he no longer posed a major security problem for the rice farmers of Duc Hue. Major Nghiem confided in me that he was much more concerned about the development of the economy of his district, its schools, and its social welfare programs. The Vietcong, he concluded with a smile, were "under control." The major added that the training of his district's militia forces remained an important priority, since it was always possible that the Vietcong could be reinforced in the future. Concerning the political leanings of "his people," the major conceded that each village had "a few families" who supported the Vietcong, but he insisted that fully 95 percent of Duc Hue's twenty-nine thousand people were progovernment.

I was thus thoroughly confused by the end of my first week in Duc Hue. Apart from Colonel Weissinger's instinct and a single Vietcong document praising Tan My village, there seemed to be precious little evidence to support the conclusion that Duc Hue district was infested with Vietcong. True, Hau Nghia province had traditionally been a revolutionary hotbed, but wasn't it possible that Colonel Weissinger was confusing past events with present realities? After all, there had been no major military conflict in Duc Hue for almost twelve months. Major Eby drove almost everywhere in the district accompanied only by his dog, and the last time the district headquarters had been fired upon by the enemy was July, 1969, almost eighteen months ago. The Vietnamese officials in Duc Hue seemed convinced that pacification was proceeding admirably, and dismissed the notion that Tan My village was a revolutionary stronghold.

But in spite of the evidence to the contrary, I had an uneasy feeling that I had landed in the middle of something that stunk—and that something was Tan My village. As a newcomer to the district, I didn't know enough to confirm my suspicions. However, I had already noticed that virtually all village, hamlet, and district officials in Duc Hue slept either in military outposts or in the district compound. I had met several of Tan My's hamlet chiefs during my visit to the village office; all of them were conducting their hamlet business there, far from the actual hamlets they represented. The more I received the smiling reassurances of the Vietnamese in Duc Hue that the local Vietcong were defeated and demoralized, the more uneasy and suspicious I became. Was it possible that the Vietnamese were trying to get me on board for twelve months of barbecued duck and curried eel—and no waves?

After two weeks in Duc Hue, I received orders to attend a one-week Phoenix advisors' school in Vung Tau. Before departing, I spent several days in the Phoenix office, trying to learn for myself the complex system of cards and dossiers on which Colonel Weissinger had warned me that Lieutenant Furumoto had squandered his tour. My enlisted assistant was Sfc. Eddie Shelton, who had already been in Duc Hue for a number of months. Shelton guided me through the impressive maze of colored file cards and folders that were all aimed at the goal of establishing "target folders" on identified Vietcong politicians. From what I could tell, the Duc Hue Phoenix operation would have earned high marks for its paperwork. Unfortunately, Sergeant Shelton noted wryly, the impressive files had not yet resulted in the launching of a single specifically targeted operation against a single Vietcong agent. The only members of the so-called shadow government who had been killed or captured in Duc Hue during 1970 had been the victims of conventional military operations. Shelton, a bright young black NCO with considerable intelligence experience, summed up the Duc Hue Phoenix program pointedly: "They just go through the motions to please the Americans, sir."

A police officer named Phung was the nominal head of the Phoenix office. During my first visit to his office, he had proudly displayed the results of a recent inspection of his operation. The Duc Hue Phoenix office had received a satisfactory rating in all areas from inspectors of the Saigon Phoenix Directorate. I was beginning to realize why Colonel Weissinger was so cynical about Phoenix. Before boarding the helicopter for Vung Tau, I told Major Eby that I was confident my time at the Phoenix school would be well spent. The Duc Hue Phoenix was a sick bird, and I hoped to return from Vung Tau with the medicine to revive it.

A twinge of regret swept over me as the Huey helicopter circled the high promontory that overlooked Vung Tau's beaches. No wonder my friend in the States had urged me to pursue an assignment here. My usual luck had not held, and I was stuck on the Cambodian border, surrounded by Vietnamese of questionable competence and sincerity and answerable to the the demanding Colonel Weissinger. If I had had a morale problem upon arriving in Hau Nghia, it was nothing compared to how I felt when I saw what I had missed in Vung Tau.

Approximately twenty-five military intelligence officers attended the Phoenix school that first week in February, 1971. Most of my classmates were captains like me, assigned to Phoenix offices in districts all over Vietnam. Hence it didn't take me long to learn that our problems in Duc Hue were not unique. Almost all of my new friends reported similar frustrations with the elusive Phoenix bird.

The Phoenix program made good sense conceptually. Since the Vietnamese government had several organizations in each district that were somehow engaged in the gathering of information on the Vietcong, why not open a central office in which all of these organizations would be represented? Each organization would then be responsible for funneling all of its information on the Vietcong insurgents into this office. As the information on hand about a given individual accumulated, a file or dossier could be opened on him. Eventually, the amount of information on the "target" would assume such proportions that the police or the military would be able to capture, kill, or recruit him (to defect or to remain in place as an informant). In the Phoenix lexicon, these options were collectively known as neutralization.

This was the theory behind the establishment of the Phoenix offices in each of Vietnam's 247 districts. Each Phoenix office was supposed to house representatives of the national police; the district S-2 (intelligence officer); the Military Security Service (MSS, the military intelligence organization responsible for a variety of missions, including counterespionage and countersubversion); the Rural Development cadre (a kind of domestic Peace Corps whose members frequently learned much about Vietcong activity as they built schools and dikes in the villages); and finally, the S-3 (the operations section of the district staff which—in theory—planned military operations based upon the targets generated by the Phoenix effort). A functioning Phoenix office was thus no more than a place where the various Vietnamese agencies shared their intelligence on the enemy. The goal was simple. If the Vietcong agent was a "legal cadre," one who carried a government identity card and lived overtly, the Phoenix office would mount a police operation to arrest him. If the Vietcong was an "illegal cadre," one who lived in a bunker by day and operated covertly at night, then the Phoenix office would plan a military operation to kill or capture him. Since the "illegals" always traveled with an armed military escort, the chances of capturing them without a fight were slim. Phoenix offices also spent considerable effort attempting to convince the Vietcong to surrender voluntarily to the government under the terms of an official amnesty program known as *Chieu Hoi*, or "Open Arms."

Our instructor in Vung Tau confidently pointed out that all we had to do in our districts was to get the Vietnamese talking to one another and the structure of the local shadow government would spring into focus. Other features of the program included "Wanted" posters on Vietcong cadre (who were civil offenders rather than prisoners of war if captured, which meant that they served relatively brief jail terms rather than perpetual confinement "for the duration" in a POW camp); the establishment of "blacklists" of important Vietcong in each village; and the classification of Vietcong political cadre by position as Category A, B, or C. Category A Vietcong were the key members of an organization, such as the Vietcong village chief, whereas category C persons were low-level support cadre, such as women who shopped for medicine at the marketplace for the Communists. When captured, the length of the jail term that a Vietcong could draw was partially determined by his category.

As I waited for the helicopter that would take me back to Duc Hue, I wondered whether it was possible to cure the paralysis that afflicted our Phoenix program. How could we get our counterparts to work smoothly together in the manner described by the instructor? Major Eby's Tan My dilemma weighed heavily on my mind, for I knew that when I returned, Colonel Weissinger would be looking more than ever for results. Somehow, the Phoenix concept must contain the answer. As the helicopter took off, the beaches of Vung Tau once more came into view, and I cursed my luck at drawing an assignment to Hau Nghia. The night before, three of us had spent a memorable evening downtown, highlighted by an elegant lobster dinner for less than two dollars apiece. The rice paddies and bamboo thickets of Duc Hue had seemed a million miles away as we sipped our "33" beer on the patio of Cyrno's restaurant and watched the fishing fleet return to port with its catch. Now, in little more than an hour, I would be back at Duc Hue, sleeping under a mosquito net and waking up with a start every time the Vietnamese artillery section outside my window opened fire.

Back in Duc Hue, I reported to Major Eby on my experience. Full of optimism from my week's schooling, I told the major that I suspected we had possessed the information needed to attack the Vietcong shadow government all along—the problem was one of simple communication. We needed to get the two key organizations—the police and the military —to work together. Major Eby no doubt had his reservations about how simple the problem was, but he nonetheless encouraged me, promising that he would attempt to get the district chief to support whatever steps I might recommend.

I arrived at the Phoenix office the following morning determined to shake things up. With the exception of Sergeant Shelton, there was no one in the office that morning—or any morning—at 8:00 A.M. I took advantage of the time to outline my plan to the sergeant. To begin with, he and I would work in the office during normal duty hours to demonstrate a renewed American commitment to the Phoenix program. Hopefully, this would prove more effective than Major Eby's recent camping trip to Tan My village. We would hold a meeting of all Phoenix personnel as soon as possible. Our mission: to get Mr. Phung of the police and Lieutenant Bong of district intelligence to share their information with one another—if indeed they had information—or at least get them talking to one another about the attack on the Vietcong organization.

Sergeant Shelton flashed his easygoing smile. He didn't think much of my school-hatched plan. He had already seen several similar attempts to revive the Phoenix effort, and he told me directly that he didn't think we could revive a beast that had never been alive in the first place. I wasn't too pleased with his forecast of failure, but at least I couldn't accuse him of being a yes man.

The big meeting had to be postponed until the following day. Mr. Phung lived in Saigon on weekends and didn't make it back to Duc Hue on Mondays. I was beginning to conclude that the Phoenix program's problems and Mr. Phung were one and the same.

The following day Phung arrived at the office at 10:30 A.M. Disguising my dissatisfaction ("Don't make a Vietnamese lose face," our instructors at Fort Bragg had warned), I arranged for our meeting at 1:00 P.M.

The appointed hour came and went with no sign of either Lieutenant Bong or Mr. Phung. All the other Phoenix personnel were still enjoying their midday siesta, sleeping on their desks. This ritual lasted until 2:00 P.M. daily, the grinning Sergeant Shelton explained. Finally, sometime after two, we had our meeting. I carefully explained the urgency and importance of our mutual task, and outlined my plan to increase the flow of information between the various Vietnamese organizations.

I was pleased with the reactions of Phung and Bong. Both men smiled, took notes, and nodded enthusiastic agreement with the concept of sharing information more openly. Neither man voiced any problems with my plan for intensifying the attack on the Vietcong. However, after the meeting, just as I was congratulating myself for the good start, Lieutenant Bong called me aside. He warned me that although our plan was a sound one, it would surely be hindered by the national police. Their chief was an alcoholic, and most of the other personnel assigned to Duc Hue by police headquarters were losers—men who had been exiled to our district as a form of punishment. Naturally, the lieutenant concluded with a winning smile, he would cooperate fully, but I would have to do something about the police.

I expected Mr. Phung to hold some sort of meeting that afternoon to kick off our new approach. Instead, he simply disappeared (to Saigon, it turned out). By now, my patience had worn thin. Since the Phoenix typist worked for the advisory team, I asked her to begin a discreet record of Mr. Phung's comings and goings. If Phung would not cooperate with me, I would take steps to have him removed. Within two days, I learned that Phung was upset that I was spying on him, and planned to send a report on me to his superiors in Bao Trai. In the meantime, it was business (or no business) as usual in the Phoenix office. It was as if our meeting had never taken place.

I was learning my first lesson in dealing with the Vietnamese. Don't judge their reaction to events by the smiles on their faces or by appearances of agreement. Mr. Phung had given every indication (by American standards) of agreement with my plan. In fact, he regarded me as a meddler and had no intention of cooperating. It was becoming clear to me (for reasons I still didn't understand) that revitalizing the Phoenix effort in Duc Hue was not going to happen as a result of an instant cure imported from Vung Tau.

Colonel Weissinger had warned me about wasting my tour shuffling papers. I decided that I had just wasted a precious two weeks and that the potential for still more lost time in the Phoenix office was great. For this reason, with no fanfare, I put an end to my career as a Phoenix advisor. I told Sergeant Shelton that I had a pair of special projects that would take me out of the Phoenix office, and instructed him to "carry on." How he resisted the world's loudest "I told you so," I'll never know. Later, during the final month of his tour, Shelton exposed a network of ping-pong fanatics in the Phoenix office. As I went about my duties, I often heard the sounds of competition coming from that direction. No one could beat Sergeant Shelton, nor could I fault him for his sporting inclination. I had stuck him with Phoenix after becoming fed up in less than two weeks. And I knew that when Sergeant Shelton returned to the States, he would not be replaced; his job was a victim of the Vietnamization program. Hence, when he departed, there would be no American in the Phoenix office, since I had decided to have nothing to do with it.

I had really wanted to be a successful advisor. For this reason I had been disturbed by Colonel Weissinger's impatient demand that if the Vietnamese were not up to the task of eliminating the Vietcong organization, we Americans should do it for them. I believed firmly that one of the major shortcomings of our overall approach in Vietnam had been the tendency to do things ourselves rather than to train the Vietnamese to do them. President Nixon's Vietnamization policy was thus a step in the right direction—however overdue. The American role in Vietnam reminded me of the proud father who bought his three-year-old son an electric train. When the son proved to be too young to operate the complex toy, the father had taken it over and run it himself. Months later, the son still couldn't run the train because the father became so wrapped up in the toy that he never bothered to teach the boy. In Vietnam, we had been guilty of this mistake. For several years, American units had fought the war and given little more than lip service to training the Vietnamese to "run the train." But, unlike the three-year-old in the story, the Vietnamese were quite capable of running the train all along.

I went to Hau Nghia determined not to make this mistake, but wound up ill equipped to cope with the frustrations of advisory duty. Accordingly, I threw myself into two projects. Both involved the exploitation of Vietcong defectors.

II

COMRADE HAI CHUA

He was tired, frightened, and fed up with the need to hide in a mosquito-infested swamp from both government troops and his former Vietcong comrades. He had resigned his post as Communist village chief seven months earlier, pleading ill health as a cover for his loss of nerve, and had lived in fear ever since. Thus he had come to surrender to the government under the terms of the Chieu Hoi amnesty program shortly before my arrival in Duc Hue. His real name was Nguyen van Dung, but he went by the party alias of "Hai Chua." Chua had been the village secretary of Hiep Hoa village, which made him the highest-ranking Vietcong cadre to defect in Duc Hue for some time. Under the terms of the amnesty program, the South Vietnamese government extended amnesty to any returnee who truthfully revealed his identity and the position he had held as an insurgent. As a "rallier," Hai Chua would receive several months of "vocational training" in the Chieu Hoi Center, located in Bao Trai. Actually, much of the time spent here would be devoted to extensive political reindoctrination to prepare him for a life as a loyal citizen of South Vietnam.

Government military and political authorities had little use for ralliers, whom they regarded with suspicion and contempt. In following the Communists and then defecting to the government, a rallier had, after all, been a traitor two times over. There was little sympathy in Duc Hue for the notion that a properly handled Communist returnee could be a priceless source of information. When I suggested to Lieutenant Bong that we needed a cooperative defector if we were to ever get a good insight into the Vietcong's local organization, the lieutenant replied that defectors could not be relied upon to cooperate because the revolution did not take kindly to traitors. Bong then showed me a captured Communist document that outlined the Vietcong's policy toward ralliers.

> Comrades who weaken and abandon the revolution because of the enemy's treacherous Chieu Hoi program fall into three categories. Category I are those former comrades who contact the enemy's police and intelligence organizations and give information harmful to the revolution for their personal gain. Such comrades are traitors and should be eliminated. Category II are those comrades who have brief contact with the enemy's police and intelligence apparatus, and who give a small amount of information not greatly harmful to the revolution. Such comrades should be recontacted with caution, and evaluated for possible reeducation and return to the revolution. Category III are those former comrades who do not cooperate in any way with the enemy. Every effort should be made to recontact and reactivate such comrades.

Lieutenant Bong told me bluntly that all ralliers were untrustworthy and a waste of time.

But the fact that Hai Chua had been the senior Vietcong official in Hiep Hoa village intrigued me. After all, Duc Hue district headquarters was located in the middle of this village. What better way could there be to follow Colonel Weissinger's advice to "get totally involved" with the enemy situation than to pump the brain of the man who until recently had been the leading Vietcong in the very village where I now lived? If Hai Chua would open up and discuss the course of the revolution in Hiep Hoa, we could gain some understanding of how the situation had come to where it was in February, 1971. Colonel Weissinger's logic was compelling—if we could grasp the roots of the insurgency, if we could understand the motivations of the young men who had volunteered to serve the Vietcong over the years, then we could function more effectively as we struggled to cope with the complexities of the insurgency. Each time I met the strong-willed Colonel Weissinger, he reiterated his dissatisfaction with the lack of involvement of most Americans in Vietnam—their failure, as he put it, to ask the right questions about the Vietcong movement. "Naturally," the colonel argued, "we need to know the answers to such questions as 'How many Vietcong are there in a given village, and who are they?' But it is equally important to know why they are out there, and what goes through their minds as they hide in their bunkers." The colonel was convinced that his advisors had a shallow grasp of the real reasons for the Vietcong insurgency, and he was thus receptive to my proposal to debrief Hai Chua on his life as a Communist.

I attacked my new mission enthusiastically. The colonel authorized the use of a discreet, comfortable facility in Bao Trai where I could carry on an extended dialogue with Chua. I had access to a modest amount of funds to reimburse him on an hourly basis and to pay for cigarettes, food, or whatever else it might take to gain his cooperation. The colonel even agreed that I could wear civilian clothes during the debriefing sessions if I thought this might make Hai Chua a little more comfortable.

Now that I had gained official sanction for the project, the next step was to find out what it was that motivated Hai Chua. How could I gain his confidence? I had met the man only once, shortly after he had surrendered. The meeting had taken place at Major Nghiem's house in Duc Hue. For more than an hour, the major had attempted in vain to get Chua to talk openly about the situation in Duc Hue. During the interview, Chua had smiled nervously and displayed little inclination to discuss the details of his life as a Vietcong. Much to Major Nghiem's chagrin, he had politely answered, *"Da, khong biet"* ("I don't know, sir") to most questions concerning Hiep Hoa village's remaining Vietcong cadre. Several times during the interview, Chua had explained apologetically that he had been expelled from his post as village secretary several months earlier, and for this reason, he didn't know much about his former comrades' situation. It had been evident that he was afraid to talk. This interview had convinced my counterparts that any further time spent on Chua would be wasted, and he had been sent to the Chieu Hoi Center for training.

Before contacting Chua, I embarked on a cram course to learn everything possible about Hiep Hoa village's Vietcong movement from other sources. If I was to succeed in establishing a meaningful dialogue with Hai Chua, I would have to be knowledgeable about the revolution in Hiep Hoa. Otherwise, I would not be able to ask the right questions, nor would I be able to distinguish truthful responses from lies. It was essential to gain Chua's respect at the outset of our relationship if I expected to gain his cooperation. The more I knew about Hiep Hoa at the onset of our discussions, the more I would be able to learn.

Fortunately, one of our night ambush patrols in Hiep Hoa had recently ambushed a Vietcong courier. The lucky man had escaped with his life, but he had dropped his document pouch as he fled. Among its contents was a notebook that clearly belonged to the village's Vietcong security chief. This fascinating document contained page after page of status reports on Hiep Hoa's revolutionary committee. On one page appeared the names of the village guerrilla unit members and how much rice each man had been issued. Still another page listed several villagers whom the author suspected of being government informants. One entry even listed the names of the key members of the village revolutionary committee. The notebook was a godsend that would allow us to cross-check much of what Hai Chua would tell me once our discussions commenced. I was also able to contact another former Hiep Hoa Vietcong, a man who had once been one of Chua's subordinates and who had rallied some months before him. I arranged to debrief both men simultaneously, which would enable me to double-check what I was hearing. This man agreed to talk to me on two conditions: First, we must be discreet; and second, I must "sympathize" with his economic plight (a classic Vietnamese way of indirectly requesting reimbursement).

The project was thus shaping up. Hai Chua was easy to contact since he was still a resident of the Chieu Hoi Center. I had learned that he had told his counselor there that he would like to go to work for the Americans—a piece of information that enabled me more easily to solicit his cooperation. Chua automatically assumed when I sought him out that his cooperation was the price of a good job with the American advisory team. Hence, he readily agreed to meet with me, on the condition that we conduct our relationship discreetly. We established a meeting arrangement that would allow me to see Chua each morning, then meet with the other man in the afternoons. Neither man was aware I was in contact with the other.

For the next two months, I immersed myself in the drama of Hiep Hoa village. Our discussions ranged from the days of the Japanese occupation of the village during World War II to the return and eventual defeat of the French—and finally to the eventual arrival of the Americans. It was not a pretty story, dealing as it did with nearly thirty years of subversion, suspicion, and military conflict. Nor was it easy to draw out of the two men the many facets of the story that would make it meaningful for the American reader. The villagers of Hiep Hoa had been submerged in conflict for so long, and had seen so much violence and duplicity, that such things were almost taken for granted by the actors in the drama. The world Hai Chua and his former subordinate described could not have been more alien to me, conditioned as I was by the rules of existence in middle-class America.

I quickly learned that I had to spend considerable effort cross-checking the two men's words against one another and against the many documentary sources that had fallen into our hands over the years. If the project was to succeed, both men needed to know from the beginning that they could not get away with lying, nor with the old trick of feigning lack of knowledge. Predictably, each man attempted early in our relationship to lie—with no success. Armed as I was with the capability to cross-check most of what they were saying, it was not difficult to establish a no-nonsense relationship with them.

Out of our marathon discussions emerged an intriguing chronicle of the formative years of the Vietcong movement in Hiep Hoa village. Hai Chua, for example, was able to recall the brief but ruthless Japanese occupation of his village in the closing days of World War II.

The Japanese had ruled Hiep Hoa brutally, Chua recalled. If a farmer objected to the heavy crop levies, the occupiers had simply burned his crops. These tactics had quickly led to the formation of a village resistance movement. As the war drew to a close, speculation had mounted as to whether or not the French would return. Many of the villagers believed that the French would never give up their hold on Vietnam, and so, as word of the impending surrender of the Japanese spread, a bargain had been struck between local resistance leaders and the Japanese commander. A "raid" had been conducted against the Japanese arms depot which, by arrangement, the Japanese garrison did not resist. Thus, when the first Frenchman returned to Hiep Hoa, most of the Japanese arms were in the hands of the men who would soon become known as the Vietminh.

Hai Chua's father had served from 1946 to 1950 as Hiep Hoa's deputy village chief under the reestablished French administration. This had been an increasingly dangerous job as the Vietminh escalated their efforts to defeat the French. The Vietminh had labeled those Vietnamese who served the French *Viet gian*, "Vietnamese traitors." I asked Hai Chua how his father had been able to cope with this delicate situation. His reply:

> My father was a clever man. He whittled the stick at both ends. He did not really like working for the French, but he was afraid that if he quit, his successor would not look out for the people. His first concern was always for the people of Hiep Hoa. Therefore, even though he worked for the French, he was also friendly with the resistance. He cooperated with them just enough so that they did not want to eliminate him because they were fairly certain that his successor would be worse.

Chua explained that his father had been able to walk the delicate path between the two sides partly because he had grown up in the same hamlet with the village's first resistance leader. This phenomenon of unofficial accommodation between the early Vietminh and government officials was something that I would encounter repeatedly as I delved into the realities of the war in Hau Nghia. As Chua described his father's role under the French, much of his story tracked uncannily with what we had begun to learn about our current situation. In the space of twenty-five years, history was repeating itself.

Hai Chua described the attempts of the French to reimpose their control over the rural areas of Hiep Hoa. They had attempted to administer the government at the village level with an exclusively Vietnamese bureaucracy. In Hiep Hoa, for example, the only French nationals had been the manager of the sugar mill and the priest in the Catholic church. Chua explained that the French had been caught in a dilemma. On the one hand, they knew they would never be accepted or be able to function at the village level. Still, in attempting to run the country from the towns and cities through local officials, they were out of touch with the people. Vietnam, Chua reminded me, was and remained a village-oriented society. Outsiders who lived in the towns were the prisoners of information fed to them by their Vietnamese "henchmen" (as the people referred to many of the French-installed officials).

In 1947, after French-led government troops arrested several resistance leaders and sent them to the dreaded Con Son Island prison, the resistance movement had been forced to adopt stricter security measures. Of necessity, all resistance work went underground. The shadow government was born.

Chua explained that the Hiep Hoa peasantry had been divided over the issue of violent resistance against the French. Virtually no one liked the French—they were westerners. Even the Vietnamese bureaucrats who were benefiting from the system by working for the French didn't like them. But most people were neither virulently proresistance nor anti-French at that time. Hiep Hoa's rice farmers just wanted to farm their paddies in peace.

But would the villagers report to the government about the covert activities of the resistance? Hai Chua smiled at my question and then patiently explained to the naive American the Vietnamese way. Regardless of how politically involved or apathetic the villagers might be, almost no one would ever report to the government about the activities of the resistance. To do so would be to subject a fellow Vietnamese to arrest, torture, or even death at the hands of westerners. Virtually no one would do such a thing. It was "them" against "us."

But surely, I argued, there were people who supported the government who would defy this code.

Chua insisted that most villagers held the French and their Vietnamese supporters in such contempt that they could be relied upon to protect the resistance leaders from capture. And those few who might be tempted to violate their obligations as Vietnamese were aware of the risks of such a betrayal. There were no secrets in a rural Vietnamese hamlet, and everyone understood the meaning of the words "revolutionary justice."

Both men insisted that an ingrained dislike of foreigners was central to the Vietnamese outlook, and that this fact had played a key role in their village. Chua had described this phenomenon with reference to the French but had made it clear that he believed that it extended to all westerners. I began to seek confirmation of this assertion, and when I raised it with my government counterparts I quickly learned that it was a most delicate issue. One South Vietnamese intelligence officer smiled and told me to "pay no attention to such allegations by a Vietcong traitor." Hai Chua, he explained, came from a revolutionary hamlet where his mind had been warped by Communist propaganda. But others replied differently. Referring to the centuries-old Vietnamese struggle against foreign domination, they confirmed that Vietnamese xenophobia was very real. Foreigners, they explained, often overlooked this because the "Vietnamese way" dictated that such feelings be concealed. The polite smile and the seemingly obsequious behavior of many Vietnamese was a mask that often concealed contempt for the foreigner. One of my more candid counterparts, who had been trained at an American intelligence school on Okinawa, summed up the situation by reminding me that "you can't help it if you're an American, but you should always remember that very few of our people are capable of genuine positive feelings towards you. You must assume that you are not wholly liked and trusted, and not be deceived by the Asian smile."

I was intrigued by the fact that Hai Chua's father had been a civil servant for the French. Here was a former Communist village chief whose father had performed virtually the same duties in the same village for the hated French. What had happened to cause the son to steer such a radically different course?

Chua smiled. He would have preferred to remain neutral in the struggle, but the situation in Hiep Hoa had not permitted this. The Vietminh had grown stronger and stronger as the French continued their futile attempt to govern the countryside from the towns and cities. The government did little for the people other than levy taxes and was increasingly perceived by the peasantry as an outside power of little or no use. The people had to contend more and more with the resistance, which was continuously represented at the all-important village level. Chua recalled that, by 1949, each hamlet in Hiep Hoa had its own "self defense group," a unit of unarmed volunteers that gave early warning in the event government forces approached. Later, these units became the nuclei of the armed hamlet guerrilla forces of the Vietminh.

It had become more and more difficult for Chua's father to coexist with the Vietminh. As resistance against the French grew, a new Vietminh leader appeared in the village. This man was a North Vietnamese who had come south with his family at the urging of the French—lured by promises of great economic gain to anyone who would migrate south to work on the rubber plantations. The French promises had proven to be hollow, and the Vietminh had found many dedicated recruits among these displaced and disillusioned northerners.

By 1949, this Vietminh leader was demanding more and more help from Hai Chua's father, who could not comply without risking French retaliation. Faced with this dilemma, and plagued by failing health, he had retired. The Vietminh promptly declared the old bureaucrat to be a traitor and attempted to have him eliminated. Hai Chua's last memories of his father were of the harried old man hiding in the bamboo every time the Vietminh approached the hamlet.

Chua was nineteen when his father died—just the right age to serve as a soldier for either the French or the Vietminh. In his words, "After my father's death, I became concerned with staying home to look after my mother and sister. To do this, I had to become an accomplished draft-dodger." Chua's reaction to his father's fate had been predictable. He wanted nothing to do with the politics of either side, nor did he want to be netted by the recruiting cadre of either side, both of whom regularly swept through the hamlets of Hiep Hoa in search of military-age males. For almost three years, the wily Chua succeeded in avoiding a commitment to either side of the escalating conflict.

But as the resistance flared into a full-scale war, it had become impossible to remain neutral. Faced with the need to choose sides, the pragmatic young peasant had volunteered to work as an entertainment cadre for the Vietminh—a job that required him to serve as a guitar player in a troupe of artists that entertained the troops with songs and skits extolling Vietminh victories. By 1954, Chua related, most of the villagers in Hiep Hoa "leaned toward the Vietminh." Here is how he explained the shifting political sands in his village to me:

At this time, the people of Hiep Hoa fell into four "religious" groups. There were Catholics, who tended to support the French. Many of the Buddhists supported the Vietminh. The *Cao Dai* also tended to support the French.* The fourth religion was what I call the "U" group. These were the "yes" people, the people who blew with the wind. These people were the ones who realized that the French were trying to control the country from the cities, and that this tactic could not succeed. The adherents of this fourth "religion" were Catholics, Buddhists, and Cao Dai. I would say that 80 percent of the people fell into this category. In my own case, for example, as a Cao Dai and the son of a former colonial administrator, I should not have been a convinced supporter of the Vietminh. And, in fact, I was not. But I must admit to being a member of the "yes" group, in that I had the feeling that the French were going to lose. This was why I had begun to lean towards the Vietminh. I think in this respect, I was typical of most of my neighbors.

Chua hoped that his decision to join the Vietminh would preempt any problems that a Communist regime might cause for him and his family because of his father's service for the French. The opportunistic Chua also conceded that the defeat of the French at Dien Bien Phu had influenced him and his neighbors. Until General Giap's stunning defeat of the French, the villagers had extended only cautious support to the Vietminh. After the French defeat and subsequent withdrawal, Chua recalled that "the people listened a little more carefully to the Vietminh message."

The message, which the Vietminh propaganda machine kept hammering home, was that when elections were held in two years, as provided for in the Geneva Accords, Vietnam would be unified under the leadership of Ho Chi Minh. The peasants of Hiep Hoa believed that lasting peace had finally come to their village. Not so Hai Chua and his fellow Vietminh cadre. For several months after the signing of the Geneva Accords, they worked day and night in what was known as the "cleaning up" task. During this period, Hai Chua and hundreds of others carried all of the Vietminh's weapons and ammunition to storage caches in neighboring Cambodia. This was the last major task before the local Vietminh organization became dormant. Chua remembered it this way:

The reason for the hiding of the weapons was explained only to the village's Vietminh. We were told that Ho Chi Minh believed that the imperialists could not be trusted to allow the promised elections in 1956, and that we thus had to prepare to fight once more for our

*The Cao Dai are one of several religious minorities in Vietnam.

goals if necessary. This was explained only to us. As far as the people knew, the future held nothing but peace.

Several of Hiep Hoa's most dedicated Communists left the village at this time, "regrouping" to the north under the terms of the Geneva Accords. Several years later, they would return to their village to rekindle the insurgency. But Hai Chua and hundreds of other rice farmers who had united to resist the French returned to their primary occupations in the paddies that surrounded Hiep Hoa.

The first several years after the Geneva Accords, under the new President Ngo Dinh Diem, had been a time of relative peace and contentment. Hai Chua remembered that "the life of the people of Hiep Hoa during that period was much better than it is today." The insurgency was dormant, and the people enjoyed the first real peace in more than a decade. The Saigon-appointed village chief proved to be a popular and fair man who was accessible to the people and successful in bringing government money to the village. What then, I asked, had happened to turn Hiep Hoa into a revolutionary hotbed by 1964?

At first, Chua replied, the Communists had launched an intensive indoctrination campaign in the village. The refusal of the Saigon government to allow the elections in 1956 had given them a theme to exploit. Nightly political rallies became common in Hiep Hoa's hamlets as disciplined Communist political officers struggled to overcome the fact that the villagers were basically content with the current situation. Again, in Hai Chua's words:

The theme of these meetings was always the same. We were told that the imperialists had double-crossed the Vietnamese people once again. After World War II and the Indochina War, the French had owed so much money to the Americans that they couldn't pay it all back in cash. Therefore, the French had made a bargain with the Americans, who had agreed to take Vietnam as a payment for the French debt. We were told that this was the reason why the elections had not been held.

We also learned that because the Americans had observed the French defeat, they knew that they could not run the country themselves. For this reason, they had decided to control the country using a Vietnamese puppet government. The Diem regime in Saigon was working for the Americans, and its real purpose was to exploit the wealth of Vietnam for its American masters.

Hai Chua admitted that this explanation had made sense to him and to many of his friends and neighbors. After all, had not Uncle Ho warned in 1954 that the imperialists were not to be trusted? Still, it was difficult for me to fathom why the peaceful, apolitical peasants of Hiep Hoa would flock to the Communist banner merely because of a smooth-sounding propaganda line. Or had the Communists managed to gain sway over the people by threats and terror, as many of my superiors believed?

Chua shook his head. Terror and the threat of "revolutionary justice" had always played a role, but only a minor one. A more significant role had been played by the Diem government itself, whose policies had actually driven many of the villagers into the arms of the Vietcong.* The relentless Communist propaganda campaign could not have been effective if the Diem government had not done things to lend credibility to Communist allegations. Hai Chua's recollection of this period illustrates the dilemma faced by President Diem:

> First, the government forced many of the people to move to central locations called "strategic hamlets." We were told that this was for our protection from the Vietcong, but at this time, the people of Hiep Hoa did not yet feel the need for such protection. The program caused many hardships as whole households were uprooted and moved to settlements near the main road. The Communists capitalized on this unpopular policy by pointing out that the government was trying to sever the people's ties to their ancestral lands.
>
> Then the popular village chief was replaced in 1960 by a selfish man. This man was inaccessible to the people, and it was commonly believed that he was dishonest. He looked out for the rich people in the village and no one else. Since the villagers' view of the government was based largely on its local representative, the prestige of the Diem government suffered because of this man, who eventually absconded with the village funds.
>
> Another reason for the decline in the government's popularity was the so-called Decree 10–59. This law stated that all people who had worked for the Vietminh could be imprisoned, or even executed. This law alienated many of the villagers who had fought with the Vietminh against the French, but who were not Communists. Many of these people had engaged in nothing more than peaceful farming since 1955, but now they had to fear reprisals from the government.

*Vietcong: a shortened version of *Viet Nam Cong San*, Vietnamese Communist.

The Hiep Hoa Vietcong were quick to take advantage of this, and they urged all former Vietminh to join them and assist in ousting the regime that was so unfairly treating them.

If the Diem regime's heavy-handed attempts to combat the growing insurgency backfired, its land reform policies fared little better. Hai Chua recalled that no one welcomed the government's land reform program more than the Vietcong:

> In 1952–53, the Vietminh had confiscated land from rich landowners and given it to the poor people of the village. Our one acre was augmented by an additional half acre, compliments of the Vietminh. We tilled this land until 1961, when the Saigon government redistributed all land in Hiep Hoa. This plan had the effect of dividing up all the land among both the poor and the rich, whereas the Vietminh had taken from the rich and given to the poor. As a result, many Hiep Hoa farmers lost land that they had tilled for a number of years. Even worse, some of this land was given to rich landlords who did not even live in the village. In some cases, they did not even bother to work the land, and it lay fallow. In other instances, a farmer was faced with having to pay rent on land that he had owned the year before.

Gradually, but inexorably, these government blunders and the accompanying Vietcong propaganda campaign had begun to take their toll. As the people's attitudes shifted, Communist guerrilla units were reborn in the hamlets and government officials became less and less visible in the village. Hai Chua estimated that by 1962, more than 50 percent of Hiep Hoa's rice farmers had come to accept the Vietcong's version of political reality, while most of the remaining villagers remained largely noncommittal. The reborn Communist organization employed the selective use of terror and assassination to freeze the government out of the village, and continued its relentless indoctrination efforts. By 1963, the revolution enjoyed a virtual monopoly position with the people in Hiep Hoa's rural hamlets. By now a man of thirty-one, Hai Chua once again tested the political winds and made his move.

"I realized," he confided in me with a sheepish grin, "that if I did not act quickly, I would sooner or later wind up being a soldier on one side or another." Convinced that the Vietcong would ultimately triumph, the timid but crafty Chua volunteered to serve as a Vietcong political officer, confident that this would shield him from the dangers of military service.

Initially, all went well. The revolution's strength was growing daily, and Chua's duties as a propaganda cadre were not demanding or dangerous. Chua became a full member of the Communist party by the end of 1964 and received a promotion in the village hierarchy. By early 1965, Vietcong hamlet and village guerrillas had been reinforced by new, well-armed "main force" units, and Hiep Hoa's small government militia platoon stayed more and more in its outpost near the sugar mill. At year's end, Hiep Hoa village was firmly in the Communist camp, and the people had begun to pay harvest taxes to the Vietcong. "At this time, it was not necessary to use threats or terror to obtain such support," Chua remembered. "It was given willingly because the people were nearly certain that the future lay with the Communists." Once again, I detected the unabashed pragmatism of the peasantry when it came to political loyalties.

The Vietcong's popularity in Hiep Hoa peaked in 1965–66, when the Communists enjoyed support that Chua described this way:

> The most important form of support was not the recruits or even the money. The critical thing was that the people were willing to cover for us at all times. They would not report our activities or locations to the government forces if they came into the village. Sometimes they would even volunteer misleading information about us. Without this form of support, we could not have gotten along. As for the 30 percent or so who did not support us, most of these people were either Catholic or Cao Dai, or they had relatives serving with the government forces. But even these people lent their support in the sense that they did not reveal information about our movements and activities. They knew that to do so would have not been healthy.

Hiep Hoa's villagers greeted the 1965 new year enthusiastically as the "year of total victory." The "puppet" South Vietnamese 25th Division had begun to operate in the area by that time, but its morale was low and its initial operations sloppy and ineffective. Hai Chua and his comrades saw the position of the Saigon government as similar to that of the French in 1954. Hiep Hoa's hamlets were virtually "off limits" to government officials, the "revolutionary morale" of the people was high, and victory was at hand.

It was during this critical period that the first Americans began to appear in Hiep Hoa. At first, there were only a few Green Beret advisors, but these men were followed by others who began to advise the South Vietnamese 25th Division. By the beginning of 1966, the American 25th

Infantry Division had begun to operate in the Hau Nghia area, supported
by large numbers of helicopters. The security of Hiep Hoa's hamlets
began to evaporate, and the fainthearted Hai Chua suddenly found himself in the front lines of a new war. The "Second Indochina War" had
begun. Chua remembered this vividly:

> The government troops did not pose too much of a problem at first,
> but the Americans with their helicopters and artillery changed the
> face of the war overnight in Hiep Hoa. I was forced to spend more
> and more time in hiding, and my wife became increasingly dissatis-
> fied. Casualties among the people of Hiep Hoa mounted, as did
> property damage from the fighting. The people began to draw away
> from us and to fear our presence, knowing that we would attract
> government forces and more fighting.

In 1965, the drive from Duc Hue district to Bao Trai was too dangerous to undertake without a military escort. Exploding mines and Vietcong ambushes along the roads were daily occurrences. Government
militia units had been powerless to cope with the rapidly growing Vietcong military machine, but the arrival of American combat troops in the
province transformed the situation and checked the momentum toward
a Communist victory.

Hai Chua and his comrades reported to their superiors that the inexorable American buildup was threatening the very existence of the
revolution at the grass roots level. Something had to be done. As the
Americanized war intensified throughout 1966 and 1967, the desperate
Communist high command was compelled to take drastic measures to
salvage the revolution's eroding position. This was the purpose of the
1968 Tet Offensive. In Hiep Hoa village, preparations for this offensive
were intensive. Communist tax collectors implored the people to make
even greater sacrifices for the promised "general offensive–general
uprising," while Hai Chua and his propaganda teams pledged that the
coming offensive would "crush the puppet government and end the
war."

But the Tet attacks failed to deliver the peace that the villagers of Hiep
Hoa had been promised. For Hai Chua, the ill-fated Tet Offensive was a
watershed event. "It was after the Tet attacks," he confessed, "that I
began to doubt that we had any chance of defeating the Saigon government and its American ally. This defeat and the failure of the general
uprising to materialize badly hurt our credibility in the village." Casualties among soldiers of both sides and among the peasantry had shot up

dramatically as the fighting escalated. In Hai Chua's native hamlet, nearly a hundred people died between 1967 and 1969, out of a total population of less than seven hundred persons. Chua recalled bitterly that after Tet "popular dissatisfaction with our efforts in Hiep Hoa rose sharply."

But the defeat had its brighter side. The heavy casualties among the Vietcong cadre during the Tet attacks and their aftermath created new advancement opportunities for the surviving party members. Hai Chua was among the first to benefit. He was promoted to village secretary in January, 1969, at a time when the situation in Hiep Hoa was almost out of control. He recalled that his marching orders were quite explicit:

> The party directed me to wage a three-pronged attack on the enemy; military proselyting, civilian proselyting, and military pressure. But in reality, I had all I could do to keep the village organization from falling apart. From January to July, enemy military operations in Hiep Hoa had escalated greatly. The government constructed new outposts in our safe areas, and the military pressure became so great that we could not operate at all without incurring the risk of being ambushed. We spent most of our time avoiding the enemy's forces, which now used helicopters to appear without warning almost anywhere in the village. As a result, during the summer of 1969, many of our village guerrillas fled to Cambodia where our forces were still in complete control. This was the beginning of an exodus that I could not prevent.

The virtual dissolution of his village organization was more than Hai Chua could handle, and the neophyte village secretary soon lost his nerve. He had become a political cadre to avoid military violence, and he was simply not strong enough to follow his orders to "stick to the people." At the end of August, 1969, Hai Chua said good-bye to his wife and his mistress and followed his comrades to the safety of nearby Cambodia.

This was the beginning of the end of Chua's career as a Vietcong. Cambodia was crowded with frightened cadre like himself, all there to escape the fury of the new war in their villages. Within a few weeks, Chua had been contacted by the party and ordered to attend a series of "study sessions." He remembered these sessions with bitterness:

> We were told that the Saigon government was pursuing its own three-pronged policy that consisted of burning the people's houses

and crops, killing the people, and destroying the countryside with chemicals. It was explained to us that the enemy had been forced to rely on this negative strategy because we had crippled him with our successful attacks during Tet of 1968. According to the party, the result of the Tet attacks was that the people no longer had any confidence in the puppet government.

The study group leader explained to us that the United States was on the verge of total capitulation, as proven by the fact that the Americans had come to the conference table in Paris. The Americans, we were told, would soon withdraw, leaving the puppet government to defend itself, which it could not do without the Americans.

Hai Chua could not relate to this depiction of reality. He believed that he had barely escaped from Hiep Hoa with his life, and could not accept the notion that the Tet disasters had been a victory. The study group leader, he concluded, was a typical rear area type who did not know what he was talking about. "I could not," he commented, "believe that the government was as weak as he claimed, any more than I could accept his claim that the United States, which had just put a man on the moon, was a deteriorating power."

The dispirited Hai Chua managed to hide out in Cambodia for more than five months, during which he decided to retire from service with the revolution. Pleading ill health as a pretext, he informed his superiors that he was returning to Hiep Hoa to turn over his duties to a new man. In early February, 1970, Chua returned to Vietnam and declared his intention to step down from his post.

But leaving the service of the revolution was not as easy as joining, and Chua found himself embroiled in a bitter dispute with his former subordinates. His successor denounced him as a contemptible coward, and called a meeting of the village committee to decide the issue. At this meeting, Chua learned that he had been expelled from the party and relieved of all duties. The party cited two grounds for his dismissal. He had left his post without authorization, and he had violated the party's rules of conduct by taking a mistress. Hereafter, it was decreed, he would be permitted to carry on the work of the revolution as an untitled, low-level cadre.

Chua smarted at this treatment and declined the "lenient" offer, politely pleading ill health once again. "Had I shown my anger," he confided, "they would have worried that I might rally to the government, and I probably would have been marked for elimination."

Chua could read the handwriting on the wall. "I had to become an outsider," he recalled, "but I didn't know where to turn." He considered turning himself in to the government, but he was plagued by fears that he would either be imprisoned or forced to relocate far from Hiep Hoa village. He also knew all too well the revolution's attitude toward defectors. And so, the victim of his own propaganda, the frightened Chua hesitated until he could wait no longer. When he learned that his former comrades had decided to eliminate him, he made his decision. Fearing assassination, Hai Chua ended his career as a Vietcong and turned himself in to the government on February 19, 1971.

Our journey into the history of the revolution in Hiep Hoa village had been a fascinating and an eye-opening experience. At first, Hai Chua had impressed me as a dull-witted country bumpkin who had become involved in a high-stakes game for which he was ill prepared. Chua seemed to lack the forceful personality and other attributes that one normally associates with exceptional leadership ability. One of his former colleagues characterized him as a man of mediocre talents who rose in the party hierarchy due to the heavy attrition of cadre rather than because of his own abilities.

But Chua could not be entirely blamed for his failure in Hiep Hoa. He had become village secretary at a time when great leadership and courage were required, but he possessed neither of these attributes. What he did possess was a formidable sense of cunning and self-preservation. Having studiously avoided military service for years, Chua had twice opted to serve as a political cadre. When life in this role had become too risky, he had rallied to the government, but only when he sensed that his defection would guarantee him more security than his life as a defunct cadre. I prefaced my report to Colonel Weissinger with this assessment of Chua's motivations:

At present, Hai Chua is convinced that the government will eventually defeat the Vietcong. If he should ever become convinced that the Communists are about to emerge victorious, he would probably rally to them if he felt he could get away with it. Such an action would be befitting a member of the "U" or "yes" religion to which he has confessed adherence. In this respect, he no doubt remains typical of most of his friends and neighbors in Hiep Hoa village.

During my conversations with Chua and his colleague, I repeatedly cautioned myself not to accept at face value the perceptions of two disaffected Vietcong. Could I reasonably expect the picture that they would paint of the revolutionary movement in their village to be accurate?

Yet I could not ignore the similarity of the two men's accounts of life in Hiep Hoa. Both described a rapidly changing situation in the village during which the Vietcong had been subjected to intense military pressure once the Americans had arrived in force. In fact, both men admitted they had lost faith in the revolution when they realized that the military reversals of 1968 and 1969 portended the future.

Initially, I experienced a sense of wonder at the revelation that the Vietcong could experience fear too. The dreaded enemy, "Ol' Charlie," was human after all. Dating from my Fort Benning days, I had unconsciously formed a mental image of the Vietcong as hard-core, fanatical, clever men who were somehow exempt from normal human frailties. That Vietcong could experience fear, take mistresses, or scheme for "secure" jobs had simply not entered my mind. As my tour in Duc Hue progressed, I would find it increasingly difficult to dehumanize our adversaries.

Hai Chua's vivid description of the 1968 Tet Offensive made a deep impression on me. Prior to our conversation, all I had known about Tet was that havoc had been wreaked in South Vietnam's cities by fanatical Vietcong troops who had absorbed heavy losses in the process. When Hai Chua recalled Tet, he described the unforgettable slaughter of the exposed Vietcong light infantry by American and South Vietnamese firepower. As a Vietcong cadre in a tiny village near the Cambodian border, Chua could not fathom the psychological forces that the Tet assaults had triggered in the United States. To him, Tet had caused the people to lose faith in the Vietcong and precipitated a drop in the "revolutionary morale" of the insurgents themselves.

Similarly, I had always associated the 1970 cross-border operations into Cambodia by American and South Vietnamese troops with the controversy over Cambodian neutrality—or with the tragedy of Kent State. But to Hai Chua and his Vietcong friends, these operations had meant something quite different. The destruction of their Cambodian sanctuary had been disastrous for the Hiep Hoa Vietcong. Overnight, Chua and his comrades had been denied the convenience of their medical facilities, schools, ammunition dumps, and food storage sites. Cambodia (Chua called it *phia sau*, "the rear") had been a place to go to escape the pressures of "the front" *(phia truoc)*. The denial of these facilities had brought home to Chua and his fellow cadre that there was literally "no place to hide" from the increasingly lethal war.

Through Chua's eyes, I had my first look at the remarkable organizational talent of the Vietcong. Even on the village level, the stress on the absolute need for a disciplined organization was evident. The Hiep Hoa village Vietcong had a clear chain of command, carefully compartmented so that one member's knowledge of the hierarchy was often limited to one contact man. Village cadre were under continuous pressure to establish "revolutionary presence" in every hamlet to insure that missions generated from above could be accomplished countrywide. Presence in a hamlet might mean in good times an established hamlet guerrilla unit, such as Chua described in Hiep Hoa. Or, if the balance of military power did not permit this, then a single Vietcong agent in the hamlet might suffice. Either way, there was intense pressure on the village revolutionary committee to insure that no "white hamlets" be permitted to exist in South Vietnam's twenty-five-hundred-odd villages (a white hamlet was one in which there was no Vietcong presence). Because of this, one of the distinctive features of the Vietcong movement in Hau Nghia and elsewhere was the omnipresence of the Communists. The Vietcong weren't literally everywhere as their propaganda would have liked people to believe, but their organization was sufficiently developed so that one could never be certain whether or not there was a Communist agent in a given group. This organizational achievement enabled the Vietcong to accomplish many feats that would have been otherwise impossible—the most significant of which was the control of the country's rural population by a relatively small elite.

The more I learned about the revolution, the more I was struck by the unenviable position of the villagers of rural Vietnam. Hai Chua was not the only Vietnamese teenager who had grown up to learn the art of draft-dodging. The village-oriented Vietnamese did not have much use for central governments of any persuasion; yet, since 1946, war had been raging in their land over who should sit in Saigon. Hai Chua referred often to the mistake of the French in trying to run the countryside from the district capital, and his words conveyed the clear message that the peasants in his hamlet considered the sugar mill to be a faraway place. In fact, it was in the district town, little more than two or three kilometers from Chua's native hamlet. The world of the Vietnamese peasant ended at the entrance to his village.

The task of the Vietcong and the government was thus a formidable one. Both struggled to secure the loyalty and cooperation of the traditionally politically apathetic peasantry. For the Vietcong, this task was complicated by the fact that South Vietnamese law made them criminal

offenders. As the political "outs," they could be hunted like animals—
and they were. Hai Chua graphically described what this meant to the
life-style of those who supported the revolution.

How did the Vietcong manage to mobilize volunteers in the face of the
Americanized war and the new dangers posed by the Phoenix campaign?
What kind of a fool would choose to serve such a cause, particularly after
the Tet debacle? I learned in Duc Hue that the typical Communist recruit
was a poor or landless peasant who could more easily accept the Communists' unique depiction of Vietnamese history.

According to this history, the Saigon government consisted of "country-selling puppets" who represented foreign interests. Communist political officers explained that Vietnam was one country, temporarily divided
by the Geneva Accords. The people in the northern half of the country
lived in peace and harmony under socialism, while their southern brethren were enslaved by the Americans and their "corrupt puppets." Since
the stubborn imperialists had refused to allow the reunification of the
country by free elections in 1956, armed struggle was the only way to
liberate the "oppressed" southern half of the country. But the southerners
themselves had been corrupted by the Americans and frequently did not
understand how miserable they actually were. Hence, they had to be
"educated" concerning their own plight so that they could unite under
the banner of the revolution to rid the country of foreign domination.
Hence, to the Vietcong cadre who accepted this dogma, a sacred mission
—a country-saving endeavor—was the justification for the personal risks
involved in challenging the Saigon government.

Political reality also shaped up in black and white to the non-Communist southerner. He and his fellow rice farmers wanted no part of Ho Chi
Minh's socialism. Like their Communist adversaries, they too did not like
foreign influence in Vietnam. Virtually all Vietnamese of any political
stripe would admit to anti-French, anti-Chinese, anti-Japanese, and, if
pressed, anti-American sentiments. But the non-Communist southerner
viewed the American presence in South Vietnam as a necessary, temporary condition—to be tolerated only as long as required. The Vietnamese
knew that they had big enemies and that they therefore needed a big
friend. No one in Saigon needed reminding that the Soviet Union and
China stood behind North Vietnam, the Vietcong's "great socialist rear."

Many of South Vietnam's most virulent anti-Communists were ethnic
North Vietnamese Catholics who had fled to the south following the
1954 Geneva Accords. (Approximately nine hundred thousand northerners migrated south during this period. Most of them were Catholic. Communist cadre say that these people were "tricked" or abducted when

Catholic priests allegedly told their flocks that the Virgin Mary was going to the south and that the faithful should follow. The refugees themselves state that they had no use for Ho Chi Minh's brand of socialism in the north.) These North Vietnamese Catholics formed the nucleus of anti-Communist sentiment in South Vietnam. They rejected communism on religious grounds and because they saw the Communists as purveyors of a foreign ideology—Soviet and Chinese Marxism-Leninism. Many South Vietnamese peasants resented the Vietcong's advocacy of collectivized agriculture; the expropriation of private property was viewed distastefully as un-Vietnamese by both the middle-class peasantry and the small but growing class of city dwellers. Virtually all South Vietnamese had heard of the revolt of the North Vietnamese rice farmers in 1956 when Ho Chi Minh's new regime had attempted to force collectivization. Like the Vietcong, the non-Communist southerners saw the many flaws of the Saigon government. The difference was that most South Vietnamese preferred the endemic corruption of the purse of their government to the corruption of the spirit of Hanoi-style communism.

And so the struggle progressed, with the hapless rice farmers of Hiep Hoa caught forlornly in the middle. By night, disciplined Communist political officers explained over and over to the villagers the realities of their "plight," while during the day, government civil servants laid down barrages of anti-Communist exhortations ("Don't listen to what the Communists *say*, but pay close attention to what the Communists *do!*"). Both sides recruited for military manpower relentlessly, and both sides equally demanded the loyalty of the peasants. Thus, a rice farmer in Hiep Hoa could easily find himself sitting under a banner at midnight, participating in an antigovernment rally during which he might play the role of an outraged and exploited peasant, under the watchful eye of a Communist propaganda cadre. The following morning, the same farmer could send his children to the new, government-built school and then walk to the village office to vote in a local election—this time under the watchful eye of a government hamlet chief. The village Vietcong would boast in their report that ". . . sixty outraged farmers of our village attended a rally to protest the policies of the puppet regime. Brother Ba Den expressed his fervent hope that the 1971–72 Dry Season Offensive will result in the liberation of his village. So far, 90 percent of the villagers have actively thrown their support to the cause of the revolution." At the same time the Hiep Hoa village chief would inform his superiors that "more than 95 percent of the villagers voted in the recent election, with anti-Communist candidates receiving the near unanimous support of the people."

My first exposure to a Vietcong document had been a report on the situation in Hiep Hoa village. The report was a detailed account of the state of the revolution in the village, and depicted the people as increasingly resentful of the "dark schemes" of the Saigon government. Page after page of statistics described the "revolutionary spirit" of the villagers. Entries included attendance figures for propaganda meetings; the number of families that had paid the rice tax; the number of government soldiers who had been urged that month to resist their superiors; how many families had paid the livestock tax; and how many families had helped to erect propaganda signs. These categories were covered in that report and virtually all others like it, and for the novice, to read such reports was to be alarmed. But I soon learned that one couldn't fathom the real meaning of such rhetoric unless one understood the position of the peasantry between the two sides. In this sense, it was essential to grasp one key concept—the meaning of the word "support."

Hai Chua chose to describe 80 percent of the people of Hiep Hoa as members of the "yes" group, which was his way of describing the apolitical sentiments of his neighbors. Put another way, the vast majority of the people of Hiep Hoa were quite capable of supporting whichever side seemed to be winning the political-military struggle. Thus, as the French position in the village began to weaken, Chua pointed out, support for the Vietminh rose sharply. Similarly, in the waning days of the Diem regime, many Hiep Hoa villagers found it convenient to cast their lot with the Vietcong. Vietnamese villagers had become adept at playing the role of the political chameleon. Hence, much of the statistical evidence of support that appeared in both government and Vietcong documents was actually no more than a meaningless recitation of actions taken by the peasantry to accommodate *both* sides. Both sides could and did claim extensive popular support in the countryside based upon the actions of the world's most flexible peasantry.

Under such circumstances, it was little wonder that we Americans were often mystified by the events that unfolded around us. American confusion over the meaning of the peasantry's behavior caused considerable difficulties during the war. For example, it was axiomatic that villagers were "VC sympathizers" if they stood by passively as American or South Vietnamese troops entered a booby-trapped area. One infamous bit of television newsreel footage even shows a U.S. Marine setting fire to a peasant's home because enemy sniper fire had come from the village. On the sole occasion when an American infantry unit operated in Duc Hue during my tour, Major Eby had experienced difficulty in convincing its commander that he simply could not "blow away" one of our hamlets if his unit took sniper fire from that direction. The commonly accepted presumption, of course, was that people who permitted snipers to use their homes, or who "didn't know" about Vietcong activities in their village were certainly either Communists or Communist sympathizers. The connection made sense to thousands of young Americans who struggled to complete their twelve-month hitch and return home in one piece. Most of them had no way of knowing that the widespread refusal of the Vietnamese peasantry to get involved in the war that raged around them was really a testament to the Vietcong's organizational effectiveness. The Communist apparatus extended down to the hamlet level and gave the revolution the leverage that was so crucial to its survival.

By 1965, the villagers of Hiep Hoa had been fought over by Communist and government forces for nearly twenty years. The rules of survival in this environment had thus long since become clear. Rule number one was "Never inform the government of Communist activities." In Hiep Hoa, most of the villagers were well aware which families were revolutionary families and who constituted the village's party committee. But no one could be certain of the loyalties of every one of his neighbors. Each Vietcong village committee had civilian and military proselyting officers whose jobs were to recruit agents and sympathizers in the village. Virtually every hamlet in Vietnam had at least one clandestine informant who would not hesitate to report to the Vietcong the name of a farmer who warned the Americans about a booby trap. The Vietcong's organization was thus the major device by which the revolution insured the silence of the people—and this silence was sufficient to frustrate our efforts.

Little wonder that we had difficulty in understanding this environment. The intrigue and duplicity of the insurgency escaped us, as did the real meaning of living under the ever present threat of a violent death at the hands of one's neighbors. For most Americans in Vietnam, the dynamics of the Vietnamese villager's dilemma were impossible to grasp, and the barriers to understanding posed by the linguistic and cultural differences between our two peoples were insurmountable.

III

NGUYEN VAN PHICH

Colonel Weissinger was pleased with the results of the Hiep Hoa project and seemed convinced that I was not wasting my tour shuffling papers. But Major Eby was a different story. The Hai Chua interviews had yielded interesting information, but it was of little direct use for our most immediate task—the identification and destruction of the Vietcong shadow government. To Major Eby, this meant only one thing. We must eliminate the Vietcong organization in Tan My village.

The first major break in the Tan My case had actually occurred just prior to my arrival in Duc Hue. Forty-three-year-old Nguyen van Phich, the executive officer of a Vietcong local force company, became fed up with his life as a revolutionary soldier and rallied to the government. Phich was a native of Tan My village—a landless peasant with five children. Faced with perpetual poverty, he had been the perfect recruit for the revolution. Attracted by the Vietcong's promises of land reform, Phich had worked himself up through the ranks during a six-year career carrying a rifle as a guerrilla soldier. Much of this time he had spent living in bunkers and fighting against the Americans and the ever growing South Vietnamese army. Encouraged by his superiors' assurances of an impending popular uprising, Phich and his comrades attacked Duc Hue district town in 1968. The attack failed, the promised general uprising never materialized, and the twice-wounded Phich began to wonder whether there was any hope for a Communist victory. Almost 90 percent of his men had been killed, wounded, or captured during the abortive Tet attacks.

Like Hai Chua, Phich had been dismayed at the 1970 invasion of Cambodia and its destructive impact on Vietcong sanctuaries. At the

41

same time, he noticed that even the Saigon government's militia platoons had been rearmed with the M-16 rifle, whereas his own troops were so short of ammunition that they were under standing orders to avoid combat.

But the disheartened Phich couldn't bring himself to accept the government's offer of amnesty. Like Hai Chua, he suspected a trick and feared that if he gave himself up, he would be tortured and sent to prison. Ultimately, Phich's wife had played a key role in reassuring him that ralliers to the government were being well treated, and he had surrendered himself in Bao Trai in late 1970.

Phich's wife had been right. The government had received him civilly, if not warmly. But the Vietcong were not to be so forgiving. The Communists began to send him warnings through his neighbors, threatening both him and his family if he refused to "return to the revolution." Phich's response to the Vietcong intimidation was to lead government troops to a cache of precious small arms ammunition. In this way, he burned his bridges and became irrevocably committed to the defeat of the Vietcong.

Colonel Weissinger had taken an instant liking to Phich. The colonel had generously assisted Phich, who was penniless, as the former Vietcong leader strove to adjust to his new role as breadwinner for his long-neglected family. Phich and the colonel had spent long hours talking about the revolution. Thus, by the time I arrived on the scene, Colonel Weissinger had already accomplished the first step in the art of defector exploitation—the establishment of rapport with the subject. In fact, the colonel had already recruited Phich to work for our advisory team. His job was to convince other Vietcong in Tan My village to join him as a rallier.

Major Eby had launched Phich on the Tan My project several weeks before my arrival. With the grudging consent of Major Nghiem (who didn't trust any rallier), Phich was composing letters to his former comrades and delivering them through their families in Tan My village. Phich was actually illiterate, which necessitated that he dictate his thoughts to one of the team's interpreters, Sergeant Trung. Trung, a former journalist, would then compose the actual letters. In these letters, Phich assured his old friends that he was being well treated, and urged them to "return to the republic" and resume normal lives with their families.

Phich and Sergeant Trung visited Tan My several times each week to deliver the letters to the Vietcong families. During these visits, the two men would do their best to urge the Vietcong women to assist in "saving" their husbands. After a short visit ("Don't stay in the village too long"), the two men would return to Duc Hue. Phich would immediately immerse himself in *ba xi de* (Vietnamese rice whiskey), while Trung would report to Major Eby on the results of the day's operation.

One of the first steps taken by the major when I arrived was to introduce me to Phich and Trung as their new boss. Eby had emphasized at the time how important it was for Phich's efforts to yield at least one defector from Tan My. Such a break would please Colonel Weissinger and give us additional leverage in the village itself. Major Eby never tired of reminding me that he expected results in Tan My.

My first inclination was to put Phich on the wagon, since he seemed perpetually drunk. Sergeant Trung advised against this and assured me that Phich was sufficiently disciplined to dry himself out prior to each foray into Tan My. According to Trung, Phich's cooperation in the project was difficult to retain. Depriving him of his beloved rice whiskey could mean the end of our efforts. Since the last thing I wanted to do was to jeopardize my new project, I dropped the subject reluctantly.

I also learned that my new operative's needs went beyond alcohol. Phich had to be supplied regularly with American cigarettes, fed in our mess hall, and given weekly subsidies of his cash flow—especially after our interpreters lured him into one of their nightly card games. My initial impression of Mr. Phich was thus not very positive. I couldn't picture him as a combat leader of the Vietcong, no matter how hard I tried. Later, however, I was to change my mind.

Phich and Trung wasted no time in relating to me their frustrations as they attempted to convince the Tan My village Vietcong to defect to the government. Trung showed me copies of the letters they had sent and explained that none of the Vietcong women would admit to having seen their husbands for months, or even years. Instead, they insisted that "he went to Cambodia in 1967," or "he was killed by an air strike during Tet of 1968." Phich, of course, knew better. In most cases, he had even talked with the letters' addressees just before he had rallied. One unforgettable young wife always insisted with a twinkle in her eye that she hadn't seen her husband for two years, even though she was six-months pregnant and had a nine-month-old son on her breast. During all of the visits, the pattern was the same, and the women never rejected the letters. Phich was certain that the recipients were actually reading his words.

Sergeant Trung was dissatisfied with the project from the beginning. He simply did not believe that any of the Tan My village revolutionaries would heed Phich's call, and he regarded the repeated trips into Tan My as both futile and risky. Trung openly told me that he had no desire to be

the target of a Vietcong ambush while on a postal mission in Tan My.
When I asked him what it would take to allay his fears, Trung smiled
and, in the typically indirect way of the Vietnamese, explained that
what was required was not available. I countered with typical American
directness by insisting that he level with me and let me worry about the
availability of resources. I will always remember his reply as my first
lesson in the dynamics of the advisor-counterpart problem that so
plagued us as we struggled to assist the Vietnamese.

"You see, sir," Trung began, "what we need in order to continue our
Tan My visits safely is an escort of four or five soldiers from one of the
militia platoons in Tan My. They are local men and wouldn't alienate
the people. But only the district chief can authorize this, and he has
already turned down Major Eby once before when asked, claiming other
operational commitments. In fact, sir, Major Nghiem could easily spare
a few soldiers to escort us, but he doesn't want to. He resents our project
because if we succeed in Tan My, our success will underscore his failure.
We are paid with American money, and Phich smokes American cigarettes. Major Nghiem treated Phich poorly when he rallied and continues
to snub him. He has told me that he thinks our trips into Tan My are a
waste of time, while at the same time he smiles at Major Eby and pre-
tends that he supports the project. It is the same with the Tan My village
officials. They are afraid of what Phich and I might accomplish because
our success will make them look bad. So Phich and I are in the middle.
We work for you, but we must live with our people. You must understand that most Vietnamese want to defeat the Vietcong, but they are
proud and want to do it in their own way. They often don't realize that
this attitude is dangerous and really helps the Vietcong. Nothing in Duc
Hue will work without the support of Major Nghiem, sir, and we don't
have it. That's why I think it is best that we forget the whole project, get
Phich a job in Bao Trai, and move him and his family to where they will
be safe."

Phich had sat quietly during Trung's comments on their plight. Since
Phich didn't speak English, Trung had punctuated his comments with
brief Vietnamese explanations of what he was saying. Phich had nodded
enthusiastic agreement each time. When Trung finished, Phich added his
opinion.

"Colonel Weissinger has been good to me, Dai Uy, and that is why I
agreed to this project in the first place. I want to help him, and I will
continue to cooperate. As you know, I am a poor man who needs money
to take care of his family. But you must try and make your superiors
understand that the answer to the problem of the Vietcong in Tan My

village is not to be found in polite letters. The only way to solve the problem of the Communist rule of Tan My is to drive them out of the village."

Did Phich really believe that the Vietcong ruled Tan My? After all, I probed, had he not agreed with the accuracy of the Phoenix office's list of Tan My cadre—a list that contained only a handful of names? How then could he say that the Vietcong ruled Tan My's five thousand citizens when there were over five hundred government soldiers permanently stationed in the village?

When sober, Phich was not a demonstrative person, but he laughed aloud at my questions. "Dai Uy, it's a joke to say that there are only a handful of Vietcong in Tan My village. The list in the Phoenix office is only a small part of the whole picture."

But why hadn't he come forth at the time and given a complete list of the Vietcong currently operating in Tan My?

"You must understand, Dai Uy, that my unit operated in villages all over the district—not just in Tan My. So I am not completely familiar with every Vietcong in the village, especially the political cadre. When I rallied, I didn't trust anyone, and I was not inclined to volunteer information. No one asked me about anything other than village-level cadre in Tan My, so I was content to answer only that question."

—Phich then launched into a description of the situation in Tan My village that erased any doubts about who was the authority in its hamlets. If there was such a thing as a "model revolutionary village" in Duc Hue, then Tan My was it.

Phich explained that Tan My had always been a perfect place for the Communists to operate. During the war against the French, the Vietminh were so strong in Tan My that the French built an underground fort for the village's garrison. The fort's remains were still being used at this time as the headquarters of the government militia unit in the village. One of the major reasons why the insurgents favored Tan My was the terrain. The village was surrounded on three sides by swamplands which provided excellent hiding areas. Only one road connected the village's interior to the main road, a feature that simplified the Vietcong's military planning.

Phich estimated that the people of Tan My were at least 10 percent Vietcong sympathizers. Progovernment families numbered 20 percent or so, but these people all lived on the main road and in the vicinity of the village office. Thus, in the village's six outlying hamlets, more than four thousand people lived, of whom well over 10 percent had good revolutionary credentials. Most of the other families were neutral, which meant that the government could not rely on them to assist in its efforts to bring the insurgency under control. For this reason, it was easier for the Vietcong to operate in Tan My village than in other areas of Duc Hue. In Tan My, the people would warn the Vietcong of government ambushes by placing signal lamps in their windows. Revolutionary families sheltered the village's guerrillas and brought them food when they were forced to hide in their secret bunkers. Food and medicine were procured at the local market for the guerrillas and political cadre by teenaged girls, who quite often were in love with the men whom they were helping.

Most of the people paid taxes to the Vietcong revolutionary committee. Frequent nocturnal political rallies were held by the insurgents to persuade the villagers to support the revolution. Phich explained that Tan My village was also a favorite place for high-ranking Vietcong cadre to visit when they wanted to check on the status of the movement at the "front." Tan My was often chosen to receive visitors because the village organization could almost guarantee the security of the visitors; hence the title "model revolutionary village." Phich himself had often provided security troops from his company for these visitors. He recalled that such missions were fairly routine, and simplified by the fact that the government forces in the village tacitly cooperated with the Vietcong. Even though the government's 58th Regional Forces (RF) Group conducted daily day and night operations in the village, these posed no problem for the Vietcong. The government unit had been in Tan My long enough to know what areas of the village to avoid in order to prevent any bloodshed. Ambush patrols usually went to the same site several nights a week, while daytime operations consisted of sweeps through the hamlets that carefully skirted the heavily booby-trapped Vietcong hiding areas. Lest there be any doubt about which areas were unsafe, the Tan My Vietcong had thoughtfully marked them with warning signs. These signs had a skull and crossbones emblem and were inscribed *Tu Dia* or "Death Area." They served a dual purpose: the local people were thereby warned of the danger—especially the children, and the RF soldiers were neatly guided by them around the perimeters of enemy hiding areas.

Under such circumstances, the Tan My Vietcong had long been able to move freely about the village. For this reason, Phich concluded, we would not be seeing too many defections from their ranks. Phich repeated that Major Nghiem would have to exert intense military pressure against the Tan My revolutionary organization on its own soil. This would deprive the insurgents of their sense of security and increase our chances of getting additional defectors from their tightly knit organization.

Colonel Weissinger had made a wise move the day that he had hired Phich. Until this conversation, I hadn't even been certain that Tan My was heavily penetrated by the Communists. All I had to go on was Colonel Weissinger's insistence that this was so, backed up by the infamous captured document in which the village had been lauded. Phich's description of his native village confirmed for me what Colonel Weissinger's intuition had told him several months earlier. The Tan My organization was an extensive one—a ripe target that was long overdue to be attacked. And the man who had just described it was the main weapon for such an offensive.

Phich had said that he wasn't certain about the details of much of the Tan My organization, but he had also insisted that he could learn more about it if given secure access to the village's hamlets. I produced a map of Tan My, and Phich began to educate me on the nuances of the Vietnamese extended family. Jumping from hamlet to hamlet, he began to name his many cousins, aunts, uncles, nieces, and nephews who lived in Tan My. Phich was related to virtually half of the population of Tan My village. Here was the key to unlock the Tan My puzzle. To step up the pressure on the Tan My organization, we needed specific information on every Vietcong in the village. Who were they? In which hamlets did they operate? Who hid in which base areas, and who carried food and medicine to them? How many higher-ranking cadre were normally in the village, and which of the six hamlets did the Communists regard as the most secure? Could not Phich learn the answers to these and other questions during his sorties into Tan My? In short, if Major Eby could procure the district chief's consent to provide a military escort for Phich and Trung, couldn't we use the letter delivery missions as a cover for the two men's efforts to develop and exploit a village-wide network of informants?

Both Phich and Trung agreed that this change in the thrust of the Tan My project was feasible, but neither of them seemed enthusiastic about the idea. Sergeant Trung bluntly told me that he was an interpreter, not a spy. Project Tan My was an improper use of his services, and I should understand that he had a wife and children. Trung also argued that even if the project did succeed in bringing the Tan My Vietcong structure into focus, the district chief would take no action on any information that he and Phich might uncover.

Phich nodded his agreement to this latter statement. He personally wasn't worried about the risks of the project—the Vietcong had already marked him for elimination. But, like Trung, he had no confidence in either Major Nghiem or the government troops in Tan My.

Ultimately, both men agreed to undertake the project on the condition that they receive an escort for their missions. In addition, Trung would have to be compensated for the heightened risk involved in the project. He was the stabilizing influence on Phich, without whom the whole endeavor would fail.

As always, Major Eby was as enthusiastic and cooperative as one could hope. He promptly secured Major Nghiem's reluctant consent to provide an escort for the team during their daily journeys into Tan My. At Sergeant Trung's insistence, we deliberately avoided telling the good district chief of the new direction that the project was about to take. Had Major Nghiem known that the two men were collecting intelligence for the American advisors, he would have been displeased.

After less than three weeks in Duc Hue, I had already begun to regard our Vietnamese counterparts as adversaries in the effort to defeat the Vietcong. I had fallen victim to every pitfall our instructors at Fort Bragg had described. As an American military man, schooled in the direct, aggressive approach to problem-solving, I was going to get the job done, with or without the help of the Vietnamese. As such, I had become a perfect disciple of Colonel Weissinger, whom I had faulted for this attitude a few short weeks earlier.

Phich and Trung finally commenced their intelligence-gathering missions into Tan My in the spring of 1971. Capitalizing on Phich's many relatives and contacts in the village, the two men quickly succeeded in developing a healthy network of informants throughout the village. By tapping into this source, we were able to fill in the details of the Vietcong structure that Phich had described earlier. Each evening, the two men would report the results of the day's operations to me and receive instructions for the next mission. Phich and Trung cross-checked with their sympathizers all references to Vietcong personalities that had appeared in the many Communist documents that had fallen into our hands during the past year. "Who is Brother Sau?" "Is Sister Bay a cadre or a guerrilla—or are there two people with the same name?" Names quickly began to fall in place, as did the specific areas of operation of the individual insurgents. As the picture began to take shape, it became clear that we had opened the proverbial Pandora's box in Tan My. The "handful" of Vietcong politicians and the "squad" of guerrillas began to emerge as an organization of considerable size operating, as Phich had said, under the noses of the village's government soldiers. If anything, Phich's original depiction of the Tan My organization had understated the extent of revolutionary activity in the village.

After only two months of the two men's operations, their efforts enabled us to state confidently that the Vietcong did in fact control Tan My village, to the extent, we learned, that the revolutionary committee had even become involved in the adjudication of land disputes among the peasants of one hamlet. In my first full report to Colonel Weissinger, I summarized what we had learned from Phich's and Trung's efforts:

Activities of the Vietcong Infrastructure: Including subregion and district-level cadre, at least twenty confirmed cadre operate regularly in the village, and we have a way to go before it will be possible to state with assurance that we know who most of the Tan My Vietcong are. However, our picture of Tan My is the clearest of our four villages. We know that systematic taxation is carried out by the VC in five of the village's seven hamlets, with 90 percent or more of the people contributing. Civilian and military proselyting activities are carried out on a large scale . . . the people have been "educated" against the government's land clearing program, the PSDF (People's Self Defense Force—a government militia composed of teenagers and old men), and South Vietnamese military involvement in Cambodia. Recruitment, although a weak spot of the Tan My VC, is far from nonexistent. Since 1 February, eight teenaged members of the PSDF have been recruited by the Tan My VC, of whom four are currently operating as guerrillas in the village. One of them has been killed, one captured, and two have rallied. The VC have offered a 10,000 piaster reward to any member of the PSDF who brings his weapon to them. Security operations in the village have been particularly effective. Recently, several government informants have been discovered and either warned or killed.

In summary, Project Tan My has revealed an extremely healthy, effective infrastructure that is performing those tasks levied upon it by Vietcong higher headquarters. Its operations are being carried out with the tacit and sometimes the express consent of the people, who almost universally deny the government information about Vietcong activities. One reason for this is that the government has not provided adequate security for the people. However, in Tan My, the reasons run deeper than this. The people of one hamlet have said that the VC have one big advantage over the government, and that is leadership. The Vietcong leaders in Tan My are in many cases older men who are respected by the villagers. They are almost always natives of the hamlets of Tan My. Many of the government officials, especially the hamlet chiefs, are younger men who are not natives and who spend little or no time in the hamlets.

This report also detailed the names of many Tan My Vietcong, their organization into cells, and which cells operated in the village's different hamlets. Short of pinpointing exact bunker locations, the report could not have been more specific. Phich and Trung winced when I told them that Major Eby had given a copy of the report to Major Nghiem, and for good reason. For after the major had smilingly accepted it from Major Eby, he had called Phich and Trung into his office and chastised them for their disloyalty in passing information to the Americans. And as Phich and Trung had predicted, he took no measures in reaction to the information contained in the report. The following day it was business as usual in Tan My village.

Faced with this situation, the ever impatient Colonel Weissinger perceived the perfect opportunity to solve both the problems of Major Nghiem and Tan My. He was thoroughly fed up with Major Nghiem's obstructionism, and he seized upon this opportunity to discredit him. He did this by making a copy of the Tan My report available to his counterpart in Bao Trai, the new province chief—Major Nghiem's boss. Colonel Weissinger had decided that the removal of Major Nghiem was essential if we were to make any progress in Tan My village. With his long tour in Hau Nghia drawing to a close, the determined colonel was resolved to clean up the Tan My mess before his departure.

The province chief was an ethnic North Vietnamese named Thanh. Colonel Thanh had only been in Hau Nghia since the beginning of the year, but he had already impressed Americans and Vietnamese alike with his directness and courage. Bespectacled and diminutive, Colonel Thanh was given to donning a pair of black pajamas and riding a Honda motorbike into Hau Nghia's villages. In this way, Thanh boasted that he was able to acquire a good feel for what the people were saying. Colonel Thanh's solitary sojourns into the villages also enabled him to learn what his government officials were (or were not) doing. More than one unfortunate government bureaucrat had been surprised and humiliated by this "peasant" who turned into the province chief.

Thanh had a wife and ten children, and he was widely respected as a decent man of humble means. We American advisors could hardly believe our luck at having an honest, aggressive, and hard-working officer in command. Surely here was the man to end the Vietcong menace to Hau Nghia.

Shortly after I had forwarded the Tan My report to Colonel Weissinger, I received word to proceed to Bao Trai. Colonel Thanh had invited me to dinner and desired that I come prepared to discuss the enemy situation in Duc Hue district. I was cautioned not to inform anyone at the district other than Major Eby of the invitation. Colonel Thanh did not want Major Nghiem to know that he was tapping American advisory personnel for a clarification of the situation in Duc Hue.

As I drove my jeep over the rutted road to Bao Trai, the prospect of getting some action in Tan My dominated my thoughts. If only we could win Colonel Thanh's confidence, we had enough information to make life uncomfortable for the Tan My village shadow government.

I was one nervous young captain when I followed Colonel Weissinger through the front door of Colonel Thanh's aging stucco villa. Thanh himself greeted us and introduced me to his wife, an attractive and young-looking woman at thirty-nine, in spite of having borne ten children. The fare was Vietnamese, served by Mrs. Thanh and an enlisted orderly, and I took advantage of the rare social occasion to practice my Vietnamese with the hostess.

After dinner, Colonel Weissinger politely excused himself, pleading that he had a backlog of paperwork awaiting him in his quarters. Mrs. Thanh disappeared into the kitchen, and the province chief unfolded a large map and laid it on the table.

"Now, we talk," he directed firmly. He had read my report on Tan My and wanted me to discuss Duc Hue's other three villages.

Still nervous, I began slowly, using a grease pencil to make notes on the map. We talked for almost two hours, during which I quickly learned that Colonel Thanh was every bit the dynamic, straightforward person that I had heard about. He seemed genuinely interested in hearing what I had to say, and he interrupted me repeatedly with questions that showed he was grasping the gravity of the situation in Duc Hue.

Colonel Thanh admitted to me that Major Nghiem had not truthfully reported the situation in Duc Hue. Nghiem had consistently described the Duc Hue Vietcong as a weak, disorganized, "platoon-sized" force— the same thing he had told me when I arrived. Nghiem had concealed the fact that the villages of his district actually harbored virulent Vietcong organizations complete with guerrilla units, security cadre, and other supporting forces.

I emphasized to Colonel Thanh that we believed our information on the extent of the Vietcong organization to be extremely incomplete. If we knew about sixty to seventy-five Vietcong operating in Tan My alone, then it was most likely that the actual number was considerably higher. Hence, we suspected, but could not prove, that our other villages were equally heavily penetrated. Only in Hiep Hoa village were the Vietcong in any difficulty.

Colonel Thanh's face betrayed his disappointment and anger. He explained that he was experiencing difficulties with his new job, particularly in discovering which of his subordinates he could trust and which he should watch carefully. Then he asked me what I thought of Major Nghiem.

The question took me off guard, and I hesitated. Thanh sensed my discomfort and hastily assured me that our conversation was off the record. He added with a satisfied smile that it was my duty to share my thoughts with him openly.

I had accepted Colonel Thanh's invitation knowing full well that he was going to pick my brain on the enemy situation, and I had come to Bao Trai prepared for that. I was not prepared to be grilled on the friendly situation, even though it had become glaringly evident to me by that point in my tour that the friendlies in Duc Hue were tacitly aiding the Vietcong just as surely as if there were a cease-fire in our district. I sensed that Colonel Thanh and I were getting along well, and feared that an evasive response to his pointed query would destroy whatever rapport we had established. And so, with a silent apology to Major Eby, I proceeded to analyze his counterpart.

Major Nghiem, I ventured, was a good and well-intentioned man. He seemed to lead a humble life-style, quite different from the stereotype of the corrupt district chief on the take. Unfortunately, he did not seem to be approaching the war in Duc Hue at all correctly. The major had even told me that he believed his primary responsibility was to "take care of his people," which meant to him that he should avoid rocking the military boat. Major Nghiem thus had a distaste for any military operations that would disrupt the lives of the people of Duc Hue, even though such operations were sometimes required to eliminate the Vietcong. Major Nghiem was reluctant to expose his militia troops to the dangers of enemy fire or booby traps. He refused to run military operations near Buddhist pagodas because the ground was sacred, but the Vietcong knew this and hid in those places. I told Colonel Thanh that Major Nghiem was a compassionate man who was simply ill suited for the job of wartime district chief. He had good intentions and seemed to want to eliminate the Vietcong, but he did not want to pay the price for success.

I also suggested to Colonel Thanh that it was inconceivable to Americans and Vietnamese alike how Major Nghiem could order almost a thousand troops to the field on a seven-day "high point" campaign during which time the results would be 100 percent negative. Not one friendly soldier was wounded by a booby trap, not a single enemy was sighted—let alone engaged—and not a single bunker or cache was discovered during Duc Hue's most recent "offensive." Such a box score could only mean that accommodation was the order of business in Duc Hue. Major Nghiem's soldiers knew the location of the enemy base areas and carefully avoided them. Their leaders, from Major Nghiem on down, put no pressure on them for results. If this were not the case, it would not be possible for government operations in our district to be consistently uneventful "walks in the sun." And the Tan My village Vietcong could not have multiplied as they had if Major Nghiem's forces were genuinely committed to the defeat of the insurgency. It had been almost a year since the last encounter with the Vietcong in Tan My village.

Thanh nodded his agreement and shifted our discussion to the question of remedial actions. What should he do to correct the situation?

I replied that I was an intelligence officer, not a tactician, but that I was certain we were ignoring one of the best possible weapons against the Vietcong—defectors. A week earlier, I had accompanied a government unit on an operation in which a Vietcong defector had led the troops to an enemy bunker complex. When a search revealed that the bunkers were abandoned, the government troops had turned angrily on their guide. I felt certain that, had I not been present, he would have been beaten. The troops had good reasons for disliking former Vietcong, but this should not be allowed to interfere with the proper use of these men. Many defectors were both knowledgeable and aggressive. Given proper treatment and a little incentive, such men could be a valuable asset in our struggle. After all, much of the information that had enabled us to piece together the Tan My village situation had come from Phich, who had been poorly treated by Major Nghiem.

I suggested to Colonel Thanh that he send the province Armed Propaganda Team platoon to Tan My with the mission of eliminating the Vietcong organization there. This unit consisted of some two dozen former Vietcong led by a somewhat unscrupulous but daring former guerrilla named Det. I had recently talked with Det, himself a Tan My native, and knew that he and his men were itching for an assignment more challenging than guarding the perimeter of the Chieu Hoi Center in Bao Trai.

As I bid Colonel Thanh good night, I told him that my favorite trick when playing a losing tennis match had always been to abruptly change my tactics—the assumption being that my current approach was producing defeat. Since I was losing anyway, I had nothing further to lose by a change in game plan. In Tan My village, I reminded the colonel, we were losing.

IV

REVOLUTIONARY JUSTICE

Colonel Thanh's reaction to Major Nghiem's smokescreen was not long in coming. Within a matter of days, he assumed personal responsibility for the restoration of security in Tan My village. Thanh's first move was to implement a recommendation that Colonel Weissinger had repeatedly made. Hau Nghia's crack 305th RF Battalion replaced the ineffective 58th RF Group in Tan My. The commander of the new unit was instructed to report directly to Colonel Thanh rather than to Major Nghiem. At the same time, Colonel Thanh issued M-16 rifles to Det's Armed Propaganda Team platoon and challenged them to clean out Tan My village.

Things began to happen almost immediately in Tan My. On the second day of the new unit's operations in the village, Major Eby and I learned that fighting had broken out in Tan My. We exchanged surprised glances. A daytime contact in Tan My village? No one had seen a Vietcong in the daytime in Duc Hue for months. We rushed to the scene of the action in our jeep, arriving just in time to hear two loud explosions and a chorus of cheers. By the time we pulled up to a group of soldiers next to a bamboo thicket, Colonel Thanh had already landed and dismounted from his helicopter and was examining some documents that had been taken from the bodies of three very dead Vietcong.

Thanh was jubilant as he explained what had happened. Det and his group of plucky ex-Vietcong had joined up that morning with a company of the 305th Battalion on a sweep of one of the enemy base areas that had been described by Phich. The heavily booby-trapped area had always been avoided by the troops of the 58th Group, but not so with the newly arrived 305th. Led by scouts from Det's platoon, the new unit had penetrated the thick bamboo growth and tripped a booby trap in the process. One man had been slightly wounded by the detonation. Several Vietcong had then opened fire on the government troops before fleeing deeper into the undergrowth to a hidden bunker complex. Two of Det's men had gone right in after them, and the brief clash had ended when one of the men had crawled up to the mouth of a bunker and lobbed in two hand grenades.

The three Vietcong had died instantly. Documents found on their shattered bodies identified them as "security cadre" attached to the Tan My village revolutionary committee. Their duties were to perform escort missions for ranking Communist officers and to mete out "revolutionary justice" to traitors. One document of interest was an after-action report of a recent assassination mission. Two of them had stood by the side of the road wearing government uniforms, armed with American-made weapons. When their target appeared, they had merely shot him off his Honda and then melted into the hamlet.

Colonel Thanh proudly pointed out that one of the three men's names appeared on the list of Tan My Vietcong that Phich had given us. The other two men were strangers, proving that the "iceberg theory" was as valid as ever. If we knew about sixty to seventy-five Vietcong in the village, then there were most likely many more.

Major Eby dreaded his next meeting with Major Nghiem. The district chief had lost considerable face during the last two days. Colonel Thanh had been in operational control of the Tan My effort for only a brief time, yet he had already achieved striking results. It was the beginning of the end for Major Nghiem's tenure as district chief.

I didn't have to tell Phich and Trung about my session with Colonel Thanh on Tan My village; the Vietnamese grapevine did it for me. Both men were elated at the turn of events that was symbolized by the transfer of the 58th Group out of the village. Relieved of the fear that their efforts would produce no tangible results, they began to increase their efforts in Tan My, making as many as five trips a week into the village. Concerned for their safety, I cautioned Trung that the establishment of a daily routine in Tan My could lead to their undoing. Trung replied cockily, "Don't worry, Dai Uy, the people will take care of us. We have friends in every hamlet. If the Vietcong try to make trouble, someone will warn us." With that, he and Phich loaded their jeep with clothes and toys for the children of a Tan My Vietcong cadre and headed out of the compound.

Colonel Thanh's troops pressed their attack on the Tan My village Communist organization. Secret bunkers were compromised, clandestine meetings raided, and base areas destroyed. Huge "Rome Plows" of an American land-clearing company erased many of the enemy's tradi-tional hideouts. Det and his men continued to haunt the village's outlying hamlets, areas that had always been considered secure by the Vietcong. Colonel Thanh's confidence in the accuracy of the information we were providing him grew, and he began to react immediately to our daily reports on Tan My. One evening, we reported that Phich's cousin had seen two Vietcong hiding in a swamp on the village perimeter. Within an hour, Colonel Thanh had ordered the entire 305th Battalion to cordon off the swamp. Swift reaction of this type insured that our efforts in Tan My would continue to bear fruit.

Needless to say, the turnaround in Tan My pleased Colonel Weissinger and Major Eby. The colonel had seen in Tan My the opportunity to demonstrate that the war could indeed be won by the Vietnamese with-out the American military. He firmly believed that the key to victory was a more direct and aggressive approach to the war by the Vietnamese. The Tan My project seemed to prove him correct.

Colonel Weissinger visited us in Duc Hue several times before depart-ing in late May. During one such visit, we sat on a bench outside the team house and reflected on the events of the past ninety days. As the sampans floated by on the brown waters of the Vam Co Dong, the colonel recalled how dramatically the security situation in Hau Nghia had improved during his tour as province senior advisor. He was clearly a satisfied man. He saw the Vietcong as an enemy on the verge of defeat, and he puzzled over the obstinate refusal of the remaining cadre to rally to the government.

"Don't they realize how strong this government is? Don't they under-stand how hopeless it is to keep struggling when confronted by so much power and strength?" I can still remember his questions and my inability at the time to provide satisfactory answers. From my association with Vietcong prisoners and defectors, I too sensed by mid-1971 that the revo-lution in Hau Nghia was in great trouble. Even Tan My, the "model revolutionary village," was rapidly becoming too dangerous for the Viet-cong. But even as Colonel Thanh's forces continued to whittle away at the Tan My cadre, I had asked Phich if he felt the dwindling number of village cadre would ever break discipline and surrender. Phich had shaken his head firmly. If their plight in Tan My became unbearable, he explained, the survivors might flee the village, but they would never sur-render. They might hide in the safer base areas along the river, or even flee to Cambodia, but they would never surrender. They were simply too dedicated to give up. I had shared Phich's view with Colonel Weissinger, who shook his head in awe and disbelief at what seemed to him to be such a foolish waste of dedicated lives.

When Colonel Weissinger finally departed Hau Nghia in mid-May, many of the men on Team 43 breathed a sigh of relief. Demanding, impetuous, impatient, and short-fused, the colonel had been a difficult taskmaster. Major Eby probably had the best reason of anyone to desire the colonel's departure, so great had the pressure been on him for results in Tan My. Personally, I had begun my tour with a game plan that involved placating Colonel Weissinger until his departure. Since Major Eby was under the gun from the colonel to achieve results in Tan My, I had had no choice but to direct my efforts toward that goal. My initial motivation had thus been to protect Major Eby from the wrath of Colonel Weissinger—and thereby myself from Major Eby. If this involved the destruction of the Tan My Vietcong, then so be it.

On the eve of Colonel Weissinger's departure, Major Eby and I communed over two tall gin and tonics and agreed that Colonel Weissinger had not been such a bad sort after all. We were pleased that, during his last month, the colonel had begun dropping in on us at Duc Hue in search of good news and stimulating conversation—a part of his eternal quest for answers on the nature of the revolution. Later that night, in a cassette message home, I reported to my parents that I was sorry to see Colonel Weissinger leave. "He was a most perceptive man," I reported, "whose unpopularity stemmed from the fact that he was extremely demanding. He forced me to put out one or two notches above what I might have done under an easier man, with the result that I have become familiar with the situation here much quicker than would have otherwise been possible. Without his personal interest and encouragement, I would have accomplished less since my arrival."

Our new boss was Lt. Col. Gerald T. Bartlett, a young armor officer whose reputation as a "water walker" had preceded his arrival. Virtually all army units have a grapevine that provides the troops with advance intelligence on matters of importance, and the Team 43 scuttlebutt artists had outdone themselves in their advance work on Colonel Bartlett. The new boss, we learned, was variously reported to be a "five-percenter," (that is, promoted early to his present rank); the number one graduate in his Province Senior Advisor Class at the Foreign Service Institute; extremely "hard-core" in the Weissinger sense; and a gentleman who would reverse Colonel Weissinger's restrictive policies and allow overnight passes in Saigon to enable team members to tend to "personal affairs."

We briefed the new colonel in Duc Hue shortly after his arrival. My first impression was that he was in many ways Colonel Weissinger's opposite. Whereas Colonel Weissinger's physical presence had always been intimidating, the new colonel somehow made me feel comfortable. He was a big man—well over six feet—but trim and youthful. His dark hair was trimmed in a not-so-stylish crew cut and already beginning to show some gray. Thinking back, I can't recall exactly why Colonel Bartlett came across so positively at that first meeting—although I suspect it was the sense that he was above all a gentleman. His lead card was politeness and consideration for others, and I received the impression that he was a man whose inner toughness was no doubt formidable—but a card that he seldom had to play.

Our briefing of Colonel Bartlett went smoothly. Major Eby explained his efforts to assist in the training and upgrading of Duc Hue's RF and PF militia units and summarized the status of the district's many social and economic programs. I followed with a village-by-village review of the Vietcong organization that concluded with a description of our Tan My village project.

The colonel was interested in the Tan My project, but he was also curious and concerned about the status of the Vietnamese Phoenix effort. I had telegraphed to him my negative feelings about Phoenix by including only a cursory mention of the program in my briefing—even though I was the Duc Hue Phoenix advisor. We soon learned that Colonel Bartlett considered the Phoenix effort to be essential to the success of the overall pacification program. For the duration of his eighteen-month tour in Hau Nghia, he would strive valiantly to secure Vietnamese cooperation in implementing Phoenix. Later, in his end-of-tour report, he would write that no single area of endeavor had caused him more concern and frustration than Phoenix.

As Team 43 adjusted to the new style of leadership of Colonel Bartlett, our local Vietcong began to show signs of life. Following reports that the enemy was about to make moves designed to "bolster sagging revolutionary morale," Vietcong forces launched a series of attacks in Hau Nghia which told us that they had recovered from the 1970 raids into their Cambodian sanctuaries. Communist units attacked several outposts in Duc Hue one evening in late July, overrunning one post in An Ninh village with the help of a traitor in the government unit. At a prearranged time, the traitor had signaled the attackers by lighting a cigarette and then opened the gate to admit the enemy troops. Taken by surprise in their sleep, the outpost's defenders suffered almost 50 percent casualties. Many of the groggy troops escaped in their underwear by fleeing through the barbed wire perimeter designed to keep the Vietcong out of the outpost. After raising the liberation flag and raiding the garrison's arms room, the Vietcong troops had marched their prisoners into the darkness. This incident was a grim reminder for us of the damage that Vietcong political cadre were capable of inflicting, for it had been a military proselyting cadre from the An Ninh village "shadow government" who had recruited the traitor responsible for the government defeat.

As the summer of 1971 drew on, we were to learn repeatedly that Hau Nghia's proximity to Cambodia made all military planning more complex. Colonel Bartlett and his counterpart were haunted continuously by the stark reality that the Vietcong could reinforce Hau Nghia literally overnight by merely inserting new units into our area from across the border. The danger was particularly acute for the villages located along the Vam Co Dong River. There, enemy units could enter a village, attack a government installation, and quickly withdraw to the west side of the river.

Colonel Thanh spent that summer desperately looking for the correct combination of leadership and force deployment to cope with this threat. With the assistance of Colonel Bartlett, who proved to be a born advisor, Thanh "shifted and lifted" so many unit commanders that we advisors had a difficult time keeping track of who was commanding which units. If an officer's unit was not killing or capturing Vietcong, that officer was likely to find himself unemployed without warning. Colonel Thanh was no diplomat and had little use for excuses. On one occasion in midsummer, an officer who had been relieved of his command entered the office of Thanh's chief of staff and shot the unfortunate man to death as he sat at his desk. There was no doubt in anyone's mind that Colonel Thanh was serious about converting his militia forces into an army that could withstand an assault by main force North Vietnamese units, if required.

In the meantime, the 305th RF Battalion and Det's platoon were completing the destruction of the Tan My village Vietcong. Each time they scored a success in Tan My, Colonel Thanh would reward their efforts and challenge them to further achievements. Phich and Trung became difficult to restrain as they warmed up to the prospects of success. Soon they were making twice-daily trips into the village as the pragmatic Tan My villagers became more communicative with the decline of the Vietcong's fortunes. Trung and Phich no longer returned from their missions laden with Vietcong propaganda banners—evidence of nocturnal propaganda meetings. The two men's fears of entering the village finally evaporated, and they ended their reliance on a military escort for each trip.

Conditions in Tan My had so ameliorated by midsummer that I found myself playing Sunday afternoon volleyball with the teenagers of Phich's native hamlet and attending Catholic or Vietnamese holiday celebrations in the hamlet as a guest of the people. One memorable afternoon found me at an outdoor feast at Phich's humble straw and mud home, where a large crowd had gathered to honor the hundredth day since the death of Phich's father. It was a community function to which each family brought some delicacy, and we consumed a sumptuous banquet of duck, roast pig, sweet rice, and shrimp rolls—all washed down with large quantities of Phich's cherished rice whiskey. This was my first encounter with *ba xi de*, an insidious local concoction that apparently erodes the memory cells of one's brain. All I can remember about that June afternoon is that I was having a good time until I woke up in my bunk back at the team house. Judging from the pictures that Sergeant Trung took, the affair had been a great success. Back at Duc Hue, Trung recalled for me how he and I had staggered our way to Major Eby's jeep for a ride back to the compound. Major Eby had arrived too late to participate in the repeated gracious toasts of our hosts and had thus been mercifully spared my fate. Phich, in a stubborn, drunken mood, had insisted on remaining overnight with his family in the hamlet.

A full day later—it took that long for my brain to clear—I rebuked myself for my behavior. A few months earlier, the idea of even entering Tan My without a military escort was unthinkable. Now, sipping iced tea in the shade of the broad-leafed banana trees that abounded in Phich's native hamlet, it was difficult to keep in mind that there was a war going on. Sensing the danger of such complacency, I made a mental note to warn Phich yet again about his tendency to let his guard down and reminded myself that getting soused anywhere in Duc Hue was not too bright.

Word reached us in July through our informants that the Tan My Vietcong organization was in disarray. Deprived of their traditional base areas, most of the surviving village cadre and their guerrilla security force had fled the village. According to Phich's contacts in the village, the frightened Tan My survivors were hiding in the Vietcong base areas along the Vam Co Dong River. Ironically, they had informed their superiors that they would not reenter Tan My without a military escort of main force troops.

One Tan My guerrilla turned himself in to the government. A teenager who had joined the Vietcong a few months prior to Colonel Thanh's Tan My campaign, the young returnee explained that the Tan My insurgents had split up in disagreement over how to cope with their new situation.

One small faction, led by an old revolutionary named Tam Thay, had insisted on following party directives to "stay close to the people." The other group, which included most of the village's remaining cadre, had argued that the new conditions required a tactical retreat. These men argued that rigidly adhering to the party's orders would result in the total annihilation of their organization, and it was they who had fled the village. The others, led by the dogged old Tam Thay, had holed up in a swamp on the west side of the village to rethink their situation.

Tam Thay's military escort consisted of three guerrillas, led by a nineteen-year-old named Nhanh. Nhanh had been Phich's neighbor when growing up, and I knew him as the son about whom his mother and father talked with great pain. They were a Catholic family and disgraced that their impetuous oldest son had run off to follow "Uncle Phich," as the boy called Phich. During my Sunday visits to the hamlet, I had often played volleyball with Nhanh's brothers. Phich felt guilty over his part in Nhanh's decision to follow the revolution, and nurtured hopes of wooing Nhanh back to his family. We were therefore deeply disturbed to hear that he was among the hard core of the village organization who had refused to flee.

The Tan My drama unfolded still further with the capture of a batch of Vietcong documents in a night ambush. Among the papers seized was a report on Tan My written by a Vietcong security officer who had been sent to the village to investigate the breach of discipline there. Noting that effective operations in the village had ceased, the author concluded that "the traitor Phich is working against the revolution and is responsible for the current setback." The report contained no recommendation, but one was hardly needed. Phich was in extreme danger. If he didn't alter his habits, he would most certainly fall victim to a Vietcong assassin. It was time to execute the final phase of our operation—the relocation of Phich and his family to the relative safety of Bao Trai and the procurement of stable employment for him.

The Team 43 payroll was not the answer to our problem, since it was evident that American presence in Hau Nghia would soon be a thing of the past. Vietnamization in Hau Nghia meant the almost daily shrinking of Colonel Bartlett's command. Colonel Thanh had benefited the most from Phich's anti-Communist vendetta. It was now time for an expression of his gratitude. When he learned of our intentions, Thanh promised that he would take steps to place Phich in some sort of a government job in Bao Trai—no small task in view of Phich's past Communist affiliations. With the province chief's support assured, Sergeant Trung and Phich could begin house hunting in Bao Trai.

Phich was by then under strict orders to sleep only in the Duc Hue advisory compound. Major Eby and I had tried to convince him to avoid Tan My village entirely, but Phich had insisted that he needed to visit his wife periodically—she was by then pregnant with their sixth child. At Major Eby's insistence, I warned Phich that he was not to sleep at home —no matter how safe it seemed.

On the morning of August 8, Major Eby's agonized cry confirmed that our worst fear had materialized. "Oh my God, they got him! Phich's dead! They killed Phich!" Phich had been assassinated while he slept in his home in Tan My village the preceding evening. Sergeant Trung and I were horrified at the news and dumbstruck how such a thing could have happened. Major Eby, deeply shaken, explained that Phich had somehow fallen asleep at home instead of going to the nearby government outpost to bed down. There he had been killed in his sleep by a Vietcong assassin. Details were still sketchy since the report had just been radioed in from the Tan My village office only minutes before.

Sergeant Trung wanted to go to Phich's immediately. We tried to dissuade him, fearful that he could be easily ambushed on the single dirt access path to the house. A compromise was reached. Trung would drive to the outpost and pick up a military escort there for the short walk to Phich's house. I volunteered halfheartedly to accompany Trung on his sad mission, though I didn't feel that my presence at that time would contribute anything. I was overcome with the sick feeling of being responsible for Phich's untimely end and fearful of bringing more trouble to his neighbors. Trung sensed my discomfort and mercifully insisted that it would be best if no American entered the hamlet that morning. Phich's assassination was the first violence in his hamlet in well over a year, and there was no way to predict how its citizens would react to the tragedy. I could wait until Phich's funeral to offer my condolences to his family.

Trung returned to Duc Hue later that afternoon with the details of poor Phich's demise. His voice quavering with rage and grief, the ashenfaced sergeant described Phich's last hours.

Phich had gone home that afternoon to visit his family. As was his custom, he and a couple of his cronies had consumed their usual quantity of rice whiskey. Phich's cautious wife had reminded him repeatedly that it would soon be dark and that he should return to Duc Hue to sleep. But the stubborn Phich had insisted on staying, assuring her that he would sleep in the outpost. As darkness fell, a drunken Phich left home to walk the three hundred meters to the outpost. He never made it. When he stopped at a neighbor's house for a short visit, he fell asleep on the family's large, bamboo bed. There he lay until around one in the morning,

when three Vietcong entered the open-fronted house. Their leader shined
a flashlight at Phich's face. When the woman of the house awoke and
called out, the Vietcong leader ordered her sharply to be quiet and make
no move. Then he called out Phich's name three times, keeping the light
in his eyes. The doomed Phich woke up—although mercifully he was
probably too drunk and groggy to know what was happening. It was
over in a second. One bullet in the forehead, and two more in the chest
for good measure—followed by several smashing blows of the rifle butt
to the face. This was the revolutionary justice of the Tan My Vietcong.
The shots were muffled by the wet night air and not even heard in the
nearby outpost—or so its occupants claimed in the morning. The Vietcong leader then warned the terrified woman to forget what she had seen
and disappeared into the darkness. The shaken old woman had run
immediately to Phich's house and aroused his widow. The grief-stricken
woman and her friends spent the rest of the evening in vain attempts to
undo the damage to Phich's face caused by the assassin's blows. By the
time Sergeant Trung had arrived on the scene, Phich's body was already
laid out in a yellow-painted pine casket and incense sticks were burning
on a makeshift altar at his feet. Phich's wife was stoically mourning her
loss, still in shock over the brutal disfiguring of Phich's body by his
assassins—an act that had violated a Vietnamese taboo. The entire
hamlet was turning out with expressions of sympathy, offers of assistance, and plates of food. The woman in whose home Phich had met his
end was vainly trying to wash all traces of his blood out of the bamboo
bed and mat, and angrily chastising the troops in the outpost for allowing the assassins to execute Phich virtually under their noses.

Trung spoke with the government platoon leader, who explained that
the previous evening's security patrol had been on the other side of the
hamlet and that the Vietcong had entered and left as though they knew
the area well. Then he visited the sole witness to the killing, who by this
time had settled down sufficiently to talk about her experience. Of course
she had recognized Phich's assassin, and why shouldn't she? It had been
the boy, Nhanh, whom she had known since he was born two hundred
meters down the trail. The woman had watched the young guerrilla kill
Phich and maim his corpse, then pause briefly to remove his victim's
wristwatch. It was a Timex that Major Eby had given Phich earlier in
the year. "Uncle Phich" wouldn't need it anymore.

Several days after his death, Phich struck his final blow against the
Vietcong. In response to the last report generated by Phich's sympathizers, Colonel Thanh ordered Det and his men into the swamps to hunt

down Tam Thay and his cell of die-hard guerrillas. Det and his men waded into the mosquito-infested no-man's-land and promptly flushed four Vietcong from a reed shelter. In a brief firefight, all four of the Communists died. Among the victims were two guerrillas, a female military proselyting cadre, and the dedicated old Tam Thay. Det himself had killed Thay as he attempted to flee in a sampan.

At the Tan My village office, Det and his men laid out the corpses of the Vietcong on straw mats—to be seen by anyone tempted to follow the Communists and to be claimed by their relatives. Det stood by the bodies with a somber look on his face—a far cry from his usual jubilation after such a victory. One of the victors explained that Tam Thay had been Det's uncle. I clumsily tried to console Det, for we both knew that had the tables been turned, Tam Thay wouldn't have hesitated to kill him as well. Still, I was inwardly shaken by the ugliness that I had seen that day and thankful that my family in the States was insulated from such horrors.

Phich's execution forced me to rethink my assumptions about the Vietcong movement. The Tan My organization had been badly crippled, but it had still managed to carry out the orders of its superiors and eliminate Phich—in spite of the fact that Phich's hamlet was relatively remote from their swampy hideouts and inhabited by unsympathetic Catholic farmers. A single cell of determined guerrillas had made a mockery of the government's efforts to provide security for the people. When I next visited Phich's hamlet, I detected an unmistakable chill in the people's attitude toward me. It was as if they were saying, "We trusted you to keep the war away from our homes, and you failed us. If you can't deliver an end to the Vietcong terror, then at least stay away from us so that both sides will leave us alone."

It was only after the tragedy of Phich's death that the stakes of our efforts in Duc Hue began to prey on my mind. I had originally regarded Tan My as a problem that had to be solved to placate Colonel Weissinger. Later, I had continued the project as a job that needed to be done, while still writing home that I was hoping for a "Christmas drop" that would get me home in time for the holidays. I was still very much the dove who had not wanted to go to Vietnam in the first place. After the death of Phich, I found myself looking less at the calendar and thinking more about my work. Gone was my preoccupation with the Christmas drop. Somehow, getting home just didn't seem that important anymore.

What had happened to me had happened to many American advisors before me. As the months of close and continuous contact with the Vietnamese passed, the advisor was constantly submerged in an atmosphere of daily physical danger, shared hardship, and repeated exposure to emotion-charged events. In time, many of us found ourselves undergoing an irresistible tendency to identify with our counterparts. We even came to regard their districts and villages as our own, and to resent the Vietcong interlopers just as much as if they were penetrating the parks in our own hometowns and threatening our own wives and children, rather than the rice farmers of a land thousands of miles from home. This process was a subtle one—one that I realized was under way only after it had already run its logical course and I had volunteered to remain in Duc Hue rather than return to the States. In April I had written my parents that ". . . I have yet to see anything here that makes me want to urge President Nixon to do anything but withdraw from this country and let the outcome—whatever it may be—take place. If the South Vietnamese want democracy badly enough, fine. If not, then so be it." By September, I was still giving lip service to the Christmas drop, but I had begun to write differently about what I was witnessing in Duc Hue— something that was easily picked up at home.

> Even this tour, however much sadness and tragedy I have seen, I have still been able to meet another people, communicate with them in their language, and learn a little more how very much alike all people are, in spite of what appearances or sociologists say. Vietnamese men like dirty jokes, seventeen-year-old Vietnamese girls flirt, children get crushes on adults, and married couples argue over money. These people are fighting inflation like you and I, grumbling about high taxes, and condemning their politicians roundly. And so forth. It's really another phase of one's education to live among such poverty and tragedy as surrounds me here, to see how little it can take to make someone happy or comfortable. I only wish that you could see for yourselves.

I had gone to Vietnam to fulfill an obligation to the Army—it was my turn to go. But by the end of 1971, I had been inexorably drawn into the struggle that gripped Duc Hue's villages, and I was serving in Vietnam to fulfill a different sort of obligation. Phich's assassination was undoubtedly a pivotal event in my conversion, but there was more to it than that. I had found myself more and more burdened by the inescapable feeling that all of the sacrifices I was witnessing were the product of our country's promise to stand beside the South Vietnamese in their resistance to North Vietnamese Communism. Without our help, the South Vietnamese could not possibly have withstood the military pressure from their Soviet-

and Chinese-backed northern cousins. We had entered the war in 1965 with the commitment that we would not permit South Vietnam to be absorbed at the point of a North Vietnamese gun. The hardships and suffering of the war that ensued demanded that we not experience a late-inning change of heart. I had learned that to actually experience war was profoundly different than to philosophize about it in a seminar room.

The war in Hau Nghia escalated sharply after Phich's death. Fresh Vietcong units began to enter our hamlets almost nightly to support the rice collection efforts of their tax collectors. The "rice war," the fight for a share of the harvest, was upon us. One evening, an entire North Vietnamese company gathered the residents of one hamlet in a schoolyard only four hundred meters from a government outpost. While the khaki-clad North Vietnamese troops lined up in an impressive formation, their political officer reminded the villagers that in spite of the proximity of the government unit, it had failed to protect them. The message was clear. The government troops are powerless to stop us, and the people must support the revolution.

In Tan My village, the Vietcong appointed a new village secretary and charged him with responsibility for rebuilding the village organization. The new man was given a squad of North Vietnamese soldiers to perform the security tasks normally done by village guerrillas—a measure that underscored the depth of the revolution's problem in Tan My. The new village secretary was not a Tan My native, and the use of northern troops in the village was bound to alienate the people. Still, I was learning yet another lesson about the Vietcong's tenacity. The Communists saw our victories in Tan My as a temporary setback—two steps forward, one step backward. The damage done by Phich could and would be repaired—regardless of what steps would be required. Individual Vietcong might be inclined to fade into the jungle and surrender in the face of adversity, but not the revolution itself. The peasants of Hau Nghia province would be liberated—whether they wanted it or not.

V

SENIOR CAPTAIN HAI TIET

Even though Duc Hue district was a violent place during 1971, the war was little more than a smoldering insurgency compared to what had gone before it. As I traveled Duc Hue's roads with Lieutenant Bong, he would relate hair-raising anecdotes about the days when the U.S. 25th Infantry Division had operated out of the nearby Cu Chi base camp. Bong recalled the days when government forces had been forced to fight their way through battalion-sized Vietcong ambushes on the road from Duc Hue to Bao Trai. He remembered one dark day several years earlier when Vietcong troops had overrun the compound where we both lived in Hiep Hoa, taking several American green beret troopers prisoner in the process. Now, with just the two of us moving freely about the district in our jeep, those days seemed more remote than ever. The war in Duc Hue had become one of small unit clashes—a war in which our militia forces fought the Vietcong guerrilla units that protected the enemy's political cadre. It was a strange war—one in which whom we killed was far more important than how many we killed. Very few of our contacts with the Vietcong in 1971 involved enemy units greater than a platoon (twenty-five to thirty men) in size.

Hence, the appearance in Hau Nghia of larger enemy units signaled that the Communists had completed their rebuilding phase. We began to capture enemy documents that spoke of the need to "consolidate gains and be prepared to strike heavy blows against the puppets in 1972." These documents invariably described the war as entering a "new phase." The Americans were retreating, a disgrace that had been forced on Washington by the "repeated victories of the liberation forces."

With our local Vietcong crying out for help and with a clear enemy buildup under way, we realized that the scale of hostilities in Hau Nghia was about to escalate still further. Colonel Thanh's reorganized militia troops would soon be tested, of this we were virtually certain. We faced a renewed war, and we needed to know how badly, and where, we could expect to get hit. The best way to acquire the details of the impending offensive would be through a good human source—ideally a high-ranking defector with knowledge of the Communist 1972 Dry Season Plan.

He was a short, wiry man with a Charlie McCarthy smile etched permanently on his face. On December 21, 1971, he stepped out of the jungle and stopped a Honda on the road to the Duc Hoa district headquarters. Even though he was dressed in faded olive drab fatigues like those of any South Vietnamese soldier, something about him bothered the Honda's driver, for the stranger was wearing the black rubber sandals of the Vietcong, and his shirttail barely concealed the Chinese pistol he was carrying in a brown leather holster. And so, when the stranger requested a ride to Duc Hoa, the Honda's owner tried to protest that his machine was too weak to carry a second passenger. The stranger reacted by drawing his pistol and, still smiling, demanded that he be taken to Duc Hoa to surrender to the district chief. Sr. Capt. Hai Tiet, Commander of the C1 Duc Hoa Local Force Company, and Vietcong Deputy Chief of Military Affairs for Duc Hoa District, had decided to end his career as a revolutionary.

Within two hours, Hai Tiet led a government unit to the bunker complex that housed the troops of his company. A fierce firefight ensued when none of his confused troops heeded their former commander's call to surrender. When the action subsided, four of Tiet's men were dead and three prisoners had been taken. Numerous blood trails and bandages left behind by the retreating survivors attested to the fact that the C1 company would no doubt have to withdraw to Cambodia to recover from its misfortune.

I was in Bao Trai when word reached me that Hai Tiet was in our hands. Here was the intelligence break that we needed to complete the picture of the coming offensive. A man of Tiet's rank and position would most certainly be knowledgeable about the enemy's plans for the next phase of the war. When Colonel Bartlett heard the good news, he expressed his concern that our new arrival receive an appropriate welcome. The last thing that we needed was for some low-ranking Vietnamese interrogator down in Duc Hoa to get his hands on Hai Tiet and alienate him by a heavy-handed interrogation.

Colonel Weissinger would have been pleased to hear that Hai Tiet had rallied to the government. Tiet had been one of the first recipients of a letter from Phich at the beginning of the Tan My project. Phich had described Tiet as an affable fellow who was unlike many of his more dogmatic colleagues. Tiet was an easygoing native of the Mekong Delta, widely known for his charm with the young girls of Duc Hoa's hamlets. He had been one of the only targets of the early letter-writing campaign whom Phich had felt he had even the remotest chance of influencing.

We needn't have worried about Hai Tiet's reception. Colonel Thanh himself welcomed the ex-Vietcong to Bao Trai as if he were a returning hero. It was an unlikely scene—Hai Tiet, Vietcong, smoking a huge cigar (a luxury he most certainly hadn't indulged in for some time), trading war stories with his former adversary as if they were old friends. This was the most critical phase of defector exploitation. If Hai Tiet could be won over in the first hours after his surrender, he could prove to be a gold mine of information. Colonel Thanh understood this and outdid himself with the warm reception, a tactical move that reaped great rewards for us in the coming months. For just as Phich's defection had been a watershed event in the Tan My case, so would Hai Tiet's timely assistance be a turning point in our efforts to cope with the renewed war in Hau Nghia.

By the time I arrived on the scene, our new arrival was flushed with pride in his new status as a returning hero. Tiet was an alert and dynamic personality, a man who clearly possessed leadership ability that would permit him to ask the impossible of his men and be confident that they would have a go at it.

Tiet grasped my hand tightly in both of his when we were introduced by Colonel Thanh. "I know all about you. You're the Phoenix captain from Duc Hue." Then he grinned triumphantly at Colonel Thanh, clearly proud of his memory.

I managed to retort, "I know you too. You are from My Tho, and you have a girl friend in a village in Duc Hoa." This was all I could remember of what Phich had told me about Tiet's background.

We sparred with one another for the next hour. Tiet explained that he had learned of Phich's operations in Tan My village by midsummer, including the fact that Phich was working for a Vietnamese-speaking American captain at Duc Hue. He also confessed that his company had originally been ordered to provide security for the mission to assassinate Phich but that he had convinced his superiors that a small team of village guerrillas would have a better chance of infiltrating the hamlet undetected. This was why Nhanh, the teenaged guerrilla, had been the trigger man that fateful evening. Tiet spoke fondly of Phich, whom he referred to as "Brother Nam," and admitted that he had received several letters from Phich urging him to rally to the government. Had he been influenced by the letters? Tiet shook his head. He had not even considered such a step at that time. Since then, however, events had taken place that had forced him to surrender.

Hai Tiet was the eldest of four brothers, the son of a poor farmer from the delta city of My Tho. Two of his brothers had fought for the government; one of them had died in a Vietcong ambush. Hai Tiet had thrown in his lot with the revolution in 1965, over the objections of his father. At the time, he had been married both to a woman who had borne him two children and to the poverty that went hand in hand with his status as the son of a landless peasant. Like Phich, Hai Tiet had been swayed by the revolution's call for social justice.

Tiet was a self-confident young man, and he had risen rapidly from village guerrilla to his present rank. But like Hai Chua and Phich, he had become discouraged at the repeated demands of his superiors for continued sacrifice and their hollow promises of light at the end of the tunnel. By 1968, his wife had left him for another man, and he had been wounded three times. Tiet recalled bitterly that his superiors had rejected his request to work in his native village and sent him instead to Cambodia to work as a bodyguard for a ranking Vietcong officer. It was this assignment that had cost him his wife and children, for when he had returned, he had found another man living in his house.

Tiet had reestablished contact with his father after his reassignment to Duc Hoa. In a jungle clearing close to Bao Trai, father and son had held regular meetings for the past several years. Tiet's father had done his best to get him to rally to the government, but the stubborn streak in the son had always prevailed. Finally, two events had occurred during the summer of 1971 that propelled Hai Tiet into our grateful hands.

First, he was passed over for promotion to Chief of the Duc Hoa Military Affairs Section. Tiet had worked hard as the number two man in this section, a duty that he had performed concurrently with his responsibilities as combat leader of the C1 company. Hardly a modest sort, Tiet flatly stated that he knew the Duc Hoa area better than anyone and should have been promoted when his superior was transferred to Cambodia. When it was announced that an outsider—a North Vietnamese—would assume the post, Tiet had felt betrayed at being passed over. From the day he had learned of this decision, his heart had not been in his job.

If Tiet's heart was not in his work, I soon learned where it was. Her name was Tam, she was twenty years old, and she lived in a village in

Duc Hoa district. Hai Tiet was in love, and he had grown weary of the need to rendezvous with his sweetheart during clandestine visits to her hamlet under military escort. Tiet had already lost one family because of the revolution, and he was determined not to let this happen again. Hence, when his father had urged him to rally during their last meeting, he had paid attention. Now, having thrown in his lot with the government, Tiet announced to me that we had a lot of work to do. If he was to be on the government side, then he would dedicate every ounce of his energy to the defeat of the Vietcong.

Here was an intelligence officer's dream. A willing source, zealous as only a recent convert could be, begging to be debriefed, and itching to lead military operations against his new enemy. Colonel Bartlett urged me to take advantage of Tiet's zeal, and concurred that we should not allow him to be "abducted" by either American or Vietnamese higher headquarters. Once Tiet was turned over to our superiors, we would almost certainly not be able to retrieve him before most of his information had become dated and useless. This problem was the perennial nemesis of the lower-level intelligence officer in Vietnam. Every time a good source came along, a helicopter from some higher headquarters would swoop out of the sky to spirit him away to the rear for interrogation—from whence neither source nor information ever seemed to return. I was determined that this should not be allowed to happen with Hai Tiet.

Predictably, our province national police advisors agreed to put up Tiet in one of their guest rooms that evening, thus giving them first crack at debriefing him. Tiet and I agreed to meet the next morning to begin our collaboration. I hoped to convince Colonel Bartlett to allow Tiet to move in with me in Duc Hue, which would enable me to debrief him at night on targets that we could then exploit the following day.

I drove to Bao Trai the following morning filled with optimism. If Hai Tiet performed as well as he talked, we were about to commence one of the most productive operations of my tour. As I maneuvered my jeep down Bao Trai's main street, throngs of peasant women were on their way home from their daily trip to the central market. Some carried live ducks by their bound feet, while others labored under the burden of heavily laden tote sacks full of fresh vegetables and fish from the nearby river. Hau Nghia's peasant women were excellent subjects for any photographer. Uniformly clad in the black satin pants and pastel blouses of the rural peasantry, they exuded a certain strength that their Western sisters somehow lacked. The older women were particularly intriguing subjects. They usually wore two blouses—to combat the early morning chill and to frustrate pickpockets. (Their tightly rolled wads of piaster notes and their government ID cards were secreted in the pockets of the inner blouse.) As I passed the three-wheeled Lambretta scooters that shuttled them to the outlying hamlets, I wondered how much longer they would be forced to assume the roles of both father and mother at home — a social condition that was the legacy of almost thirty years of warfare.

The piercing horn of an olive drab military truck interrupted my thoughts as one of Colonel Thanh's headquarters troops hogged the road on his way out of the headquarters compound. Chickens, school children in blue and white uniforms, Hondas, and jeeps all scattered in recognition of Vietnam's fundamental law of the road—the bigger the vehicle, the greater title its driver had to the right of way. I pulled up to the gate of the police compound, which was cheerfully opened by a guard.

My national police contact greeted me with a concerned look on his face. Hai Tiet had left shortly after dawn in the company of a Vietnamese sergeant from the Corps Interrogation Center in Bien Hoa. This was the worst possible news. The interrogation methods of this particular office were a throwback to the Spanish Inquisition. A Vietcong was a Vietcong, and all of them were liars, was the view of the interrogators who worked for Colonel Sinh, the commanding officer of the center. Here, as elsewhere in Vietnam, the use of force to intimidate sources was widespread. Countless American advisors had struggled over the years to convince the Vietnamese that brutality and successful interrogation did not go together, but in Bien Hoa, as in Hau Nghia province, we still had a long way to go. The prospect of our carefully cultivated source falling into the hands of one of Colonel Sinh's interrogators was totally unacceptable, and within the hour I was on my way to Bien Hoa with instructions from Colonel Bartlett to liberate Hai Tiet.

Two hours later, I was sipping tea with Colonel Sinh in his office. Like so many South Vietnamese officers, Sinh was an ethnic North Vietnamese—a Catholic who had come south during the great migration of 1954. Sinh was a rotund, loquacious man whose ego required that he play the "I know something that you don't know" game with every American he encountered. I was in no mood for such games; my mission was to spirit Hai Tiet back to Hau Nghia that same day. As the road to Hau Nghia through Phu Loi was not very secure, the earlier we got started, the better.

Colonel Sinh was his usual, overbearing self. While his enlisted orderly brought more tea, he coyly related the latest information he had gleaned from a "high-level source." Seeing my opportunity, I remarked that with so many good sources in his stable, Sinh surely didn't have the assets to waste on a low-level district cadre like Hai Tiet. (One of Sinh's captains had already tipped me off that Tiet was sitting in a cell and would not be interrogated for several days.) I appealed to the intelligence officer in Sinh, explaining that we needed Tiet in Hau Nghia for several days, since he possessed information that we could use to strike blows at the Vietcong. Then I played my trump card, mentioning matter-of-factly that I was going to stop at the PX on my way back to Hau Nghia. Sinh, who could be depended upon to need something, warmed up as he saw the opportunity to mount a PX penetration mission. The stereo and other artifacts in his office testified to the fact that he had long since mastered this tactic.

But this time around I was to get off easily. The good colonel was running out of pipe tobacco. Within fifteen minutes, Hai Tiet and I were on our way back to Bao Trai, but only after I solemnly promised Sinh two cans of his favorite tobacco—and the return of Tiet to him within three days.

One look at Tiet told me that my arrival in Bien Hoa was none too soon. For the first time since he rallied, he wasn't smiling. As we headed across the Dong Nai River on an old iron bridge, an outraged Hai Tiet told me that he had been mug-shot like a criminal, placed in a cell, and fed rice gruel. Alone in his cell, he had nonetheless overheard the whispered conversations of his neighbors, whom he assumed were prisoners of war. Their words had convinced him that he would be brutalized by Colonel Sinh's men. Tiet's smile returned as he clasped my shoulder and thanked me for my timely rescue. I made a mental note to tell Colonel Bartlett what we had encountered. Colonel Sinh's people were doing more harm than good as they reinforced the images of life under President Thieu's regime that all Communist soldiers and cadre were hearing from their political officers.

By now, we were speeding through the most dangerous part of our return trip—the Phu Hoa corridor. Actually a stretch of road through the jungle where there were no government outposts, the corridor was another traditional Vietcong invasion route to Saigon that had been used in 1968. I nervously pressed the accelerator to the floor. Dusk was approaching, and here I was driving a jeep down one of Vietnam's most dangerous roads. For security, I had one former Vietcong company commander, armed with my M-16 rifle.

It was dark when we arrived in Bao Trai. The last three miles of our trip had been nerve-wracking for both of us. We had sped through Cu Chi district's infamous Muoi Lon hamlet and across the large swamp that separated Bao Trai from Highway 1, arriving at the barbed wire roadblock that the police erected every night at the town limits. I had not driven a vehicle after dark more than two or three times during my tour thus far. To do so was to offer some local guerrilla the chance to be a hero. Each time I had done this, I had arrived at my destination with sweaty palms and the feeling that I had just done something dumb. That night was no exception, and I rebuked myself for not staying overnight in Bien Hoa.

Colonel Bartlett reacted angrily to the news of Hai Tiet's narrow escape from Sinh's interrogators. Then he noted with a smile that possession was still nine-tenths of the law and instructed me to keep Hai Tiet in Hau Nghia for as long as possible. To preserve future cooperation with the touchy Colonel Sinh, the colonel would have Colonel Thanh legitimize this arrangement through proper channels. The colonel emphasized the importance of the next few days. Tiet would have to provide us with information that would lead to a successful military operation quickly. This would provide Colonel Thanh with the ammunition needed to convince his superiors that the rallier Hai Tiet was too valuable to sit in a cell in Bien Hoa.

We had no difficulty convincing *"Anh Hai"* ("Brother two"—meaning that he was the eldest son; "one" was reserved for the village chief) that he should remain in Bao Trai. He wanted no more to do with Bien Hoa, and he immediately grasped our strategy. "Since we need prompt results, Dai Uy," he remarked, "you must take me to the province jail." There, he explained, one of his former soldiers was imprisoned, awaiting transfer to a POW camp.

The prisoner's name was Ky. He was a nineteen-year-old Vietcong soldier who had been captured during the shootout on the day Tiet had rallied. Tiet recalled that Ky had been an escort soldier on a mission six months earlier to bury a supply of ammunition. Since Tiet himself had not accompanied the expedition, he personally could not lead us to the cache site. But Anh Hai insisted that Ky was a bright young man who had committed the directions to the site to memory and could easily lead us to it. But would he agree to help the man who had betrayed him? Tiet's cocky reply to my query once again betrayed his ego and supreme self-confidence. "Don't worry, Dai Uy, he'll do what I tell him to do. After all, I'm his commander."

I rather doubted that Tiet would be able to convince the young Ky of anything after selling out his unit and causing the man's capture, but Anh Hai insisted that if he could speak to Ky alone, we would be on our way to recover the cache that morning.

At the jail, a guard brought the prisoner to us, and I would have bet a month's pay that Tiet would strike out with him. Ky was short for a Viet-namese man—five feet tall at most—and like most Vietcong troops, he needed a haircut and a few good meals. His feet were leathery, with the toes spread from years of barefoot walking. The young soldier's skin was tanned to a deep brown from over two years of outdoor living, and his only garment, a pair of blue nylon shorts, was stained with the blood of a comrade who had been killed next to him in his bunker. When he saw Hai Tiet and me, he cast his eyes down and stared sullenly at his feet. Tiet motioned for me to leave, and I complied, tugging the guard along with me.

Through a crack in the shutter, I could see Tiet and Ky squatting on the floor, face to face. Tiet was arguing his case, alternately gesturing with his hands and placing one hand on Ky's shoulder in a fatherly fashion. Ky was listening attentively, his black eyes fixed on his former commander.

When the two men emerged from their conference, Tiet was all smiles. He clasped Ky by the shoulder and announced triumphantly, "This is a good man, Dai Uy. Now, let's go!" The smaller Ky smiled nervously and shook my hand timidly. I asked him in Vietnamese if he was hungry, which produced a stunned reply.

"My god, he speaks Vietnamese!"

"Sure," retorted Tiet, "and he's a good man. You can trust him."

I signed for the prisoner and we drove to the nearby Thu Anh Restau-rant. An open-fronted, concrete block building with a blue and white ceramic tile floor, the Thu Anh belonged to the family of one of our inter-preters. They had become used to my regular visits and graciously toler-ated the menagerie of Vietcong sources whom I regularly paraded into their establishment. For the next hour, Tiet, Ky, and I enjoyed a cup of *ca-phe sua* (French coffee with sweetened condensed milk) and a bowl of *pho* (beef noodle soup with coriander)—all the while ignoring the sus-picious glances of the other patrons.

The brief interlude at the Thu Anh was well spent. Judging from the way he ate, poor Ky had been starving. And more importantly, I had the opportunity to prove to Ky that I was a human being. Like most Viet-cong troops, Ky had been filled with stories about the brutality of the Americans and what would happen to him if he ever fell into American hands.

By the end of our meal, Tiet and I were teasing Ky about his girl friend in Duc Hoa, and the young man had begun to smile for the first time. Ky the guerrilla was human too.

We linked up with the Province Intelligence Platoon and prepared to

recover the ammunition cache. Lieutenant Tuan, the commander, asked
Ky to show him our objective on the map. This produced a hasty conference between Tiet and Ky. Ky, it seemed, could not read a map, but he
could take us to the site if we could drive to lower Duc Hoa district.

Once in Duc Hoa, Ky guided us down a trail that led to the interior of
one of the villages. As our column snaked its way past the thick bamboo
groves, I asked Tiet how he had managed to transform the sullen and
hostile Ky into a cooperative mood so quickly.

"It was easy," he replied, flashing his smile. "I told him that because I
had misled him into following the Vietcong, I owed it to him to undo the
damage that I had done to his life. I reminded him that prisoners of war
were shipped to Phu Quoc Island to a camp from which many never
returned, and told him that if he would help us, I would intervene with
the Americans and get him released."

I was incredulous. "You mean that you promised him that I would
free him if he cooperated?"

"Of course," Anh Hai replied. "It was the only way I could regain his
confidence after nearly getting him killed."

"Anh Hai, I can't do that. Ky is a prisoner of the Vietnamese military.
Only the province chief has that power."

Tiet glared at me disbelievingly. "Yes, Dai Uy, but all you have to do
is to tell the province chief to do it, and it's done. Very easy!"

"Anh Hai, you don't understand. Colonel Bartlett is Colonel Thanh's
advisor, and not even Colonel Bartlett tells Colonel Thanh what to do.
We are advisors and can only make recommendations."

Tiet gave me a reproving glance. "Then, Dai Uy, you will have to
make a pretty strong suggestion. I already promised Ky, and he wants to
marry his girl friend in Duc Hoa when he is released. We must help him
now."

"Of course, I'll try my best, but it is a Vietnamese matter. If we should
find the cache today, we should get Lieutenant Tuan to send a report to
Colonel Thanh. That will help."

Tiet was skeptical. He still viewed things through the eyes of a Vietcong—and this meant that Colonel Thanh was Colonel Bartlett's puppet.

There may have been a day in Hau Nghia when the senior American
officer in the province could order his Vietnamese counterpart around in
his own country, but those days were over now. We American advisors
were invited guests in Hau Nghia and deeply conscious of the limits that
this imposed on us. Almost without exception, Team 43's advisors chafed
under this handicap that prevented us from issuing commands and
evoking the "take charge" mentality that was ingrained in most of us as

American military men. To Hai Tiet, it was axiomatic that the South Vietnamese were our docile puppets. Even after our exchange that day, I could tell that Anh Hai would require more convincing that the Americans in Hau Nghia were not running the Vietnamese train.

We arrived at the cache site in the early afternoon. Ky had led us to a spot where a straw and mud farmhouse jutted out into the paddy lands. Surrounded by bamboo and banana trees, the house was occupied by women and children only. Lieutenant Tuan greeted the woman of the house politely while his platoon sergeant borrowed two shovels and a long metal rod from the toolshed.

By now, Ky had begun pacing off a distance from a bamboo clump at the edge of the paddy. He walked some forty meters, then sighted on another tree across the paddy. Turning and walking another thirty meters or so, he came to the edge of a shallow duck pond and stopped. After exchanging a word with the platoon sergeant, Ky took off his boots, rolled up his pants, and motioned for the metal rod. Wading into the knee-deep water, he paced off another ten meters and stopped. Thrusting the rod into the pond's muddy bottom, he probed for the cache. Lieutenant Tuan barked an order that sent five of his men into the hamlet to borrow additional rods. With six men probing, it was only a few minutes before one of the probes hit a solid object with a heavy "thunk." Like a group of children on a treasure hunt, the elated platoon members unearthed ten metal boxes of small arms ammunition. Each box was soldered shut and labeled in Chinese characters. The cache contained five thousand rounds of AK-47 ammunition, enough to sustain a platoon of Vietcong for a year.

Our day had panned out well. As the truck carried us back to Bao Trai, I could sense that Tiet and Ky had suddenly become accepted members of the platoon. Earlier in the day, Lieutenant Tuan and his men had treated our guides with correct politeness, and even that had no doubt been a concession to my presence. Tuan was understandably pleased to be returning home with such booty, and he assured me that he would report Ky's and Tiet's roles in our success to Colonel Thanh. Anh Hai was also jubilant. The muddy boxes of ammunition on the floor of the truck were his ticket to an extended stay in Bao Trai, far from Colonel Sinh's interrogators in Bien Hoa.

That evening, Lieutenant Tuan invited us to a party to celebrate the day's success. The festivities took place in the G-2 office and lasted far into the night. Sitting in a circle on the floor, we played a uniquely Vietnamese version of spin the bottle. The fun centered around the head of a chicken that one of the troops had retrieved from someone's cooking pot.

Encouraged by howls of delight from his comrades, the soldier placed the chicken head in a rice bowl and covered it with his hand. Then he shook the bowl next to his ear like a dice cup and plopped it down with a flourish, lifting the bowl to reveal the chicken head. The platoon roared as the person at whom the chicken's beak pointed had to "pay" by chugging down an entire bottle of LaRue "Tiger" beer. Tiger beer came in fat, half-liter bottles and was also known as "B-40 beer" because the brown bottle resembled a B-40 antitank rocket. As each loser chugged down his beer, the others chanted *"vo, vo, vo, vo!"* the equivalent of the American "down the hatch." The vengeful chicken sought out Anh Hai early in the evening, and our new ally managed to force down the beer in spite of the fact that he was no drinker. Soon after he had downed his first bottle, Anh Hai's face began to turn red, to the delight of his new comrades. The chicken also got me several times, and I was glad I would be staying in Bao Trai that evening.

VI

"TO BE A REAL HUMAN BEING, YOU MUST BE A COMMUNIST"

The love-struck Hai Tiet was concerned for the safety of his fiancée. No one knew better than he what the Communists were capable of doing to protect the revolution. Tam lived in one of the interior hamlets in Duc Hoa district—an area that was easily accessible to the Vietcong at night. Tiet was adamant that we had to get the girl out of her hamlet—the sooner, the better. He confided in me that Tam's parents were not Vietcong sympathizers. In fact, they had steadfastly opposed the relationship that had developed between their daughter and the local Vietcong commander. Tiet had tried in vain to convince them of the justice of the revolutionary cause, but Tam's father had responded that he did not want his daughter marrying a man whose purpose in life was to overthrow the government. Thereafter, Tiet and his lover had been forced to meet secretly at a neighbor's house.

Tiet was frustrated by Tam's father's opposition to him as a son-in-law. Now that he was officially a loyal citizen of the republic, he hoped that he would be accepted into Tam's family. At this point, however, the most important task was to protect Tam from any retaliation that the Vietcong might be planning against Tiet. As he explained it to me, "They can't get me here, Dai Uy, so they may try and hurt me by abducting or assassinating her. The Vietcong can enter her hamlet any time they want. Believe me—I know." It was clear that Tiet would not be able to concentrate on anything until Tam was safe.

Tiet had a plan for an operation to rescue Tam. Lieutenant Tuan and I agreed to it. Tiet reasoned that the Vietcong might well take reprisals against Tam's family if she voluntarily left the hamlet to follow him. For this reason we would have to make her departure appear to be involuntary. One way to accomplish this was to "arrest" her.

I accompanied Tuan and his platoon on "Operation Lovebird." Tiet remained in Bao Trai. Arriving at the hamlet, we cordoned off the area around Tam's house and directed the residents to gather in the yard of a farmhouse. Tuan's men instructed everyone to bring their government identity documents with them for a routine check. Within thirty minutes, more than a hundred adults and children had assembled in the shade of a large stand of bamboo.

The first step was a quick group photograph, to be used during future debriefings of prisoners and defectors in identifying covert Vietcong cadre. Tuan's men checked everyone's ID cards and turned up one soldier from the Vietnamese 25th Division who had no leave papers. The AWOL soldier would accompany us to Bao Trai, where he would be turned over to the Military Security Service. One young girl had no ID card, but she produced a receipt to prove that she had applied for a replacement of the lost card. The soldiers also confirmed the presence of two people whom Hai Tiet had named as covert Vietcong supply cadre. Finally, we were able to identify Miss Nguyen thi Tam, Hai Tiet's lover. Tam wore black satin pants and a purple blouse, and her shiny black hair was braided into a pigtail that reached far down her back. She was a typical country girl, broad shouldered, heavy breasted, and dark complexioned. When she smiled, her beautiful face was marred (to my American eyes) by a pair of gold-plated lower teeth.

Lieutenant Tuan put our carefully worked out plan into effect. His men searched the homes in the area, paying particular attention to the property of the two suspects revealed by Hai Tiet. Tiet had assured us that the two women whose names he had given us were the regular suppliers of the C1 company. As company commander, he had parceled out part of his operational funds to them, along with a list of supplies and medicine needed by his unit. The women purchased the requested items piecemeal at the local market to avoid suspicion, then concealed the merchandise in their homes until Tiet and his men picked it up. Tiet was confident that if we carefully searched the homes of the two suspects, we would uncover incriminating evidence.

As the search proceeded, Lieutenant Tuan's platoon sergeant slipped a note to Tam. It was from Tiet, and it informed her that she was about to be "arrested" and taken away. In the note, Tiet instructed her to cooperate and to warn her parents of the impending caper so that they would not be alarmed when she was led away.

The search of the suspects' homes was successful. In one house, Tuan's men located a transistor radio that received only "Liberation Radio," the Vietcong propaganda station. One soldier uncovered a sheaf of propaganda leaflets buried in the family rice bin with dozens of vials of vitamins. In the other home, the troops uncovered twenty pairs of sandals and several lengths of gold, blue, and red cloth used to make Vietcong flags. In the wall of the same house, Tuan's men discovered an envelope containing fifty thousand piasters and a shopping list of foodstuffs and medicines. This was sufficient evidence, together with Tiet's testimony, to convict the two women under Vietnamese law.

As we prepared to depart, Lieutenant Tuan approached Tam and sternly informed her that he had orders to escort her to headquarters for questioning. The girl protested on cue, insisting that she had done nothing wrong. Tuan replied that if that was the case, then she would be home before nightfall. Nodding curtly to one of his men to take charge of Tam, Tuan dismissed the remaining civilians.

As we headed back to the waiting vehicle, the alert Tam continued to protest loudly that she was innocent, while several of the lieutenant's troops mockingly called her a "VC woman." I smiled at Tuan, who gave me the "thumbs up" gesture that meant the same in Vietnam as everywhere else in the world. Mission accomplished. I quipped to Tuan that I hoped the bridal suite in Bao Trai was ready. Tuan leered at Tam and laughed.

We were nearing the truck when I heard crying and wailing at the rear of our column that sounded like a Vietnamese funeral. An older man and woman were pursuing our column, waving their arms and calling on the soldiers to halt. It didn't take long to figure out that the distraught couple were Tam's parents. The mother overtook her daughter and threw her arms around the surprised girl. She was nearly hysterical. Tears streamed down her face as she wailed, *"Troi oi! Troi oi!* ("Dear God! Dear God!"). Tam's father quickly homed in on Lieutenant Tuan and began to berate the nonplussed officer angrily. "I am a loyal citizen of the Republic! You can't arrest my daughter. She's done nothing! Let her go!"

Tuan glanced at me for help as he tried to reason with the irate old man. Tam's father was not in a listening mood. He continued to heap vehement abuse on the unfortunate officer, to the delight of his troops. Tuan was off balance in the face of such an onslaught, and he reacted by angrily ordering his grinning men to load Tam and the other prisoners on the truck. Yelling at Tam's father that he was just following orders, the lieutenant turned on his heel and ordered the truck's driver to move out. As we got under way, Tam's father appealed to me, "Captain, please help! My daughter is not a Vietcong!" As the truck gathered speed, I had time to shout back, "Don't worry. She'll be OK."

Tam's mother, not to be outdone, chased our vehicle down the trail, wailing in Academy Award fashion. As we cleared the hamlet, I laughed at Tuan's discomfort in the face of the realistic abuse that had been aimed at him by the "outraged" father. The couple had done a completely convincing job of making their daughter's arrest a credible tragedy. Word would almost certainly reach the Communists that Hai Tiet's sweetheart had been taken away by government troops.

We reunited Tam with Hai Tiet in Bao Trai, and we all had a good laugh together as I recounted the Hollywood-like performances of Tam and her parents. Tam laughed as hard as the rest of us, especially when we recalled Lieutenant Tuan's discomfort as the victim of the staged departure. Then Tam dropped the bomb. Her parents had not been acting at all. Tam had not been able to warn them that the arrest was a ruse because they had been visiting in a neighboring hamlet when our force arrived. Thus her parents had only learned of the arrest shortly after we had departed the hamlet. Little wonder that they had reacted so realistically to our caper.

Now we were in trouble. Tam's parents were probably already on their way to complain to the Duc Hoa district chief, or worse yet, to the province chief himself. Since we hadn't coordinated our unorthodox and hastily planned operation, we were no doubt about to be called upon to do some tall explaining.

Hai Tiet thought the whole thing was hilarious. Our plan had backfired, but he had Tam, and the repercussions of the operation were mine, not his. Lieutenant Tuan blanched as he contemplated what sort of dire consequences might befall him if Colonel Thanh learned of his role in the plan. As we contemplated our next move, one of the guards announced that we had visitors at the gate. Tam's parents had tracked us down.

At the gate, Tam's father had already launched into a passionate testimonial of his family's loyalty to the republic, and the guard he had collared was listening politely. When the old man spotted me, he redirected his appeal, insisting that Tam had been forced to consort with the VC Hai Tiet because the government troops were unable to secure their hamlet at night. As he talked, his wife sobbed that Tam was a good girl, her youngest child, and definitely not a Vietcong.

To put an end to the mix-up caused by our misfired plan, we invited Tam's parents inside for a cold drink. I cringed at what would happen when they found out that Tam was with Hai Tiet. Tam greeted them at the door, which started the mother crying again. The father bristled immediately when he spotted Hai Tiet in the room. Since the whole affair had been on Anh Hai's behalf, I dumped the burden of explanation in his lap, determined to stay out of the ensuing battle. I cracked open a bottle of San Miguel beer as the fast-talking Tiet went to work.

Tam's father fired the first shot by demanding that Tam return home immediately. When Tiet attempted to protest, the old peasant interrupted him with the caustic reminder that he no longer had his Chinese pistol to enforce his will. Score one for the rice farmer. Within an hour, though, the silver-tongued Tiet had convinced the befuddled peasant that Tam was not safe in the hamlet. The old man was still a long way from welcoming Anh Hai into his family, but at least he had quit yelling and was in agreement that Tam should stay out of the hamlet for the foreseeable future. Tam's mother settled down and was listening quietly to her daughter's assurances that she was happy for the moment in Bao Trai with Tiet. By this time, iced tea had been served to everyone and the tension had finally dissipated. It had been a close call, but it appeared that we had resolved the crisis. Tiet and Tam's father were now engaged in an animated discussion of Tiet's dramatic defection.

Tam's parents finally returned to Duc Hoa and the lovebirds retired to their room. Lieutenant Tuan and I had a good laugh over the whole episode, even though the happy ending of our strange rescue mission hadn't put an end to our problems. There was still the problem of the bad feelings that our intrusion in the hamlet had caused. Tam and her family were respected and popular members of their small community, and our operation could have done nothing but harm to the government's image there. We also had to come up with an explanation for Tam's prolonged absence from the hamlet, since it was obvious that we could not allow the impression to continue that she had been jailed. (Later, we were able to minimize the damage with the cooperation of Tam's parents, who turned out to be understanding and grateful. Their complete conversion occurred several days after our operation, when a Vietcong platoon entered their hamlet one night looking for Tam. The Vietcong leader had questioned Tam's father about his daughter's whereabouts. The old man was adept at coexisting with both sides in the war, and he made up a perfect cover story on the spot. He told the Vietcong that Tam had known nothing about Hai Tiet's defection and had not seen Tiet since. She had been arrested by government security forces and questioned about her Vietcong ties, and had gone to the Delta to visit an aunt after her release. She would remain there indefinitely, her father had told the Vietcong, where she could forget Hai Tiet and avoid harassment by both sides.)

With Tam safe in Bao Trai, we could now get down to the serious business of picking Hai Tiet's brain for information on the Vietcong's plans for Hau Nghia province during the coming dry season. Tiet's posi-

tion as a high-ranking military affairs cadre made it a foregone conclusion that he knew the details of the impending offensive. Accordingly,
he and I spent the next several days closeted together in a room in Bao
Trai, with a map of Hau Nghia and Cambodia on the desk. While I wrote
as fast as my fingers would permit, Tiet shared with me his assessment of
military and political realities. His revelations during these sessions were
the most valuable and timely intelligence we were fortunate enough to
receive that year in Hau Nghia. In plain language, Tiet warned us that
the honeymoon in our province was over. Hau Nghia had been marked
for an offensive that would turn our villages and hamlets once again into
major battlefields. This is how Tiet assessed the situation:

Vietcong political and military forces in Hau Nghia had withstood
the severe setback caused by the 1970 invasion of their Cambodian base
areas—but it had been a near thing in many ways. His own company, for
example, had experienced crippling morale problems during the latter
half of 1970 and throughout 1971. Low on ammunition, forced to forage
for rice, and under increasing military pressure, they had spent most of
their time hiding from government forces. The number of hamlets that
they could safely enter at night had decreased steadily as the number of
government outposts and night ambushes had increased under Colonel
Thanh's leadership. Tiet emphasized that although the morale of his
local force troops was poor, that of the village cadre and guerrillas was
worse yet. Even villages like Tan My had become too dangerous for normal operations. The government's Phoenix program had caused a drop
in the willingness of the people to support the insurgents as fewer and
fewer of the villagers were willing to risk arrest and imprisonment by
helping the Vietcong. "Revolutionary morale" had dropped to an all-
time low. Tiet and his colleagues on the political staff of the district had
reported these facts and urgently requested reinforcements, warning of
serious consequences if they did not get help soon. They had told their
superiors that the existing forces in their district would be unable to tax
the rice harvest, that morale would decline still further, that recruitment
and proselyting activities would suffer, and that many other tasks that
were routinely levied on the local guerrilla units and political cadre of
the shadow government would go unaccomplished. In short, Tiet and his
colleagues had reported to their superiors that the revolution in Hau
Nghia was in the throws of a potentially fatal crisis. Help was desperately
needed to stave off disaster.

Just before his defection, Tiet had attended a meeting in Cambodia at
which these problems had been the main topic of discussion. He and his
fellow military cadre had been urged to hang on. Help was on its way,

their superiors told them, in the form of newly organized and equipped units that would soon be committed. Tiet and his men should "stick to the front."

Tiet warned us that both the Duc Hue district headquarters and Bao Trai would be attacked during the coming offensive. He explained that the Communist high command had assigned at least seven main force battalions to the Hau Nghia front, several of which had already deployed to base areas just across the river. When I asked if he was certain of his facts, Tiet gave me a hurt look and begged me to trust him. "I saw the orders, Dai Uy."

Most of what Tiet told us tracked with what we had been observing or hearing from other sources. We had already identified some of the units he talked about in our area of operations; others we had only known were "somewhere in Cambodia." Tiet knew the exact locations of some of these units, and even knew that they had been forced by combat losses to delay the initiation of their attacks.

For this the Vietcong could thank Colonels Thanh and Bartlett. Commencing in August, as we detected the intrusion of new enemy units into our area, Colonel Bartlett had urged Colonel Thanh to launch aggressive operations into what had formerly been the privileged enemy base areas across the river. For several months, our militia forces had roamed the west bank of the Vam Co Dong River and conducted a series of fierce battles with the enemy main force troops. The fighting had been so heavy that the Communist troops had even shot down some of our supporting helicopters. Colonel Thanh's troops had been repeatedly bloodied as they were airlifted or boatlifted across the river to search out the Vietcong before they could cross the river and invade our populated areas.

The North Vietnamese replacements who had filled up these units had fought well, in spite of their complete lack of artillery or helicopter gunship support. When two of our militia companies had encountered an enemy unit in broad daylight, they had attempted to encircle it. But the operation had faltered when our unit became pinned down by a single enemy machine gunner. The government troops finally overran the stubborn enemy position, where they found the body of a Communist warrant officer. From his shirt pocket they retrieved a regular People's Army of Vietnam (North Vietnamese) ID booklet that identified the fallen hero as Vo Dinh Phuoc, a native of South Vietnam who had been trained in the north. Other documents on his body told the rest of the story. Phuoc was a platoon leader, a full member of the Communist party who had been twice decorated for heroism. His family lived in Quang Ngai province in northern South Vietnam—famous as the home of the My Lai massacre—and Phuoc had a girl friend there who wrote him letters in beautiful script. As did most enemy soldiers, Phuoc kept a small diary. On the first page of this book, the twenty-seven-year-old Communist leader had penned these lines:

> If you are to be a flower, then be one
>   that always faces the sun.
> And if you want to be a rock, then
>   try to be a precious stone.
> And if it is a bird that you must be, then
>   by all means be a white dove.
> But if you want to be a real human being, then
>   you must be a Communist.

The dedication reflected in the young officer's poetry had carried over onto the battlefield. Our troops who fought that day all agreed that Phuoc had saved his entire platoon from destruction by remaining behind to cover their withdrawal. In a rare display of respect, they had buried him decently where he fell before their return to Duc Hue.

Hai Tiet was adamant that we could not let our guard down merely because Colonel Thanh's troops had disrupted the Vietcong's attack timetable. He insisted that when a Vietcong unit received orders to hit a target, that unit must attack that objective sooner or later unless the order was rescinded. If the attack was delayed by combat losses, then the unit would conduct a new reconnaissance and attack the target at a later date. Duc Hue and Bao Trai would definitely be attacked during the coming dry season. Tiet advised us to continue our attacks against the Vietcong units in their base areas while concurrently upgrading our defenses.

Hai Tiet came over to us in December, 1971. By the Tet holiday in mid-February, 1972, acting largely on his revelations, Colonel Thanh's troops killed more than a hundred members of the enemy main force units that had been sent to Hau Nghia to bolster sagging revolutionary morale. The plucky Tiet himself guided our militia troops to a bunker complex that sheltered an enemy water sapper unit, then steered a government operation into a major contact across the river with one of the newly arrived enemy battalions. By the eve of Tet, the long-anticipated attacks had still not materialized. Had we hurt the enemy that badly? Or was Tiet's repeated insistence that "orders were orders" an exaggeration? For the first time, I found myself doubting my smiling companion.

The Communists believed that military and political realities were inextricably linked together, and they preceded the 1972 dry season attacks with a political offensive. One target of this offensive was the People's Self Defense Force (PSDF). The PSDF units were composed of teenagers and old men, and were usually led by the deputy hamlet chief for security. Their primary purpose was to perform roving security patrols in the hamlets at night, thereby freeing the local militia platoons to perform screening missions (ambush patrols) on the approaches to the hamlets. This, in turn, freed the better-armed militia companies to engage the enemy's main force units in the province's outer areas. Since he did not believe that he could expect heavy reinforcements in the event of an all-out Communist attack, Colonel Thanh's strategy had been to upgrade the caliber of his regional force militia companies so that they would be strong enough to engage Communist regular units if necessary.

But there was a problem in upgrading the mission of the RF companies as Colonel Thanh had done. By deploying his militia companies forward in the enemy base areas along the river, the colonel had left our "rear," the populated hamlets, dangerously exposed. If an enemy unit managed to avoid detection by the militia companies while still in its base area near the river, it could then penetrate easily into the province's lightly defended interior, where it would grossly outnumber the relatively weak popular forces militia platoons. The PSDF units were of little assistance, since they were no match for any enemy unit, with the possible exception of a stray guerrilla or two. Most of the teenagers of the PSDF had little or no inclination to go to war. In spite of this, the Communists saw the PSDF program as a serious threat to the revolution's ability to gain sway over South Vietnam's youth, and they resisted it fiercely.

An alarming number of our teenaged PSDF members succumbed to the persuasive powers of Vietcong proselyting cadre during 1972. The Vietcong told our teenagers that the PSDF program was a "black plot" of the Thieu regime to turn them into cannon fodder. Vietcong leaflets reminded them that liberation forces were again ready to "strike decisive blows against the country-selling puppets." The Saigon government was "politically and militarily bankrupt," the pitch continued, and the "puppet troops" would be unable to resist the revolution now that the Americans had all but given up and gone home. Positive proof of the government's weakness, the Communists pointed out, was its need to arm sixteen-year-olds with vintage weapons and demand that they stand up and fight against the liberation forces, which were armed with the modern AK-47 assault rifle. The Vietcong urged our teenagers to resist induction into the PSDF, and called on those already in it to "return to the people," an innocent-sounding euphemism that meant something quite different.

Beginning in January, 1972, the success of the Vietcong's efforts to subvert our teenagers began to manifest itself. In Trang Bang district, teenaged penetrators in one PSDF unit allowed a Vietcong unit to enter their outpost unopposed one night. One of the teenagers then executed the deputy hamlet chief, after which the Vietcong led all forty of the young men—with their weapons—off to Cambodia. Incidents of this type began to occur with disturbing frequency, until one of my tasks became keeping track of how many PSDF and how many weapons were missing. At one time, I recall that the count approached a hundred and fifty, although we were consistently receiving reports that each incident had been perpetrated by only a small number of penetrators who had sold out their entire unit to the enemy. Events confirmed this. In virtually all of our PSDF incidents, the pattern was the same. The captives—for this is what most were—were escorted by the Vietcong to reindoctrination camps. After several weeks of "education," those who wanted to return home were allowed to leave, while those who had volunteered to serve the revolution remained for further training and eventual assignment to Communist units. Of the forty who disappeared in Trang Bang that evening, all but five were home within a month—without their weapons. Still, the number of teenagers who remained with the Communists was ominous, and the Communists crowed that the PSDF "general uprising" portended the collapse of the Saigon government.

After I extended my tour in Hau Nghia, Colonel Bartlett asked me to come to Bao Trai to serve as his G-2 advisor. I had been spending more and more of my time on these duties anyway, so the transfer would not change much—other than where I would sleep. I was finally going to get away from the two howitzers outside my window in Duc Hue.

It was 1:00 A.M. on my last night in Duc Hue when the mortar rounds began to fall in our compound. Hai Tiet's prediction that Duc Hue would be attacked had come true. Forewarned was forearmed, and my rifle and other alert gear were laid out by the bunk. I pulled on my boots and reached groggily for a knapsack full of grenades. The "crump" of the exploding mortar rounds was punctuated by the heavier "boom" of demolition charges as we rushed to our bunkers. Satchel charges! That meant we were under a sapper attack. Close by, the "whoosh-bang" of enemy B-40 rockets could be heard, along with the sporadic chatter of at least one AK-47 rifle. A distressingly weak volume of M-16 fire was coming from the perimeter. Major Nghiem's troops had been caught napping.

My bunker mate and I unlimbered our .50 caliber machine gun. If the enemy tried to cross the river anywhere to the north of us, he would have to contend with us. If he came from anywhere else, our weapon would be useless, since it could not be turned around. Aerial flares lighted up the landscape like day, but we could see no Vietcong in our perimeter. Fifty meters to the south of us, a tremendous explosion went off next to the Phoenix office. An enemy sapper had hurled a satchel charge and scored a direct hit on the Vietnamese mortar position. The explosion ignited the weapon's ammunition stockpile and killed the three-man crew.

By this time, we had our .50 barking out long bursts of tracered ammunition at the opposite river bank. The tracers cut a spectacular orange swath through the night, a reassuring sight in spite of the fact that we couldn't see anything to shoot at. After firing off several hundred rounds this way, we had to cease fire because of the cordite fumes in the bunker. I stuck my head out the back entrance to get some air but was instantly choked up by noxious fumes. Momentarily confused, I staggered back into the bunker, only then realizing that we were under a gas attack. I grabbed the field phone and called the operations bunker.

"Gas!" I gasped into the handset. "We're being gassed in bunker number two."

"Are you sure?" a voice called back incredulously.

"Damn sure!" I coughed. "If you don't believe it, stick your head outside. We need gas masks, quickly!"

The moment of realization that the Vietcong had used gas in their attack was awful. We had been forewarned by Hai Tiet of this attack, and we had prepared for over two months for it. Now, when the big event finally came, the single thing that we hadn't prepared for had happened. So unheard of was an enemy gas attack in Military Region III that Americans assigned there were not even issued gas masks. When our team medic had scrounged up a box of masks several months earlier, some of us had laughed at "old Doc, the pack rat." Now, the precious masks were stored under lock and key in the dispensary, and Doc was on R and R. No one knew who had the key.

Capt. George Benham, one of the team's few remaining officers, quickly solved our problem. Ben sprinted across the open compound and shot off the dispensary lock. Scooping up an armload of gas masks, he ran from bunker to bunker and distributed them. No more than five minutes elapsed from the moment that I first detected the gas until I donned that mask, but it was the longest five minutes of my life. If Ben had been selling masks, I would have promised a year's pay for one.

We called for artillery illumination from Bao Trai, and helicopter gunships from wherever we could get them. The enemy mortar barrage subsided, but the sky was still lit up by the secondary explosions from the mortar position where the district's mortar crew had met their end.

Soon the gunships arrived on station, putting on their own impressive display of pyrotechnics. The helicopters were armed with rockets and "miniguns," and they passed low over our compound as they delivered their ordnance on targets we called to them. Actually, by then the enemy sappers had already withdrawn, leaving behind the body of one comrade. The best that the gunships could do was to saturate the tree line to the south of our compound with fire in hopes of inflicting some damage on the enemy sappers and mortarmen as they withdrew. I spent the rest of the evening crouched in the bunker, selfishly thanking God that the Vietcong's target for the evening had been the Vietnamese portion of the compound.

The enemy had come and gone in not more than thirty minutes. The brief mortar barrage had forced our troops into their bunkers and given the three attacking sapper squads the opportunity to cut their way through the barbed wire undetected. Luckily, only one of the attacking elements had succeeded in penetrating to its target. In the compound of the militia company, several sappers had managed to toss satchel charges into an empty building. It was this squad that had lost one man in the brief firefight that had followed. His body, clad only in a loincloth, had already been laid out at the crossroads by the government troops. The second enemy squad had attempted to penetrate our perimeter near the mortar pit. It was this unit that had tossed the tear gas canisters as they tried to create enough confusion to allow them to break through to our ammunition storage area. The third sapper squad had fought a fierce battle with the soldiers of our small artillery unit and failed to break through to their target. The score for the evening was five friendly troops killed and eight wounded. It could have been much worse.

Colonel Thanh could be relied upon to visit the scene of any major night attack at first light, a habit of his that caused great concern among his staff and advisors. Hence, no one was surprised when he and Colonel Bartlett arrived the next morning to inspect the damage and debrief Duc Hue's defenders. As Major Nghiem escorted Thanh around the area, it was evident that the colonel was displeased. At all three points where the attackers had approached their targets, tall grass had enabled them to crawl undetected to within a few meters of the government positions. At the RF militia compound in particular, a close look revealed the trails that the sappers had made as they crawled through the grass. Matted-down portions of grass just outside the wire marked where they had lain, awaiting the commencement of the covering mortar barrage. So close to the sentry posts were these spots that the Vietcong must have been able to eavesdrop on the government defenders as they lay awaiting the attack signal. When the final mortar rounds had fallen, the sappers had sprinted into the compound unopposed by the defenders, who had no way of knowing that the barrage was over. The sappers had done their damage and fled before most of the government troops had realized that they were in the compound. It had been a harrowing evening, but we had been lucky. I made a firm Chinese New Year's resolution that I would never again doubt Hai Tiet's word.

I left Duc Hue the next day to assume my new duties in Bao Trai, but not without experiencing pangs of guilt at leaving just when the district seemed to be in greatest peril. As I loaded my few possessions into a jeep, Major Nghiem emerged from his house and strode across the yard. In his best English, the man whose removal had been one of my primary objectives for more than a year thanked me for my assistance and wished me good luck. A feeling of remorse swept over me as I thought of my failure to be a good advisor to the Duc Hue Vietnamese, Major Nghiem included. Then, reminding myself that there was no looking back, I climbed into the jeep and headed for Bao Trai. As I drove slowly along the canal in Hiep Hoa and past the Tan My crossroads, it was difficult to believe that it had been more than a year since I had made my first drive along that road with Major Eby. The time had flown past, but we had accomplished a lot since Colonel Weissinger had bluntly warned me not to waste my tour shuffling papers.

Looking back on the balance sheet of that first thirteen months, I could see real progress in a strictly military sense, if progress were defined as breaking the hold of the insurgents on the peasantry. The number of village guerrillas and political cadre in Duc Hue had declined significantly during the year. I could also label as progress the maturation of our militia forces under Colonel Thanh. Colonel Bartlett had certainly played a major role here, earning high marks in my book as a true advisor. The colonel was everything that I had wanted to be but couldn't be. He had patiently cultivated the kind of relationship with the impetuous Colonel Thanh that allowed him to communicate suggestions that were often accepted and usually effective. Colonel Bartlett's advice was normally transmitted to Colonel Thanh via carefully thought-out and meticulously worded written memoranda—documents which were translated into Vietnamese and given to Thanh so that he could study them at his leisure. Evidence of Colonel Bartlett's success as an advisor was Colonel Thanh's habit of seeking out his American opposite number and including him in virtually every endeavor. This was in sharp contrast to the experiences encountered by many American advisors, who were constantly trying to catch up with their elusive counterparts, who in turn were going to great lengths to shake their American "tails." By the time I moved to Bao Trai, Colonel Bartlett had established a working relationship with Colonel Thanh that was about as good as I had seen—no small achievement when one considers the linguistic and cultural barriers the two men had to overcome.

On the negative side, there was much about our situation that was cause for uneasiness. Even though we had made progress against the Vietcong in our villages, we still had to face the grim truth that the battle for the so-called hearts and minds of Hau Nghia's villagers was far from over. Our major achievement in 1971 had been to scare the enemy away by means of more frequent and improved military operations and by an unorthodox but highly successful attack on the Tan My village shadow government. This was fine as far as it went, but several problems still haunted us.

There were no indications as 1972 began that there had been any major growth in the number of people who were positively oriented toward the Saigon government. There was simply no evidence to support a conclusion that the Vietcong's losses had been the government's gains. In fact, the deeper I delved into the enemy situation, the more I became inexorably involved in the friendly situation. The Vietcong's superior organization enabled them to home in on virtually every weakness of the Saigon government, and I often thought that the revolution should have given awards to corrupt government officials for service to the cause.

Admittedly, most of what came to our attention were problems of a penny-ante nature. We once learned of a hamlet chief who was squeezing the families of fallen government soldiers for a two-hundred-piaster burial fee, although no such fee actually existed. When I began to ask questions about the reasons for the execution of one official by his PSDF troops, I learned that he had been excusing some of the teenagers from the drudgeries of guard duty—for a fee. There seemed to be no end to the imagination of some government officials when it came to thinking up ways to supplement their incomes. Sergeant Trung once warned me that the Vietnamese grapevine was buzzing with reports of my "snooping activities" and that I should be careful as I pursued my curiosity. It was widely believed that Colonel Bartlett had Colonel Thanh's ear and that whatever I could ferret out about low-level corruption would come to Thanh's attention. Thanh, everyone knew, would tolerate no such shenanigans. Hence, the Vietnamese-speaking American captain was not very welcome in some of Hau Nghia's villages and hamlets.

For my part, I was not initially interested in looking over the shoulders of government officials. I just needed to get a feel for the reasons for the continuing insurgency, and my quest for answers invariably led to the conclusion that popular grievances against the government were real and justified. Even Colonel Thanh's troops themselves, who were overwhelmingly anti-Communist, were not inclined to say much good about their own government. To be sure, they were "pro-government," if this meant that they preferred it to Communism. They could—and had and would—fight hard to prevent a Communist military victory. But it was not comforting to know that with the American withdrawal in full swing, these government forces would be faced with even greater sacrifices in the not too distant future.

Yet another dimension of the situation that was cause for concern was the growing discomfort of our Vietnamese allies with the pace of the Vietnamization process—which to them meant American withdrawal. In spite of the fact that our militia forces had developed well in 1971, all of my counterparts were aware that we had not yet encountered in Hau Nghia any of the regular divisions of General Giap's People's Army of Vietnam—the feared NVA. North Vietnam was holding a heavy fist in reserve, and the Vietnamese in Hau Nghia were uneasy as they watched our advisory team shrink from two hundred men down to forty men in the space of one year.

Communist propagandists were aware of this South Vietnamese sensitivity, and they played on it constantly. Enemy propaganda leaflets appeared in Hau Nghia that spoke of the "heavy blows" to be struck in 1972—calling up visions of a conventional invasion by the North Vietnamese Army. And lest we not appreciate the NVA's power, the Communist propaganda machine constantly reminded our soldiers of the might of Giap's legions. The favorite theme was the rout of the South Vietnamese force that had invaded Laos in early 1971. Launched without American advisors for political reasons, Operation *Lam Son* 719 had initially gone well. Well, that is, until the North Vietnamese recovered from their surprise and reinforced the battlefield considerably faster than had been thought possible by many experts. Giap's units had inundated the overextended South Vietnamese units with punishing volumes of artillery and antiaircraft fire, shooting down more than a hundred helicopters in the process. Horror stories of entire South Vietnamese battalions disappearing without a trace filled the Vietnamese grapevine, and photographs of panicky South Vietnamese troops clinging desperately to the skids of helicopters appeared in the Vietnamese press and in the American *Stars and Stripes*. Banners appeared in Hau Nghia's hamlets, boasting that the North Vietnamese had captured a South Vietnamese airborne brigade commander (they had) and quoting him as saying that the Americans had failed to support the ill-fated operation. The message was not subtle—trusting the Americans will get you into trouble. American B-52 bombers and helicopter gunships could not protect the puppet troops from the invincible People's Army of Vietnam.

This propaganda campaign had not been without its impact on our militia troops. Even Lieutenant Tuan's men began to ask me if I too was going to "throw away" Vietnam and go home. Significantly, the Vietnamese word that was commonly used to refer to our departure was *bo*, to "discard" or "throw away," rather than *rut*, which means to "withdraw." As the larger Communist units began to make their appearance in Hau Nghia, my Vietnamese friends began to ask an increasing number of concerned questions. "Why don't the Americans give us a weapon as good as the B-40, Dai Uy?" "Why do the Communists have rockets and we don't, Dai Uy?" "Why does the M-16 magazine hold only twenty rounds, while an AK-47 magazine holds thirty, Dai Uy?" and "Have you heard that the Communists are bringing tanks down the Ho Chi Minh Trail, Dai Uy?" And so the questions went, questions that were symptomatic of a basic fear that preyed continuously on the minds of our Vietnamese allies. The day was fast approaching when they would be forced to face what they perceived to be the better-armed North Vietnamese Army in a military showdown. As I contemplated my new duties in Bao Trai, I shared both their apprehension and their concern. I had not forgotten Hai Tiet's warning that both Duc Hue and Bao Trai would be attacked during the 1972 offensive. Duc Hue had already been hit. Thanks to my timely reassignment, I would arrive in Bao Trai in time for the next act of the drama.

VII

THE HUMAN DATA BANK

It was time for Hai Tiet to get out of Hau Nghia province. His three-day stay had already lasted more than two months, and there was simply no telling when his luck would run out and he would find himself the victim of revolutionary justice. After Phich's loss, none of us were under any illusion about what the Vietcong might attempt. We had already captured one enemy document that related in detail Tiet's work against the revolution. On two more occasions since December, Vietcong troops had visited Tam's parents, obviously hoping to catch her at home. Anh Hai had already exhausted his supply of ready-to-hit targets in Duc Hoa, and it was an opportune time to send him to Bien Hoa. There, he could continue his vendetta against the Communists by providing details on Communist installations in Cambodia. Friends of mine in Bien Hoa had already located a house for Tiet and Tam, and Anh Hai had reluctantly agreed to move. Had I left it up to him, he would have elected to remain in Bao Trai, hunting down his former comrades until the day when either his luck ran out or the Communists gave up the struggle. To Tiet, Bien Hoa conjured up images of Colonel Sinh's operation, and he wanted nothing to do with it. Before he departed, he assured me that he would not be happy there, and repeated his prophecy that Bao Trai would be attacked by the Vietcong in the near future.

Colonel Bartlett was anxious to commence an attack on the Vietcong political infrastructure in Duc Hoa district. He directed me to dust off our Tan My village plan and coordinate with Capt. Tim Miller. Tim was the Phoenix advisor assigned to Trang Bang district, who had already scored a legendary series of victories against the local Communist shadow government. Working closely with corps-level interrogators in

Bien Hoa, Tim and his counterparts had dealt the Vietcong a more serious setback than that we had caused in Tan My. Using an unorthodox and systematic system of interrogation, Tim and his cohorts had been responsible for the arrest of nearly two hundred Vietcong legal cadre in Trang Bang district alone.

It had become obvious that the Vietcong reaction to the increased effectiveness of the Hau Nghia militia troops had been to increase their reliance on legal cadre operatives. Hau Nghia's illegal cadre, the "bunker residents," as I called them, had been too vulnerable to military operations. Such cadre were becoming a rare species as the revolution began to realize that a government ID card was the best protection for its agents. By 1972, at least two-thirds of Hau Nghia's shadow government were disguised as loyal citizens. To counter this kind of threat, it was necessary to rely on the patient application of police investigative techniques. As the Trang Bang scorecard proved, Tim Miller had mastered this tactic.

If the enemy's dry season offensive would only let up, I would have the time to spend a few days in Bien Hoa learning the nuances of Tim's approach. If, however, Communist main force battalions continued their shuttle operations between Cambodia and Hau Nghia, then I would again be forced to concentrate on my duties as Colonel Bartlett's intelligence officer. (One of the main reasons for the new offensive was to take the pressure off the local infrastructure. In Hau Nghia, this worked. As long as we were up to our ears in sapper attacks and the like, it was difficult to find the time to root out the village political cadre and guerrillas.)

The highlight of our workday in Bao Trai was the regular morning briefing of the province chief by his staff. The briefings enabled the staff to keep Thanh informed on recent significant developments, and provided him with the opportunity to work his magic with his subordinates. One of the province chief's favorite tactics during these briefings was the ambush, usually directed at one or another hapless staff officer who had fallen out of favor. Without a doubt, Thanh's preferred target was the corpulent and corrupt Colonel Ty, the province national police chief.

One memorable morning Thanh matter-of-factly asked the puffy-faced Ty to describe the measures that his police were taking to increase vigilance at the police checkpoints on the highway approaches to Bao Trai. Since Thanh had no use for Ty and everyone knew it, Ty should have smelled danger in the innocent request. But he was too much of a sycophant to be that sensitive, and he took the bait. For several minutes, he described the elaborate measures that he had instituted to protect Bao Trai from Vietcong infiltrators. The other staff officers in the room exchanged leering glances.

What Ty did not know was that Colonel Thanh had recently tested the police checkpoints, and they had failed miserably. On the preceding day, one of Thanh's men, dressed in civilian clothes, had driven a three-wheeled Lambretta all over the province, passing through every police checkpoint at least once. On the floor of the vehicle had been a plastic bag full of AK-47 rifles—the Communist troops' issue weapon. The contraband weapons had not even been hidden, except for the opaque plastic bag, but they had not been detected by any of the police inspectors. When Ty completed his soliloquy, one of Colonel Thanh's officers brought in the bag of weapons and unceremoniously dumped them on the floor at Ty's feet.

Colonel Thanh (sarcastically): "Are these weapons invisible?"

Colonel Ty: "No, sir."

Colonel Thanh: "Then can you explain how they passed through all of your checkpoints yesterday without being detected?"

Colonel Ty (reddening): "No, sir."

Colonel Thanh (angrily): "Well, I can. The driver reported to me that only one man was working at each checkpoint while the other officer was either off sitting in the shade or drinking tea. That's what your 'extra vigilance' means!"

Ty's puffy neck turned bright crimson as he absorbed this verbal abuse in silence. The other staff officers in the room struggled to stifle their delight at the fat colonel's exposure. To me, it was astounding that Ty, a full colonel, would accept such treatment from Thanh, a lieutenant colonel. But Thanh, as province chief, was a presidential appointee, and the boss—and he never let Ty forget it.

Colonel Thanh's briefings were the only action I saw during my first month in Bao Trai. The enemy's main force units had apparently withdrawn to Cambodia to rest and to prepare for whatever was to come next. The expected attack on Bao Trai did not materialize, and I was able to spend a few days in Bien Hoa understudying Tim Miller. Colonel Bartlett would not let me forget that the Vietcong organization in Duc Hoa district was simply begging to be rolled up. If I was to tackle this mission, I needed to learn how Tim had done it in Trang Bang.

Hai Tiet liked Bien Hoa. He was bubbling over with enthusiasm for his new job as he told me about the commando raids that he and his fellow defectors were going to conduct against Vietcong installations in Cambodia. Poor Tam did not share his enthusiasm for his new work, but she too had adjusted well to city life. (Within a month, Tiet volunteered to lead a raid against a major enemy headquarters in Cambodia. He and several other defectors provided precise charts of the enemy base camp—

including the locations of the command bunkers, security outposts, and supply dumps. The operation was successful, but Anh Hai was shot through the abdomen as he led the assault on the command bunker. In critical condition, he was evacuated by helicopter to Saigon, where the intervention of American advisors got him admitted to the U.S. Army Third Field Hospital. Doctors there saved his life. I visited him in the ward. Pale and weak, he flashed his inimitable smile and asked me how many Vietcong had died in the operation. Anh Hai recovered to continue his anti-Communist crusade.)

During my visit to Bien Hoa, I was comfortably ensconced in a sumptuous penthouse apartment that the Americans had leased from the widow of Gen. Do Cao Tri. Tri had been widely regarded as South Vietnam's most skilled and aggressive corps commander before he died in a helicopter crash in 1971. His apartment was equipped with a well-stocked, padded leather bar and decorated with the various engraved plaques and memorabilia that military men tend to accumulate. My first evening in Bien Hoa, I accompanied Tim Miller to the nearby La Plage, a Chinese-owned French restaurant.

No one who was ever stationed in Bien Hoa could forget the La Plage. That evening, as the sun set over the Dong Nai River, we enjoyed a before-dinner daiquiri, followed by a giant shrimp cocktail, beef tenderloin tips in wine sauce, and a "soufflé Grand Marnier" for dessert. Bien Hoa was a different world, and even though Hau Nghia seemed a million miles away, I couldn't shake the uneasy feeling that the city's dark streets harbored danger as we drove back to my quarters. I had become accustomed to an environment in which the nights belonged to the revolution.

Across the street from the Tri House apartment, a small sign marked the location of the Kim Bar, a survivor of a different era. Since Bien Hoa city had been declared off limits to American military some time ago, virtually all of the city's bars, massage parlors, and other health outlets had been forced to close their doors. Only the Kim Bar had survived, saved by virtue of its proximity to the only remaining American civilian billet in the city. Since several of my friends in Bien Hoa had spoken fondly of their nocturnal forays into the Kim, I decided to find out what I was missing in Hau Nghia.

The Kim was like any other bar in Vietnam. Six or eight underemployed, underdressed, and overly made-up young girls were playing cards, feeding the jukebox, and even dancing with one another to combat the boredom. I decided not to reveal that I knew their language. This was a sneaky trick, but I had learned that the intelligence one could gain in this manner more than compensated for any guilt feelings about being sneaky. This was true whether the environment was operational or social. On this particularly social evening, I amused myself by listening to the girls as they argued over which one of them would approach me.

"He's mine. You got the one this afternoon."

"Watch out! He looks fierce."

"Dear God! He just looked over here like he understood that. Be careful!"

I had my usual luck of the draw and got the ugliest one. The girl who finally approached me was thirtyish, and in Vietnam, when a woman looks thirty, she's probably forty-five. Vietnamese women—at least in the cities—do not show their age. Overly painted-up and sporting two gold teeth, my companion introduced herself in pidgin English. Then she went through the ritual of asking me my name, age, marital status, and home in the States. Disappointed at my bad draw, I proved to be a difficult mark. The persistent girl desperately strove to attract my attention by the subtle device of raising her skirt closer and closer to no-man's-land —or was it everyman's land? I just hadn't been in the boondocks long enough to appreciate her dubious charms. Her girl friend in the red dress —maybe. But not her. There being—unfortunately—no diplomatic way to trade her in, I returned to the Tri House unaccompanied, virtue and wallet intact.

The next day I met Capt. Tim Miller for our first work session. In a small office with a desk piled high with file folders, its walls plastered with maps, Tim had processed the information that had enabled him and his people to decimate the Communist organization in his district. Tim looked more like a television detective than an army officer. Heavyset and stocky, brusque, and often pushy, he approached everything with intensity. He was a person whose words and mannerisms conveyed the impression that he needed thirty hours in a day to accomplish whatever it was that he was doing. Tim had become known in Bien Hoa for his boundless energy and his unique ability to fit various pieces of information together and come up with a clear picture. He was a born detective. Tim was not known for his diplomacy, a failing that he could afford in his role as an American case officer. As an advisor to the Vietnamese, Tim was about as well suited temperamentally as the departed Colonel Weissinger. Impatient, anxious for results, intolerant of incompetence, and short-fused, Tim was being well utilized behind the scenes in Bien Hoa.

The Trang Bang district success story had begun in the spring of 1971, shortly after Tim had taken over a Phoenix program that suffered from all the ills I had encountered in Duc Hue. Tim had quickly perceived the threat posed by Trang Bang's extensive legal cadre Vietcong organization, and, with the backing of Colonel Weissinger, he had embarked on an experiment. Tim knew that the key to the destruction of such an underground organization was the skilled exploitation of human sources. If he were to penetrate the cloak of secrecy that surrounded his target, he would have to obtain the cooperation of someone who had been on the inside of the Communist apparatus. Tim also knew something that we advisors had encountered difficulty in selling to the Vietnamese—that one of the keys to securing the cooperation of a source was to disarm him psychologically by decent treatment. It was nearly impossible to do a good job of winning over a source if you threw him back into a cell at the end of each debriefing. Finally, Tim realized that only the patient preparation of dossiers on each Vietcong agent could insure that, once captured, the target would be convicted under Vietnamese law. Since the Vietnamese lacked the expertise and the facilities to implement such an experiment, Tim kicked off his project as a unilateral American effort—which would be gradually Vietnamized as time went on.

Trang Bang district was a good place to initiate this experiment for several reasons. First, strategically important Highway 1 ran through the center of the district, linking the western wing of Military Region III with Saigon and Bien Hoa. Whoever controlled Trang Bang controlled this key road, and its interdiction had been a favorite ploy of the Vietcong as well as their Vietminh predecessors. Furthermore, the northern portion of Trang Bang bordered on one of Vietnam's major enemy base areas, a jungle tract over which American and Vietcong forces had fought for years. Enemy military units and political headquarters concealed in this base area had traditionally relied upon the sympathetic citizens of Trang Bang for political and logistical support. Trang Bang was the home of a strongly entrenched infrastructure that had developed and matured for years. The Vietcong regarded it as their most effectively organized district in South Vietnam, and it had been used as the case study model district at the State Department's Foreign Service Institute for several years. Because of Trang Bang's strategic location on the western approaches to Saigon, its extensive and effective enemy underground posed an unacceptable threat to the government. Tim's mission was to put an end to this menace.

The job was pure detail work. Tim spent countless hours persistently checking and cross-checking the voluminous bits of information and leads that fell his way, always hoping for the big break. As in most police operations, the successful resolution of the toughest cases often turns on a major break, and Trang Bang was no exception. The story of how Capt.

Tim Miller and his co-workers broke the back of Trang Bang's Communist underground is a classic in the annals of counterinsurgency.

Tim's break came in the fall of 1971. Nguyen van Tung, alias Ba Tung, was the Communist village secretary of An Tinh village, Trang Bang district. Compared to An Tinh, Tan My was a government stronghold. Virtually all of An Tinh's 3,250 residents were members of families with strong revolutionary ties. As village secretary, Ba Tung could look to his father for guidance—the old man had been the leader of the village's Vietminh organization in the struggle against the French. In An Tinh, revolution was a family tradition. Ba Tung himself had been an active revolutionary since he was a teenager, rising from hamlet guerrilla to the top position in the village. An exceptionally bright young man with an encyclopedic memory, Ba Tung's rise in the ranks pointed to a bright future in the revolution. Tung's father, An Tinh's aging Communist elder statesman, must surely have viewed his son's achievements with pride.

But in the fall of 1971, the usually cautious Ba Tung committed a blunder that was to change his life. He ordered the execution of his boss's nephew. It happened this way. One of the guerrillas in the An Tinh village unit had caused nothing but trouble for the revolution by his undisciplined conduct. The young soldier was given to drunkenness, and he had tried Ba Tung's patience to the limit. When Tung learned that this troublemaker had raped a girl from one of the hamlets of An Tinh, he was livid. Such conduct could not be tolerated if the revolution was to enjoy the continued support of the people. The outraged Tung then ordered the village security chief to shoot the offender and bury him. When the sentence had been carried out, the conscientious Tung dutifully reported the incident to his superiors. To his horror, he learned that the victim of the summary execution had been the nephew of a high-ranking local Communist official. Knowing that no one would ever believe that he had been unaware of the dead guerrilla's family ties, Ba Tung faced a difficult dilemma. He knew that the dead man's uncle would spare no effort to take vengeance, and that by his hasty act he had jeopardized his career and his personal safety. Faced with this situation, Tung knew that he would ultimately come out second best in any encounter, Thus, the hapless Ba Tung turned himself in to a government unit in An Tinh village. Only the government, he felt, could protect him from his new enemy.

Tim Miller was jubilant when he learned the good news. Here was the long-awaited break. Ba Tung literally had to be able to identify many of the legal cadre in Trang Bang district.

At Tim's debriefing facility in Bien Hoa, Ba Tung proved to be re-markably cooperative. He was astounded at how much his debriefers already knew about Trang Bang's and An Tinh's Vietcong organizations. Challenged by his clever interrogators to match their knowledge of An Tinh's revolutionary apparatus, Tung responded by naming no less than twenty-eight Communist agents who had helped him when he was village secretary. His memory was so good that Tim was able to produce target folders on each individual in which their names, house numbers, and other data essential to make an arrest appeared.

In early November, 1971, a secret meeting took place in Colonel Thanh's house in Bao Trai. In attendance were Colonel Bartlett, Colonel Thanh, Colonel Sinh (the Bien Hoa interrogation center commander), and Tim Miller. The purpose of the meeting was to obtain Colonel Thanh's approval of an operations plan to arrest the twenty-eight people whom Ba Tung had implicated. The concept called for a heliborne oper-ation in which Ba Tung would fly in the command helicopter, while troops of Colonel Thanh's RF would be transported in eight Huey air-craft. One helicopter would be used to swoop low and mark the target houses with colored smoke grenades, after which the troop-carrying Huey birds would descend to round up the people and sort out those to be arrested. Disguised in a wig and wearing female clothes, Ba Tung would be available to identify targets about whom any doubt existed.

Colonel Thanh gave his assent to the plan, although he privately expressed his doubt to Colonel Sinh that it would be possible to descend on the homes of so many Communist cadre and simply arrest them with-out a fight. Like mine, Colonel Thanh's experiences with the Vietcong infrastructure had been almost exclusively with the armed bunker resi-dents of Duc Hue. The idea of peacefully arresting a Vietcong was some-thing relatively new.

The plan worked to near perfection. In the space of an afternoon, the task force arrested twenty-three surprised Vietcong, ranging from supply cadre to military intelligence agents. The only hitch in the operation had occurred when Ba Tung, disguised as a female, blew his cover by urinat-ing against a papaya tree—to the delight of Colonel Thanh's troops.

Tim and his men immediately spirited the captives to Bien Hoa, where they were segregated and billeted in a "guest facility" run by the national police. A large, comfortable villa, the "National Police Convalescent Facility" could house a score or more of sources. Debriefing rooms and sleeping quarters alike were well equipped, and a full-time staff of cooks and maids maintained the facility. Its only resemblance to a jail was the fact that there were armed guards at the front gate. It was here that the first fruits of Tim's efforts were harvested. The unlucky twenty-three "guests" were confronted in turn by Ba Tung and ruthlessly played off against one another. Tim repeatedly reminded them that the only way to save themselves from government prisons was to cooperate as Ba Tung had done. Tung, of course, was always in the wings, cajoling his former comrades to join him in freedom. Some of the twenty-three men and women elected to do this. Their confessions, of course, led to more arrests, new rounds of "debriefing by confrontation," and yet another series of roll-up operations. And so it snowballed. Tim soon found himself so swamped with sources and data generated by this cycle that he became a full-time dossier man. Working ceaselessly, he produced dozens of target folders every month, all of which spawned new arrests, debriefings, and targets. The number of cooperative Trang Bang Vietcong cadre under Tim's control multiplied rapidly, and this "human data bank" virtually took the sport out of all interrogations. At one point in 1972, Tim was juggling no less than one hundred cooperative ex-Vietcong.

The damage to the Vietcong's hitherto secure organization was extensive. Tim's dragnet decimated the Communists' military intelligence network in Trang Bang and even rolled up a number of agents who worked for higher echelons of the Communist command. Shadow government functionaries from neighboring Loc Hung village were picked up during one raid, as were a number of Communist officials who worked for Trang Bang District Headquarters itself. Even though military targets were not the objective of the Bien Hoa debriefings, many enemy bases along the Saigon River were compromised by the ever-growing human data bank. During 1971 and 1972, Tim's people passed target after target to the Vietnamese corps commander, with disastrous results for Communist military units in the Saigon River base areas.

The Communist high command was alarmed by these setbacks, and it was not long before captured documents in Trang Bang began to reflect this concern. To protect Ba Tung, Tim contrived to blame much of the damage being inflicted on the Trang Bang organization on an unfortunate Vietcong prisoner named Tu Duc. Tu Duc had been the chief of military proselyting in Trang Bang district before his capture. He was a dedicated and a knowledgeable Communist who was assessed by his debriefers as "brilliant and likeable." Tu Duc could debate dialectical materialism with his captors and more than hold his own, whereas most Vietcong didn't know dialectical materialism from a rice bowl. He was also a strong-willed man who refused to be seduced into cooperating by Tim's clever interrogators. Try as they might, Tu Duc's captors could not persuade their likeable adversary to name the many legal cadre whom they were certain he knew by virtue of his position. In desperation, they attempted to break his spirit by exposing him as a traitor. The unfortunate man was forced to accompany several of the arrest operations generated by Ba Tung and other sources. By "burning" him in this manner, it was hoped that Tu Duc would realize the futility of his continued silence.

By mid-1972, the total catch from the original operation and its offspring had reached more than three hundred. Since Tim had paraded Tu Duc openly around during several of the arrest operations, the word had reached the Communists that he had betrayed the revolution. Distressed by his plight, the despondent man attempted to commit suicide one night by nearly cutting off his arm with a straight razor. Fortunately, an Australian doctor at the Bien Hoa hospital miraculously saved his life, even though his pulse had slipped to below thirty. Later, Tu Duc would see the light and throw in his lot with Tim's people, to become a valued addition to the effort. The human data bank was growing like a comic strip character.

Throughout the course of American involvement in Vietnam, Vietcong saboteurs had written an impressive record of headline-making successes in the Saigon area. The bombing of the Brinks Hotel officer billet was one example of such an operation. All over Saigon, police substations, nightclubs, restaurants, and any establishment that catered to the Americans were targets of Vietcong demolitions experts who belonged to the notorious N-10 Sapper Battalion. During his famous visit to Saigon in 1970, the antiwar Senator George McGovern was photographed by the press amid the ruins of a Saigon hotel that N-10 agents had blown up to coincide with his visit. N-10 operations were always highly political, providing as they did excellent and accessible color newsreel documentation of Vietcong "influence" in Saigon. One of the most successful operations spawned by the defection of Ba Tung involved the N-10.

One evening in Bien Hoa, after the Trang Bang roll-ups were well under way, Ba Tung and one of Tim's debriefers were drinking beer together. Tung was reminiscing absently about his days as a Vietcong when he abruptly mentioned that he had forgotten to tell his new superiors about the N-10 Sapper Battalion headquarters, which was located in An Tinh village. Thus began one of the most unheralded operations of the Vietnam War.

Tung explained that he was the only cadre in An Tinh who was privy to the location of the N-10 headquarters complex. He then described to his incredulous listener how Nam Cuong, the battalion commander, and eight members of his staff were sheltered in a complex of three bunkers in a heavily mined and booby-trapped area of An Tinh village. According to Tung, Nam Cuong and his men had only two links with the outside world. The headquarters bunker was equipped with a radio, through which the N-10 received its encrypted orders from the Communist high command. Communication with the battalion's Saigon agents was accomplished by a pretty, sixteen-year-old courier named Thi Be. Ba Tung was absolutely insistent that Nam Cuong's headquarters was completely vulnerable to attack if the attackers could only breach its protective barrier of mines and booby traps. An Tinh village had been deliberately selected as the site of the sensitive headquarters because it was a secure area relatively close to Saigon. Ba Tung also revealed that no security troops were assigned to the N-10's headquarters other than the seven men who worked with Nam Cuong and Thi Be.

From the day of these revelations, the N-10 project became priority business. Such a target was too lucrative to pass up. Tim asked Ba Tung to draw a sketch of the bunker complex, which Tung did easily. He had been born in a house not fifty meters from Nam Cuong's headquarters. On his sketch, Tung depicted the ruins of his birthplace, a nearby large banyan tree, and the three bunkers. Tim then compared Tung's sketch to an aerial photograph of the village. To everyone's delight (and no one's surprise), the photo and the sketch were a nearly perfect match. A skilled photo interpreter confirmed that the photo showed a high probability of at least three bunkers near the banyan tree. In Trang Bang, the district chief admitted to Tim that the section of An Tinh village described by Ba Tung had been "off limits" to his troops for years because of the many mines and booby traps emplaced there by the enemy.

To Tim, this all looked too good to be true. Surely, he speculated, when Ba Tung rallied, Nam Cuong must have regarded his headquarters as compromised and taken the precaution of moving to another location. Still, the aerial photographs showed signs of recent movement around the suspected bunker complex. With a "nothing ventured, nothing gained" outlook and the comforting knowledge that Ba Tung had not been wrong in anything he had revealed, Tim attended yet another meeting in Bao Trai at Colonel Thanh's house. At the meeting, Colonel Thanh gave his approval for a raid into the N-10 headquarters.

The plan called for the target area to be sealed off at dawn by Colonel Thanh's troops. Commencing at 9:00 A.M., an intensive artillery concentration would be directed against the bunkers by the banyan tree. On the ground, a young North Vietnamese sapper from Tim's coterie of Bien Hoa sources would guide the South Vietnamese through the minefield to their objective. Door gunners on the command and control helicopter would direct suppressive fire on the bunkers if necessary. The planners unanimously agreed that every attempt would be made to capture Nam Cuong and as many of his staff as possible. Colonel Thanh would brief his ground commander on this requirement. If taken alive, Nam Cuong would be a priceless addition to the human data bank.

Tim's luck held out, and the operation was conducted almost without a flaw. As the artillery lifted, the North Vietnamese sapper led Colonel Thanh's troops through the minefield, locating and disarming twenty-four booby traps in their path. Hovering over the area, the command helicopter began to receive ground fire from several enemy soldiers near the bunker complex. The door gunners returned the fire, and the resistance ceased. From the ground, the North Vietnamese sapper reported to Tim by radio that the bunkers had been overrun. All N-10 personnel were either dead or wounded, and a large quantity of documents had been seized.

By the time the command helicopter landed near the banyan tree, a tragic thing happened. The wounded Nam Cuong had surrendered to the government troops, who had promptly executed him on the spot. The sixteen-year-old courier, Thi Be, had been wounded in the thigh and would probably have suffered the same fate had not Colonel Thanh and the rest of the command group arrived. The North Vietnamese sapper was bitter and angry at what he had witnessed. Colonel Bartlett lodged a strong protest with Colonel Thanh, who apologetically explained that the Trang Bang militia troops had been tormented by the Vietcong for years. (Later, Thanh reprimanded and demoted the commander of the unit.)

A search of the bunker complex turned up seven additional bodies and more than two thousand pages of sensitive documents. Conspicuous among these documents were several scrapbooks that contained newspaper clippings describing "N-10 Victories." The wounded girl was loaded onto one of the helicopters and transported to Bien Hoa, where the Australian doctor repaired the damage to her leg. Later, surrounded by other former Trang Bang cadre, Thi Be became yet another recruit for the human data bank.

The documents seized that day proved to contain a treasure trove of information. They clearly indicated that the N-10's urban action arm in Saigon consisted entirely of legal cadre. One notebook identified more than sixty N-10 agents in the Saigon area. It contained page after page of true names, cover names, post office boxes, addresses, and instructions for the clandestine meetings and drops employed by the N-10 to control its apparatus. The same document also identified more than forty demolition-trained sappers and almost a score of support personnel. This one book alone was the key to the roll-up of the N-10.

There was also a written critique entitled "How We Blew Up the Tu Do Club," in which the female author detailed the strengths and weaknesses of a Saigon nightclub bombing that had made headlines in 1970. The troops also recovered a large scrapbook that contained the original plans for the bombing of the Brinks Hotel and newspaper clippings of Senator McGovern standing in the ruins of another N-10 triumph in downtown Saigon.

But most surprising of all was a set of documents that revealed that the chief operations officer of the N-10 in Saigon was a twenty-year-old girl named Nguyen thi Kieu. Kieu was a native of An Tinh village, as were almost all of the sixty-odd sapper cadre implicated by the documents. Most of them had been recruited right out of Trang Bang's senior high school, and they were now living in Saigon under cover names with government ID cards. Ba Tung knew Nguyen thi Kieu, as he knew virtually everyone from An Tinh. Kieu, he recalled, had served as a low-level courier while a teenager and then been sent to school in Saigon by her parents. There, the documents confirmed, she had been recruited by the N-10.

Because the N-10 apparatus was almost entirely Saigon-based, these documents were turned over to the Vietnamese special police in the capital, who would be responsible for reacting to the mass of exploitable information that they contained. Properly handled, the intelligence coup that the documents provided would enable the Vietnamese to put the N-10 out of action, not to mention the possibility of recruiting some of the compromised Vietcong cadre to work as government informants.

Several months later, a downcast Colonel Sinh reported to Tim that the Saigon police had failed to recruit a single informant, although they had succeeded in arresting fifty of the N-10 personnel. The embarrassed Sinh related to Tim how a team of Saigon special police had managed to get lost during an abortive attempt to find Nguyen thi Kieu in An Tinh village. "I am ashamed to tell you this," Sinh confessed, "but several of the prisoners were executed in Saigon—tortured to death."

Tim, angry and impatient with such blunders, organized his own operation into An Tinh, but all he and his men were able to accomplish was to obtain photographs of the girl. By now, of course, the manhunt was fruitless. Kieu had been given ample warning time, thanks to the blundering Saigon police. Later, Tim learned that she had changed her appearance and managed to avoid the police dragnet. Nguyen thi Kieu was to survive her close call and live to be acclaimed as a heroine of the revolution.

All of us were heartsick at the brutal amateurishness of the Saigon special police, for we had spent considerable effort in educating our counterparts that the use of force and torture to extract information was not effective. Even Colonel Sinh, whose Combined Interrogation Center had so frightened Hai Tiet, had gradually come around to the acceptance of our position that electric shock, water torture, and beatings were inappropriate forms of interrogation. Still, as Americans, we never seemed to be able to overcome the Vietnamese conviction that an enemy prisoner somehow forfeits his right to life itself. At times, this difference in value systems was one of the most frustrating problems faced by all of us who worked closely with the Vietnamese.

In spite of the regrettable deaths of Nam Cuong and the unnamed victims of the Saigon police, the overall results of the N-10 operation were significant. For the remainder of the war, no more major acts of sabotage were committed in Saigon. The N-10 was out of action, thanks to Tim Miller and a former Vietcong named Ba Tung.

VIII

STILL MORE REVOLUTIONARY JUSTICE

One should never argue with results, and so I returned from Bien Hoa persuaded that Tim Miller's Trang Bang experiment had shown the way to attack the Vietcong organization in Duc Hoa district. Hunting down illegal cadre in their bunkers as we had done in Tan My village had been effective, but this was simply not the way to defeat an organization that consisted overwhelmingly of legal cadre. It was these apparently up-standing citizens who were the eyes and ears of the covert village revolutionary committees. If this structure of legals could be compromised and rolled up, the hard-core bunker residents would be helpless without their support. Furthermore, in an environment where the enemy's military profile was becoming higher, it was imperative to neutralize Duc Hoa's Communist apparatus, since a goodly number of the Vietcong agents were military intelligence and military proselyting cadre. These men were the most dangerous to us in the short run, for it was they who recruited traitors in our militia units and gave the enemy detailed sketches of our outposts' defenses.

Colonel Bartlett haunted Colonel Thanh with reminders of how seriously our units were threatened by Communist legal cadre agents. He also strove to sell Thanh on the political dangers posed by the shadow government. In the event of a cease-fire, these cadre would certainly surface and attempt to challenge and embarrass the government. If this happened, the Communists could very well win by sheer organizational superiority what they had failed to win on the battlefield. The name of the game, Colonel Bartlett urged Colonel Thanh, was to stamp out this covert organization while it was still open season on Communists. With the Paris peace talks under way, there was no telling how much time we had left before our military hands would be tied.

111

Colonel Thanh was quick to appreciate the gravity of the situation. Convinced by Colonel Bartlett that time was not on our side, he began to take steps to wage war on the legal cadre apparatus. One of the first was the establishment of closer ties between Colonel Thanh and Colonel Sinh's interrogation center. Sinh's people had begun to turn out some first-rate interrogation reports as his officers began to rely more on psychology and less on force to procure cooperation. Thanh began to rely more and more on this asset at Bien Hoa, and Colonel Sinh himself began to pay regular liaison visits to Bao Trai. In time, the two men developed a close personal and working relationship. The "Bien Hoa connection" begun by Tim Miller had developed into a productive partnership.

With Colonel Thanh's support and a break or two, we felt that we could clean out Duc Hoa by the end of the summer. Not coincidentally, this was also the scheduled end of my extended tour. If we could make the kind of inroads against the Duc Hoa apparatus that Tim had made in Trang Bang, I could rotate home with a sense of mission accomplishment. The key to success was Colonel Thanh. Nowhere in Vietnam was the old adage, "What the boss doesn't check, doesn't get done," truer than in Hau Nghia. If Colonel Thanh took a personal interest in something, it got done. If not, then apathy and inaction were the most likely results. With Colonel Thanh supporting our efforts, Hau Nghia province could well develop a functioning Phoenix program after all.

But events conspired to prevent us from launching our planned assault on the Duc Hoa district Vietcong organization. As always, the problem was the refusal of the enemy to cooperate. While I was understudying Tim Miller in Bien Hoa and planning my offensive against the Duc Hoa shadow government, the North Vietnamese in Hanoi were completing plans for an offensive of their own. We were about to be given a lesson by General Giap's People's Army on the meaning of revolutionary violence —Hanoi style.

The Communists played their military trump card on March 30, 1972, when thirteen North Vietnamese divisions launched what became known as the "Easter Offensive." Hanoi's overt, conventional invasion struck in three of South Vietnam's four military regions. Virtually overnight, the South Vietnamese and their remaining American advisors found themselves engulfed in a new kind of war. The much-publicized tank-led assaults against Quang Tri province in the north and the town of An Loc north of Saigon were accompanied by several other strong thrusts, one of which was launched from the Cambodian Parrot's Beak into Hau Nghia province.

The scale and ferocity of this offensive underscored dramatically that the Communists had more than recovered from the military reversals of Tet 1968 and the 1970 raids into their Cambodian sanctuaries. Hanoi had concluded, as my sources were telling me in Hau Nghia, that the ongoing American troop withdrawals signaled a lack of resolve in Washington. The Easter attacks were thus partly calculated to embarrass the Nixon administration in an election year by discrediting Vietnamization. In January, 1972, even as North Vietnamese forces prepared for their attacks, President Nixon had announced the imminent withdrawal of an additional 70,000 troops, a move that would leave only 65,000 Americans in Vietnam out of the 543,000-man expeditionary force that was there when he was elected in 1968. The go-for-broke assaults of Hanoi's troops described in the following pages were North Vietnam's attempt to gain leverage at the stalled Paris peace talks, while at the same time providing critically needed support to its faltering comrades in South Vietnam's beleaguered shadow government—whose plight was so typified by the defections of men like Hai Chua, Phich, and Hai Tiet in Hau Nghia province.

The Communist attacks met with initial successes as tactical surprise produced early victories. The Quang Tri province capital fell, and North Vietnamese forces encircled the town of An Loc. But as the shock of the opening assaults wore off, the South Vietnamese and American response made it evident that Hanoi's leaders had underestimated the fighting spirit of the fledgling South Vietnamese army, as well as President Nixon's determination to resist military intimidation. On the ground, Saigon's armies fought fiercely to regain lost territory. In the air, both South Vietnamese and American planes mercilessly bombed the massed North Vietnamese invaders. President Nixon was scheduled to visit Moscow on May 20, but he nonetheless ordered American bombers, including B-52s, to bomb the North. The American Navy mined North Vietnam's harbors and inland waterways for the first time in the long war. This costly fighting heavily diminished Hanoi's forces in the South, while the renewed air attacks in the North brought the war home to the residents of Hanoi and Haiphong. The Easter onslaught soon bogged down into a bloody stalemate, and then became a slow, but inexorable reversal for the Communists. Hanoi's first combined arms offensive of the war was tailor-made for the firepower that American and South Vietnamese forces had so often been unable to employ effectively during the course of the war. The determined defense of An Loc by the South Vietnamese seemed to indicate that Vietnamization had been more successful than anyone had dared to hope.

In Hau Nghia province, the men of Advisory Team 43 and our Vietnamese allies were the target of a North Vietnamese division-sized feint in the direction of Saigon—an attack that led to several weeks of bitter fighting. These battles warrant little more than a footnote in the history of the war, yet, for the participants, they were a period of unprecedented violence and danger in a province that was no stranger to the sounds of combat.

Beginning on March 30, we began to receive reports of widespread, large-scale North Vietnamese attacks around the country. Particularly ominous were the bulletins that announced a tank-led Communist attack against South Vietnam's northernmost province of Quang Tri. There, North Vietnamese forces were said to be routing the newly formed and combat-inexperienced 3d Division. Hanoi's troops had employed long-range, Soviet-built 130-millimeter guns to pound South Vietnamese targets from positions in the demilitarized zone. The South Vietnamese had been helpless to retaliate, since the North Vietnamese artillery was emplaced far beyond the range of their American-supplied 105- and 155-millimeter howitzers. Radio Hanoi quickly homed in on the plight of the outgunned and outnumbered South Vietnamese. The "Nguyen Hue Offensive," Hanoi crowed, was "liberating large parts of the South," and signaled the "death knell" of the Saigon regime.*

As the events of the next week unfolded, it looked as if our worst fears were coming to pass. Hanoi had decided to go for broke and had committed its refurbished and newly equipped regular army to the struggle. Possessed of the unique advantage of being able to concentrate their forces at places where the South Vietnamese were overextended, the North Vietnamese were scoring dramatic initial successes.

These initial victories of the North Vietnamese were destructive of the morale of the South Vietnamese in Bao Trai. As the bad news continued to flow in, the officers and men in the headquarters besieged me with questions about the probable American reaction to the North Vietnamese invasion. "What will President Nixon do, Dai Uy?" was a question that I must have fielded evasively ten times a day during the first week of the Nguyen Hue Offensive.

By the middle of April, Hanoi had committed thirteen divisions to the offensive. North Vietnamese units had overrun the better part of Quang Tri province in the north, and three full divisions were assaulting Binh

*Named after the Vietnamese Emperor Nguyen Hue, who defeated the Chinese in the twelfth century.

Long province, a few hours' drive north of Saigon. The North Vietnamese attackers had encircled the province capital of An Loc and launched repeated tank assaults into the town. It was a tactical and a logistical triumph—the first time that the Communists had employed armor that far south. In An Loc, Soviet-supplied SA-7 heat-seeking antiaircraft missiles, fired from the shoulders of NVA infantrymen, changed overnight the ground rules for the use of the helicopter. The appearance of enemy tanks so close to Saigon caused an outbreak of "tank fever" among South Vietnamese troops everywhere, including Hau Nghia. (Tank fever is a highly contagious disease that affects the average infantryman in any area of operations where enemy armor is deployed for the first time. Its chief symptom is the tendency to hear, see, and smell tanks everywhere.)

Western journalists quickly labeled the North Vietnamese attacks the "Easter Offensive" and speculated that Hanoi's objective was the establishment of a so-called Third Vietnam. This was a term coined to describe the Communist desire to control a significant portion of the territory and people of South Vietnam for use as a negotiating chip. Achievement of this objective would lend credence to Hanoi's claims that the Vietcong's "Provisional Revolutionary Government" was legitimate (in that it controlled more than just vast stretches of territory only sparsely populated by tribespeople).

Whatever their objectives, the North Vietnamese attacks were cause for considerable alarm to us in Hau Nghia. Apart from their impact on our counterparts' morale, the new attacks heightened speculation that the North Vietnamese units known to be based across the border from Hau Nghia might be committed against our militia troops. To make matters worse, the last American ground surveillance radar team, which had been set up in Duc Hue, had just stood down as a part of the president's latest withdrawal announcement. If the North Vietnamese streamed out of Cambodia, we would have no warning.

Until the assaults in Quang Tri and An Loc, no one had really worried about the possibility that our militia troops might have to face enemy tanks. Now, as hundreds of Communist tanks clanked into battle, we had to contend with the reality that the ground rules of our small unit war in Hau Nghia could be rapidly overcome by events. It was one thing for Colonel Thanh's lightly armed militia troops to take on Vietcong main force battalions—which were actually only company-sized light infantry themselves. It was another for our regional force companies and battalions to lock horns with regiment- and division-sized North Vietnamese units that had given a good account of themselves against the American army earlier in the war. Hanoi's thirteen-division invading force had pinned down almost every South Vietnamese regular army division, with the exception of the three divisions responsible for securing the rice-rich Mekong Delta region. If the North Vietnamese were to strike Hau Nghia and Tay Ninh provinces—the western approach to Saigon—the defense would be up to one regular division, the 25th, and our militia forces. Since the 25th Division was one of the government's weaker units and was committed primarily in Tay Ninh, Colonels Bartlett and Thanh realized that the defense of Hau Nghia province would be in the hands of the local boys of our militia forces.

Even though as an intelligence officer I was more concerned with the enemy situation than with the state of the friendly forces, I nonetheless had my own ideas about the fighting capabilities of our militia forces. When they were well led, these troops were as aggressive and effective as any commander could reasonably desire. I therefore counted among our strengths that Colonel Thanh had spent 1971 replacing combat commanders until, in Colonel Bartlett's words, "the eight fightingest officers" were now in command of Hau Nghia's eight regional force battalions and groups. I also counted as a major plus for our side the dynamic and aggressive leadership of Colonel Thanh himself. Thanh's narrow escapes from death were legendary, and he was widely believed by his superstitious troops to be immune from death or injury. Once, in the spring of 1971, Thanh was conversing with two American officers during a land-clearing operation in Trang Bang district. When a B-40 rocket exploded a few meters away, both Americans were killed. Thanh, who was not wearing a flak jacket, as the Americans were, was not so much as scratched. News of this incident spread rapidly among his troops and added fuel to their belief in Thanh's invincibility. Even allowing for the exaggeration of the Thanh legend, we were indeed lucky to be blessed with a leader of Colonel Thanh's stature.

By the end of April, Hanoi's offensive had exceeded the scope and ferocity of the fabled Tet Offensive of 1968, and it showed no signs of fading. North Vietnamese units struck in northern Tay Ninh province, our next-door neighbor, and this convinced us that it was only a matter of time until our turn arrived. Colonel Bartlett reluctantly agreed that we would have to shelve our plans for an attack on the Duc Hoa district Vietcong organization in favor of more urgent business. My morning briefings to the colonel thereafter dealt with the tracking of several North Vietnamese regiments that we knew were somewhere in Cambodia and that we feared would soon be committed against our militia forces.

This was a frustrating period for Americans and Vietnamese alike in Hau Nghia. We watched helplessly as the North Vietnamese offensive ground on and did what we could to prepare ourselves for a possible onslaught from Cambodia. We knew that a buildup of enemy forces across the border was under way, but we had no way to unlock the secret of Hanoi's intentions for our province. Colonel Bartlett believed that since the bulk of the South Vietnamese regular army was already committed around the country, Hanoi would be foolish not to take a stab at Saigon from the west—through Hau Nghia. But the only information in our hands was Hai Tiet's somewhat dated insistence that Bao Trai would be attacked. Beyond that, we weren't even certain which North Vietnamese units were poised in Cambodia. Colonel Bartlett and I spent many evenings together in his quarters during this period second-guessing one another on what the future held for Hau Nghia. Once again, we needed an intelligence windfall to aid in clarifying the situation, but this time around there was no Hai Tiet in the wings to bail us out.

At 1:00 A.M. on the 13th of April, two loud explosions shook the walls of my bedroom. Still half asleep, I heard one of our Vietnamese guards yell something unintelligible. Then another explosion rocked the building, this one closer than the first. Bao Trai was under a mortar attack. Grabbing my alert gear and my M-16, I rushed to the ladder that led to our rooftop bunkers. By now, small arms fire had erupted all around the town's perimeter, and I knew that Hai Tiet's final prediction was coming to pass. Crouched behind the sandbags of my bunker on the roof, I could see that we were in good shape. Our villa was situated in the center of town, two hundred meters from the perimeter where the sound of gunfire told me that the fighting was taking place. Our courtyard was surrounded by an illuminated, eight-foot barbed wire fence, which was covered by two machine guns and our M-16s from the roof.

Thus secured, I rode out the first enemy attack on Bao Trai since the Tet Offensive. Several more mortar rounds impacted, one of them in the Team 43 compound across the street, injuring two captains. We had two radios on the roof, one to monitor the Vietnamese net and the other to keep in touch with the advisory team. The radio traffic told us that Bao Trai was under a sapper attack by at least four enemy elements and that our perimeter had so far been penetrated at only one location, the militia company compound about four hundred meters north of us.

Like the Duc Hue sapper attack, this one was over quickly. Within thirty minutes, most of the small arms fire had ceased, and I hurried to the province headquarters compound—a bit concerned that I might be shot by a nervous sentry. The province operations center smelled like victory. Colonel Thanh was barking orders to the artillery liaison officer for more illumination rounds east of Bao Trai, where an enemy sapper squad was retreating across the open rice paddies. Thanh's staff was all smiles, and I overheard one officer say something about an enemy unit that had been wiped out at the national police compound down the street.

Once again, Colonel Thanh's fabled luck had held out. Somewhere around 12:45 A.M., Thanh had awakened, plagued by a disconcerting hunch that something was about to happen. Unable to go back to sleep, he alerted all units that shared in the manning of the Bao Trai perimeter. Within ten minutes, troops in all units except the 773d RF Company had manned their bunkers; for some reason, the RF troops did not receive word. A few minutes later, a sergeant in the national police compound fired an aerial flare, a routine alert precaution. In the brilliant light of the flare, the shocked policemen discovered a squad of ten sappers lying prone in the barbed wire perimeter, some two meters from the ports of their bunkers. The enemy troops had been scheduled to attack at 1:00 A.M., and they were awaiting the commencement of the mortar barrage that was to provide them cover. The enemy squad leader, who was lying in the shadow of one bunker, immediately stuck his pistol through the bunker's firing port and fired one shot. The surprised defenders killed him instantly. Then a machine gun mounted in a tower swung into action and cut down the helpless sappers as they struggled to extricate themselves from the barbed wire. Eight North Vietnamese died within minutes in the wire, the victims of Colonel Thanh's premonition.

At the Chieu Hoi Center down the street, Det's Armed Propaganda Platoon repulsed another sapper squad. This enemy unit failed to get within hand grenade range of its objective. In the morning, all that could be found of them were their abandoned explosive charges and several blood trails.

Across the street, the 773d militia company had not fared so well. One of the unit's sentries had been killed by a bullet to the head, and the attackers had momentarily penetrated the compound under the cover of the brief mortar barrage. Fortunately for the government soldiers, several of the satchel charges hurled by the invaders had failed to detonate, and the damage had been minimal. The enemy unit had withdrawn as quickly as it had come, apparently unscathed.

It had not been a good night for the Communists. At the other end of town, yet another sapper squad had encountered difficulties. This unit had apparently been ordered to assault the police compound from a second direction. But, in the darkness, its leader had apparently mistaken the public works compound for the police installation immediately to its north. The enemy troops had raced through the empty compound, tossed their satchel charges through the windows of its vacant offices, and triumphantly raised a red, blue, and gold Vietcong flag on the flagpole. Having liberated one road grader and two dump trucks, one of the sappers, in a final act of heroism, had hurled his last charge at a barbershop across the street. Thus vindicated, the lucky North Vietnamese had fled across the rice paddies, one step ahead of Colonel Thanh's troops. Had they not become disoriented, they would have been slaughtered in the wire of the police compound as were their less fortunate comrades.

The whole town was alive with different versions of how Colonel Thanh had been warned of the impending attack in a dream, and how the eight dead North Vietnamese had been the victims of the province chief's mysterious powers. In the morning, curious crowds gathered at the central marketplace to gawk at the bodies of the fallen men. The dead sappers appeared to be youths of eighteen or nineteen, clad only in shorts and pistol belts. Their barefoot bodies were camouflaged with charcoal and mud, and had been horribly chewed up by the police machine gun. We searched them meticulously for some sign of a unit identification, but to no avail. The security-conscious sappers hadn't even left a name on the back of a pistol belt that we could cross-check against the captured unit rosters that we had on file.

I was in Bien Hoa when it happened, sitting in Colonel Sinh's office trying to con him into letting me interrogate a North Vietnamese lieutenant who had been captured in Tay Ninh province. The phone rang, and as soon as Sinh started to talk, I knew that something terrible had just happened.

"What?" shouted Sinh incredulously. "Who?" A brief pause, during which Sinh's face blanched. A quick glance at me, and then the bad news. "Your Colonel Thanh is dead, Dai Uy. He was ambushed this morning in Duc Hoa!"

Sinh, deeply shaken, slammed the receiver down. Biting his lip, he told me that Colonel Thanh had been killed by a mine on Route 9 south of Duc Hoa that same morning. A mine! We had not had a mining incident for months in either Duc Hoa or Duc Hue. Colonel Sinh had no further details, including any information about Colonel Bartlett. Sometimes—though not often—the two men traveled in one jeep. Colonel Sinh was no help here. He was so shaken at hearing the tragic news that he had not asked for all of the details from the caller. All he remembered from his brief conversation was that Colonel Thanh had been killed. Sinh buried his face in his hands and repeated over and over, "I told him so many times, so many times, not to ride around so much in his jeep."

On my way back to Bao Trai, I stopped briefly at Corps Headquarters, where the duty officer confirmed for me that Colonel Bartlett had not been hurt—he had been following Thanh in his own jeep. During that drive back to Hau Nghia, I knew that I would have trouble facing Colonel Bartlett. Both of us were too involved in the situation and too fond of Thanh to accept this tragedy easily.

It had happened the way one would expect. Colonel Thanh had simply gone on one too many early morning missions of mercy. The night before, the Vietcong had overrun an outpost in lower Duc Hoa district. Once again aided by a traitor in the unit, the Communist troops had walked into the outpost without firing a shot. Before the sleepy government troops could react, the attackers had overrun the unit's command post, and the battle had been as good as over. Some of our stunned troops had managed to flee by running through the wire of their own perimeter. Several had been killed in their sleep by the raiders, while still others had been captured without resisting. The company commander had been killed at the outset in the command post; his executive officer had surrendered. Before the Vietcong departed, they executed this officer and his wife. When they withdrew, the enemy troops took their prisoners and a large number of weapons and other booty with them. In a matter of thirty minutes, the Communists had inflicted the worst single defeat on Colonel Thanh's troops in more than fifteen months.

When Thanh learned of this debacle, he made plans to proceed by vehicle directly to the outpost at first light. Both his staff and Colonel Bartlett had tried to convince him to wait a few hours until the province's duty helicopter arrived, but Thanh would hear nothing of it. He wanted to be on hand at first light to rally the survivors of the shattered unit. This required that he go by jeep. The Duc Hoa district chief was ordered to mount a security sweep of the road that led to the ill-fated outpost, and, promptly at first light, Colonel Thanh had headed south out of Bao Trai, followed closely by Colonel Bartlett.

The small convoy passed through Duc Hoa town and headed west on Route 9. As they neared the outpost, the two jeeps passed the reassuring sight of the Duc Hoa militia troops pulling security on both sides of the dirt road. Arriving at the outpost, Colonel Thanh did what little he could to salvage the situation. A word of encouragement here, a directive to the Military Security Service to interview the survivors to determine the identity of the traitor, and an order for a new unit to be brought into the outpost at once. There really wasn't much of substance he could have done at that point, other than to show his troops by his presence that he cared enough to come. This accomplished, Thanh mounted his jeep for the ride back to Bao Trai.

A short distance down the road, two Vietcong waited patiently as Colonel Thanh's jeep approached. From their positions some one hundred meters from the road, a carefully buried electrical wire led to a five-gallon milk can packed with explosives and buried under the road. With perfect timing, Thanh's assassins detonated their charge just as the jeep arrived at their aiming point. The mine detonated with a roar that was heard all the way to Duc Hoa. The horrified Colonel Bartlett, following in his own jeep, glanced up in time to see Colonel Thanh's jeep suddenly propelled over three meters straight up by the force of the blast. It was over in a moment. By the time Colonel Bartlett arrived at the wrecked jeep, there was nothing he could do for Thanh. The twisted jeep lay on its side beside a smoking crater, and Thanh had died instantly from the tremendous concussion of the blast. Of the five men in the jeep, only Thanh's driver had survived, and he was badly hurt.

I can't remember much about the day or two immediately following Colonel Thanh's death. His loss had shocked me more deeply than any other single event of my tour in Hau Nghia. Even the assassination of Phich, for which I held myself responsible, did not stun me the way the loss of Colonel Thanh did. I dreaded the prospect of marching in the funeral procession and knew that I would not be able to keep my composure when I faced Mrs. Thanh at the service. I kept thinking of Thanh's ten children and of the fact that he was known as Hau Nghia's first province chief of modest means.

Colonel Bartlett and I donned khaki uniforms for the funeral. The procession was scheduled to begin at Thanh's residence, pass by the province administration building, and then proceed to Bien Hoa, where the cortege would pause at the humble house where Thanh's family lived. Vietnamese custom required that the deceased be taken on a final visit to each of his residences and places of work. From Bien Hoa, Colonel Thanh would be taken to Saigon for burial in the Mac Dinh Chi National Cemetery.

Thanh lay in state in the living room of his villa, only a few feet from the couch where I had briefed him on Tan My village thirteen months earlier. There was not a mark on him—no sign that he had died violently. I made my correct and carefully rehearsed expressions of condolence to Mrs. Thanh, who was dressed in the white muslin mourning smock that custom dictated. All of her children were at her side, similarly attired in white. I felt myself choking up and retreated to a rear corner of the room. A noise in the kitchen attracted my attention, and I glanced around the corner. A military truck had pulled up to the rear of the house, and two soldiers were quietly loading the Thanh's belongings on board. It appeared that we would have a new province chief very soon.

Colonel Bartlett and I walked in the procession behind the black, bus-like hearse that carried Colonel Thanh. As the procession moved slowly down Bao Trai's main street, it was evident that most of Bao Trai's citizenry had turned out to bid farewell to Colonel Thanh. Thanh's simple life-style and honesty had made an impression on many people. Most of the onlookers were in tears, and I could hear the nearest ones saying, "Ten children and doesn't even have a house for them to live in. What a pity." All the way to the province administration building, the procession passed grieving citizens. We had gone only several hundred meters when I felt the tears welling out of my eyes. I fought myself and glanced self-consciously at Colonel Bartlett, who was walking on my right. Looking neither left nor right, the colonel was having the same problem. It was an awful moment.

We buried Colonel Thanh that afternoon in Saigon amid the piteous graveside wailing of his widow that Vietnamese custom seemed to require. At the graveside service, Thanh's eldest son carried a large, framed picture of his father, who had been promoted posthumously to full colonel. After the funeral, we rode in silence back to Bao Trai, and I experienced a dull sense of foreboding that the loss of Colonel Thanh signaled the beginning of bad times for us in Hau Nghia province.

Colonel Thanh was assassinated because he was too effective as a military commander and not sufficiently corrupt to fit the Communist stereotype of a province chief. From the day Thanh had taken over as province chief, things had not gone well for the Vietcong in Hau Nghia.* His tenacious search for the correct combination of combat leaders and force deployment had resulted in a dramatic increase in the effectiveness of our troops—to the detriment of the Vietcong. Under Thanh's leadership, considerable progress had been made in the struggle against the Vietcong shadow government. While it was true that most of the Phoenix successes in Hau Nghia had been American-inspired, it was also true that Colonel Thanh most certainly got the credit or blame for these successes from his superiors and from the Vietcong. By the time Thanh was killed, we were finding numerous references in Vietcong documents to the problem of

---

*Colonel Thanh arrived in Hau Nghia on January 19, 1971, two days after I arrived in Vietnam. He was killed on April 20, 1972.

"white hamlets"—hamlets with no Vietcong cadre in them. Until Colonel Thanh arrived, there was no such thing as a white hamlet in Hau Nghia province. Hau Nghia had once been renowned as a safe haven for the revolution, but Colonel Thanh's aggressiveness had threatened the enemy's hold on the province's 229,000 citizens. Thanh's assassination marked the Communists' determination to put an end to the alarming erosion of their position in Hau Nghia.

Ironically, Thanh would probably never have been assassinated had he been a corrupt, ineffective, and self-serving province chief. These kinds of men—of whom South Vietnam had its fair share—were valuable assets to the revolution, since every corrupt government official perpetuated what the Communists called the "contradictions" of the Saigon regime. It was the actions of such men that insured a small base of political support for the Vietcong. Only in rare cases, when a government official was so totally corrupt and offensive that his death would be welcomed by all, would the Communists employ assassination to deal with such a person. Under normal circumstances, elimination was reserved for those whose actions were damaging the revolution's organizational integrity. In other words, the Vietcong would not help the Saigon government clean up its act.

IX

WAR COMES TO HAU NGHIA

Colonel Thanh was the proverbial "tough act to follow," and his replacement labored from the beginning under this handicap. Lt. Col. Doan Cong Hau came to Hau Nghia province from a staff job in the ARVN 25th Division, where he was famous for playing favorites among his staff officers. Hau was a handsome, if somewhat vain, officer who had a penchant for picking on his least favorite subordinates at every opportunity. I met the new colonel the day he arrived, and was not impressed. He had a way of primping like a woman and conveyed the impression that he couldn't walk past a mirror without stopping to comb his slick, black hair. I had to remind myself that no one could ever really replace Colonel Thanh and that it was important to give the new man a fair chance to show what he could do. Colonel Bartlett felt the same way, and we both resolved to withhold final judgment until Colonel Hau had had the opportunity to show us what he could do. Unless we were badly misreading the signs, this opportunity would not be long in coming.

At the time of Colonel Thanh's assassination, the Vietcong stepped up their subversion in our hamlets. Communist units broke up into small cells to facilitate movement, and these cells spread the word that the Nguyen Hue Offensive was causing the Thieu government to crumble. Communist political officers exhorted the people to support the new offensive by donating rice, and urged the teenagers of the PSDF and our soldiers to desert. In the hamlets nearest to the Vam Co Dong River, the peasants began to reinforce their household bunkers to protect themselves from the coming battles. Rice stocks normally stored in straw bins began to disappear as the savvy peasants buried their precious stocks to protect them from loss. The alarming "general uprising" of the PSDF continued when sixty-nine members of one Trang Bang district unit disappeared one night, taking 144 weapons with them. Later, forty-four of the missing teenagers returned and explained that traitors in their group had arranged for their abduction. Still, an alarmingly large number of the abductees had succumbed to the Vietcong's appeals and volunteered to remain in Cambodia for Communist military training. The combination of Trang Bang's long revolutionary ties and the impact of the fierce North Vietnamese offensive made the Vietcong's arguments more persuasive than ever to the impressionable young people. The fall of Quang Tri province and the bloody siege of An Loc were not without their impact on Hau Nghia's citizens, who must have begun to doubt the outcome of the war when North Vietnamese tanks had made their first appearance north of Saigon.

We were certain that Hau Nghia was about to be attacked, and Colonel Bartlett submitted a barrage of requests for air strikes against the suspected locations of North Vietnamese units in Cambodia. The requests were all denied. Normally, Maj. Gen. James Hollingsworth's headquarters in Bien Hoa would have supported these requests, but the general himself was spending much of his time orbiting in a helicopter over An Loc, calling in air strikes against three North Vietnamese divisions. Hollingsworth, a dynamic, action-oriented officer, had once visited us in Duc Hue. When Major Eby had shown him on our map the Vietcong base area known as the Rach Nhum Creek, the outraged general had almost suffered apoplexy. He remembered the Rach Nhum base area from an earlier tour and was astounded that no one had "done anything" about it yet. As the major attempted to explain the problem of booby traps, the irate general had interrupted him and blurted out, "You ever heard of air, major? Have you requested air strikes yet?" When poor Major Eby had tried to explain that all of our requests had been denied by the general's headquarters, Hollingsworth had thundered, "You request 'em now, Goddammit, and you'll get 'em! I want that creek turned into one giant lake!"

But now, request as we might, Hau Nghia was too low in priority to cause the diversion of vital air sorties from An Loc; we were not actually engaged with the enemy. As a result, the best we could do was to follow the growing number of North Vietnamese units that were being detected within striking distance of Hau Nghia and prepare for the worst.

Late in April, the North Vietnamese finally struck. I first realized that we were in trouble when I noticed one of the Vietnamese radio operators hunched over his microphone in earnest conversation with the Cu Chi district headquarters. Talking excitedly, the Cu Chi district chief was reporting that the people of Trung Lap village had begun to evacuate their homes. The government unit in an outpost south of the village had reported that streams of refugees were leaving the area. Entire families had loaded their rice and other movable possessions on ox carts and were abandoning the village as fast as they could.

This could mean only one thing. The enemy had occupied Trung Lap, and the people were fleeing the inevitable hostilities that would follow. I quickly alerted Colonel Bartlett and returned to the bank of radios. The duty officer had not yet dared to summon Colonel Hau, for Hau, unlike Colonel Thanh, did not appreciate being awakened at night. As a result, the duty officers were reluctant to disturb him for any reason and summoned instead his deputy.

By the time Colonel Hau learned of the situation and Colonel Bartlett could impress upon him the need for a timely reaction, it was too late. When government troops finally arrived on the outskirts of the village to engage the enemy, they came under a heavy volume of fire from the strongly entrenched occupiers. The North Vietnamese 101st Regiment had occupied Trung Lap, with orders to dig in and hold—at least until the village was destroyed.

For the next thirty-six hours, we received our introduction to a new enemy tactic. Occupying a populated area was a favorite Communist trick. The people became hostages, and the government commander then faced the dilemma of how to eject the enemy without causing undue casualties among the civilians. This tactic minimized the advantage possessed by the government forces because of their superior firepower. If the Saigon troops failed to exercise restraint, the people would blame the subsequent suffering and destruction on the government.

In Trung Lap, the North Vietnamese tried something different. Entering the village shortly after midnight, they warned the people that bitter fighting was about to take place and urged them to leave the area. Hence the exodus of ox carts that had alerted us to the impending battle. As the people loaded up their possessions, Hanoi's disciplined regulars began to dig in, emplacing antiaircraft machine guns and insuring that their positions were deep enough and sufficiently covered to protect them from the air strikes that they knew and hoped were coming. North Vietnamese troops covered the approaches to the village with automatic weapons, while the unit's mortars prepared to engage the government troops as they advanced across the open paddy lands that surrounded the village. The troops of the 101st Regiment were inviting the government to pry them out of Trung Lap with air strikes and artillery. Their objective was to force the government commander to "destroy the village in order to save it."

Trung Lap was a resettlement area populated primarily by refugees whose ancestral homes lay several kilometers to the north—on lands now controlled by the Vietcong. Trung Lap (which, ironically, means "neutral") was thus a government-controlled population center that counted among its residents an unusually large number of revolutionary families. These were not people whom one could describe as neutral. If the North Vietnamese could force the government to destroy the village, Communist propaganda cadre could then urge the people to move back to the "safe" or "liberated" areas. To many of the residents of Trung Lap, this meant returning to their ancestral homes.

Since an assault on the village's approaches would have required considerable tactical expertise and the acceptance of some casualties, the commander of the ARVN 25th Division unit that was responsible for Trung Lap's defense had elected to bomb the NVA out of their positions. Hau Nghia's disciplined militia troops, who probably could have ejected the North Vietnamese without air strikes, were not given the opportunity to try. This angered Colonel Bartlett, who observed that for the Communist unit to enter Trung Lap, it had been necessary for it to waltz undetected through the 25th Division's area of operations. Now, having failed to screen the village from enemy penetration, the ARVN commander was going to erase it with air strikes—thereby playing right into the enemy's hands.

The air strikes were awesome in their fury and accuracy, but the tenacious troops of the 101st Regiment managed to cling to Trung Lap for almost thirty-six hours. When they finally withdrew, one of the village's hamlets had ceased to exist, and the adjacent hamlets had suffered varying degrees of damage. Altogether, over three hundred families consisting of several thousand people had lost their homes to the bombing. Even if none of them heeded the Communist exhortations to relocate to their former lands, the operation would be counted a success by the enemy. At a cost of only a handful of casualties, Trung Lap had been 50 percent destroyed. While the 101st recovered in Cambodia, the Saigon government would have to care for the refugees and rebuild the destruction caused by its own air force.

I visited Trung Lap with the MSS chief, Captain Sang, shortly after the battle ended. Picking our way among the pathetic ruins of the village's wood and tin houses, we could see that our victory had been hollow. When we approached one pile of twisted tin where several women were searching for anything salvageable, one of the women looked up. Shaking her finger at Sang, she launched into a bitter denunciation of the Americans for destroying her home, not knowing—and surely not caring—that I could understand her. When she had vented her feelings,

I was stung by her accusations. It had been South Vietnamese Skyraiders that had flattened her home, not the U.S. Air Force. In that moment of tension, I lashed out at the surprised housewife, sarcastically telling her that if she didn't like the results of the operation, then she should talk to the local ARVN commander or the North Vietnamese political officer— but leave the Americans out of it. As soon as I finished my tirade, I knew that it had been senseless. To that woman, all airplanes came from America, and she didn't care who the pilots were. Her house had been flattened and her life disrupted, and no amount of political bickering could change that. The encounter left me frustrated and depressed for the rest of the day. One of the Vietcong's major strengths had just been brought home to me again. For, whatever sins the enemy might commit, however many tactical or political blunders he might be guilty of, he was still one thing I could never be—no matter how much of the language I might learn—he was Vietnamese.

The destruction of Trung Lap was a preview of things to come in Hau Nghia. I may have been appalled at my first look at the results of tactical air strikes that day, but things were about to happen that would so deeply involve us in the war that we would find ourselves not only calling in tactical air strikes, but also requesting and receiving "arc light" strikes from high-flying B-52 bombers. For on May 11, 1972, the Nguyen Hue Offensive struck Hau Nghia province.

It was four in the morning when Colonel Bartlett banged on my door and called out, "Better get up and head for the operations center, Stu. The NVA have occupied Loc Giang and An Ninh villages. It looks like we're finally getting our share of the Nguyen Hue Offensive."

"Oh God," I thought as I pulled my boots on, "do I wish Colonel Thanh were alive." If the North Vietnamese had occupied two villages, we were in serious trouble. It would take at least a regiment to attempt such an operation.

At the operations center, the entire province staff had assembled. Our counterparts were gathered around the radios, grim-faced, as they strained to keep up with the bad news that poured in from Duc Hue and Trang Bang districts. Both district chiefs had reported that a massive infiltration of their districts by North Vietnamese regulars was under way. According to the Duc Hue district chief, so many enemy troops had streamed across the border that he had been forced to order a withdrawal of the troops from almost every outpost in the northern half of his district. As he talked, we could hear the sounds of mortar, rocket, and recoilless rifle fire in the background.

The news from Trang Bang district was equally grim. Enemy troops had already entered the heart of Loc Giang village and were banging away at the outnumbered defenders of the village office with a 75-millimeter recoilless rifle. The district's militia troops had also been forced to abandon a number of outposts in the path of the advancing enemy. Trang Bang District Headquarters was under a rocket attack.

More than two thousand troops of Hanoi's 24th and 271st Regiments had invaded Hau Nghia. Armed with a week's supply of food and ammunition, soldiers of the two regiments had been ordered to seize and hold terrain at all cost. Their arrival had triggered the usual stream of refugees as the villagers fled the new combat zone. The North Vietnamese invaders were veterans of several ferocious battles in recent weeks, and they wasted no time in preparing the battlefield for a prolonged defense of their newly liberated territory. Throughout the night of May 11, they dug their positions, laid communications wire, and established observation posts. The enemy commander dispatched one platoon to set up a roadblock and cut Duc Hue off from the province capital of Bao Trai, and he ordered one of his companies to seize the An Ninh village outpost, located at a key intersection between Bao Trai and Trang Bang.

From the An Ninh outpost came a tense report. The government soldiers could hear digging noises outside their perimeter. The outpost was manned by a motley collection of militia troops, policemen, a handful of teenaged PSDF, and the civilian village chief. Outside their tiny mud fort, an entire North Vietnamese company was preparing to attack. The village chief's voice cracked as he frantically requested reinforcements.

What happened next was one of those strange, totally inexplicable events that can decisively influence how a military campaign will turn out. Having lost the advantage of surprise, the North Vietnamese unit delayed attacking the outpost for another hour, thereby giving the badly outnumbered and outgunned defenders time to prepare their defenses. At the same time, Colonel Hau ordered two companies of militia troops to prepare to move by truck to the beleaguered outpost at first light—or earlier, if necessary.

The Communist unit finally attacked the tiny outpost at around five in the morning. The assault was preceded by a mortar barrage, after which the North Vietnamese troops sprang out of their shallow foxholes and charged across the open field toward their objective. The sky was immediately lit up by an aerial flare fired by the defenders, who directed a heavy volume of fire at the exposed attackers. At least five North Vietnamese fell immediately, and the attack faltered. The stunned North Vietnamese troops pulled back to the safety of their positions to rethink the problem. The puppet soldiers had teeth.

It is impossible to reconstruct the reason for what happened next. Only the North Vietnamese company commander knows the answer, and he was not available for an after-action interview. The North Vietnamese survivors of the battle, five in all, only knew that they remained in their foxholes until dawn because they received no order to either mount a second attack or withdraw. As a result, when the sun rose, the entire Communist unit was still lying indecisively in its hastily prepared and exposed positions. The government defenders, seeing the enemy so close to their outpost, began to direct a steady stream of small arms fire at the North Vietnamese, who responded by crouching lower in their holes. By then, withdrawal would have been risky, but had the NVA infantrymen received the order, it would have been well within their capability to disengage. But by an hour after sunrise, the doomed North Vietnamese company's options ran out. Reinforcements arrived on the scene, and the battle of An Ninh crossroads was on.

Our two militia companies employed classic fire and maneuver tactics and overran the North Vietnamese positions within an hour. While one unit laid down a base of fire so heavy that the trapped North Vietnamese had to keep their heads down, the other unit ran to within hand grenade range and systematically eliminated the enemy positions one by one. In very short order, sixty-five North Vietnamese troops died in their foxholes. Only five were captured—all of them wounded. The government troops also captured one Vietcong, a nineteen-year-old An Ninh village guerrilla who was acting as a guide for the northerners. Behind a thicket in the rear of the enemy position, the victorious government troops found the unit's mortars, abandoned intact by their gunners as they fled. The company command post had apparently been colocated with the mortars, and the troops even picked up the company commander's Chinese-made binoculars, which the rattled officer had apparently dropped as he abandoned his men. Only the mortar crews and the company command group had escaped the slaughter. The rest of the company had died in their holes, awaiting orders that never came. Government casualties had been one lieutenant killed leading the assault and five men wounded. This was the legacy of Colonel Thanh's yearlong search for good combat leaders.

My counterparts and I arrived at the scene of the battle shortly after the assault. As we surveyed the carnage and captured booty, it was difficult to believe that our humble militia troops had been able to decimate a regular North Vietnamese unit so easily. Every weapon of the enemy company had been captured, and our troops had proudly stacked their impressive trophies by the road. Fifty-five AK-47 assault rifles, several machine guns, six or seven rocket launchers, and three mortars. They had even recovered the unit's field phones and the commander's map case.

Having examined the trophies, my two Vietnamese companions from the G-2 shop and I set about the grisly chore of searching each fallen enemy. The company's positions had been dug in a horseshoe configuration, one man to a hole. Each foxhole was only a foot or two deep— just enough for the NVA trooper to stay out of the path of grazing small arms fire. Stopping at the first hole, we relieved its blankly staring occupant of his mustard-colored rucksack, which we used to collect the many documents and other items of intelligence interest from the bodies. Each of the fallen NVA troops wore the same uniform and carried the same equipment: a floppy, canvas jungle hat with Russian language markings; Chinese-made black rubber "Ho Chi Minh sandals"; olive drab fatigues; oval canteen; three wooden-handled grenades on a pistol belt; a canvas tube containing several pounds of sweet dried rice; one hundred fifty rounds of AK-47 ammunition in a plastic bag; a nylon hammock; and a small toiletry kit. Each soldier also had two extra magazines for his AK-47. Including the three full magazines, each man had carried two hundred forty rounds of ammunition and three grenades—almost triple a basic load. Hanoi's troops had obviously come to fight, even though this particular company hadn't got the word. Out of almost fifty dead riflemen we checked, we could only find one who had fired all thirty rounds from his first magazine. Most of the unlucky victims had expended less than twenty rounds in the entire engagement. Further mute testimony to the firepower of our troops and the bravery of their foes was the fact that more than half of the bodies had bandages on them. Most of the North Vietnamese had been wounded, had bandaged themselves, and then kept fighting until they were overrun. Several of them had bandaged their own wounds three times before succumbing.

Among the dozens of documents we collected was a company roster. Eighty-three names appeared on the list, of whom we had just killed or captured seventy. Later in the day, I interrogated a young North Vietnamese sergeant with a head wound—the only leader of the unit to survive the battle. He wasn't very cooperative, and during the interrogation, his wound kept opening up and gushing blood, but he did shed some light on what had happened. According to him, the unit had expected the outpost's outnumbered defenders to flee rather than try to defend against such a superior force. The fierce resistance had taken them by surprise.

Asked why he and his men had not withdrawn, the dazed sergeant could only reply that no one had passed the order to disengage, and the troops had therefore held their ground.

Word of our victory spread rapidly. Within a few hours, a helicopter arrived from Saigon carrying a television newsreel team. The story of a militia force triumphing over one of Hanoi's regular units was too good for the government media to pass up. There had been precious little good news since the start of the Nguyen Hue Offensive.

The An Ninh victory transformed the outlook of our troops. It was like magic. Just hours earlier, the province staff had huddled apprehensively around the radios listening to the bad news flow in from Duc Hue and Trang Bang. At that moment, few of them would have given our forces a chance of standing up to the North Vietnamese. But the unexpected turn of events had changed everything. Our militia troops had defeated the enemy regulars without the aid of air strikes or helicopter gunships, and this accomplishment wrought an electric effect on morale. The vaunted North Vietnamese could be beaten, and now that everyone knew it, it was time to get on with the job. From that first moment of the invasion, regardless of how difficult the situation became, a confident, aggressive, winning spirit pervaded our province staff and militia forces. The spirit of An Ninh, as our counterparts came to call this phenomenon, had given our forces a timely boost in self-confidence. They now knew that they could fight and win, in spite of the loss of Colonel Thanh.

The victory on May 11 was the beginning of a three-week-long series of battles that culminated in the withdrawal of the bloodied invaders. During this period, Hau Nghia province militia forces earned the reputation of being the best in Vietnam. Only in Trang Bang district did our troops receive assistance from the 25th Division. There, the 25th committed one battalion to clear North Vietnamese forces from Loc Giang village. These troops quickly acquired a bad reputation for their bad conduct and lack of aggressiveness. During one three-day period, the 25th Division troops attempted numerous times to advance into the village. Met on each attempt by enemy mortar fire, the ARVN commander had each time ordered his men to withdraw and then spent the rest of the day randomly calling in air strikes against unseen targets, apparently hoping for a lucky hit on the enemy mortar.

While the 25th Division troops in Trang Bang struggled with their mission, the Hau Nghia militia forces continued to give the Communists trouble. The only way to relieve the pressure on Duc Hue was to drive the North Vietnamese back across the river to Cambodia. To do this, government troops had to enter the occupied hamlets and actually engage the North Vietnamese infantry. As in Loc Giang, when our troops approached the occupied hamlets, they were met by mortar and small arms fire. But the Hau Nghia troops pressed forward until they were in direct contact with the enemy, and then called in air strikes and artillery on the known enemy positions. The results were predictable. Since the fire support was directed against identified targets, it had a devastating effect on the North Vietnamese infantrymen. During the counterattacks in May to clear Duc Hue's hamlets, more than five hundred enemy troops died, at a cost of eighty-five of our own men. The 25th Division unit in Trang Bang so badly bungled its mission (it killed nineteen NVA troops in May) that the 25th Division commander, Colonel Tu, berated his commanders and threatened to send them to a Hau Nghia militia company "to learn how to fight."

By late May, our troops had pushed the North Vietnamese out of most of Duc Hue's hamlets, but North Vietnamese infantry units still remained stubbornly in place in the base areas on our side of the river. Across the river, Hanoi's troops had bypassed the outpost of the 83d Border Ranger Battalion on their way to Hau Nghia. Now they decided that it was time to eliminate the rangers, whose presence threatened their supply lines to Hau Nghia.

The first round of the North Vietnamese barrage hit the rangers' star-shaped outpost during the morning flag-raising ceremony. The 122 millimeter warhead exploded in the middle of the formation and killed twenty-two men. The siege of the 83d Rangers had begun. During the next two weeks, the Communists bombarded the isolated outpost with every weapon in their arsenal, including American-made 105 millimeter howitzers that they had seized from the Cambodian army earlier in the year. North Vietnamese sappers and infantry repeatedly assaulted the outpost's perimeter, but the rangers held. For more than a week, the pressure on the rangers was so great that they couldn't even bury their dead, and the stench of death in the air became intolerable. Finally, they buried their comrades in a mass grave inside the base camp under the cover of night.

One evening we received a panicky call for help from the rangers. Tanks were approaching their perimeter! We quickly called for a flareship to put some light on the problem for the defenders, who were reporting that a North Vietnamese armor unit was about to overrun them. It took about thirty minutes for the flareship to arrive. When the AC-119 dropped one of its million candlepower parachute flares over the besieged outpost, the surrounding terrain was lit up for a mile in all directions. Some five hundred meters to the north of the outpost, the pilot spotted a covered military truck moving hastily to the west. The North Vietnamese "tanks" were a resupply truck that was transporting ammunition to the North Vietnamese artillerymen. The days when thousands of bicycle porters had labored under their loads as they struggled down the Ho Chi Minh Trail were over. Russian-built Molotova trucks were more efficient, and they were available.

On May 27, Team 43 lost its first American since my arrival. It happened, not surprisingly, in my old home—Duc Hue district. On that day, Duc Hue militia forces launched an operation into the interior of An Ninh village. The operation was a reconnaissance-in-force along Route 7, supported by several armored personnel carriers of the 25th Division. The purpose of the operation was to determine the extent of the remaining North Vietnamese presence in the village. We knew that the battered remnants of the two invading regiments were withdrawing to Cambodia, but we did not know what forces the enemy had left behind, or where they were. The mission into An Ninh was supposed to clear up this uncertainty—which it unquestionably did.

Two advisors from the Duc Hue team, Capt. Ed Schwabe and S. Sgt. Richard Arsenault, accompanied the operation. Schwabe and our militia troops were boatlifted to the western edge of the village on the Vam Co Dong River, while the 25th Division's mechanized column approached from the east along Route 7. The ARVN unit promptly met light resistance and overran an enemy bunker. Two North Vietnamese regulars died in the brief firefight. A third man, bleeding from a face wound, was taken prisoner. The troops tied and blindfolded their captive and put him on one of the vehicles for the trip out of the village.

Farther west, the other column was moving past a graveyard when the North Vietnamese sprang a well-laid ambush. Sergeant Arsenault, who was carrying the radio, was killed instantly by the blast of a B-41 rocket. (Nothing was more feared by the North Vietnamese than an American with a radio.) The explosion knocked Captain Schwabe off his feet and peppered him with shrapnel. North Vietnamese soldiers poured heavy fire in on the stunned militia troops, who took cover behind sandstone grave markers. Several government soldiers died as the dazed and wounded Captain Schwabe struggled to gain the meager cover afforded by the cemetery. The American officer was saved from death only because a brave Vietnamese interpreter dragged his boss to safety.

I was eating lunch when word reached us of the ambush. At the operations center, I found the Vietnamese radio operators in the middle of a tense exchange with the ambushed unit. It was still under fire and was requesting artillery support as several of its men struggled to recover the bodies of their dead.

A sick sensation swept over me as I realized that Sergeant Arsenault was really dead. A Massachusetts native, the sergeant had only recently joined our team. Heavyset, gentle, and blessed with a good sense of humor, Sergeant Arsenault had made an instant hit with the people of Duc Hue by studying the Vietnamese language on his own. He was ideally suited for advisory duty and dealt comfortably with the Vietnamese, who sensed that he liked them. Now the unfortunate sergeant was a victim of the Nguyen Hue Offensive, and his body was being conveyed to Bao Trai on the back of an armored personnel carrier.

When the word of Sergeant Arsenault's death reached the Vietnamese in Duc Hue, many of them cried openly over the loss of their gentle friend —no small tribute in a district where death in battle had become an everyday event.

X

"BORN IN THE NORTH TO DIE IN THE SOUTH"

It was billed as a show not to miss. Colonel Tu, the 25th Division commander, was going to interrogate the North Vietnamese soldier who had been captured on the ill-fated Duc Hue operation. Colonel Tu was an arrogant, boisterous officer who had been Colonel Hau's superior when he had served in the 25th Division. The big event was to take place in Colonel Hau's office, and my counterparts urged me not to miss it.

Captain Sang, Captain Nga, and I arrived at Hau's office just as the prisoner was escorted into Colonel Tu's presence by one of Nga's G-2 sergeants. Most of the province staff had crowded inito the small room to witness the spectacle.

The prisoner was about five feet four inches tall; his crew cut had grown out, and his face showed the strain of combat. Nonetheless, he held his head up as he strode into the room. He wore olive drab fatigues with no insignia, and his left cheek was caked with dried blood from a small shrapnel wound below his eye.

The North Vietnamese was not permitted to sit, and the room fell silent as Colonel Tu lit a cigarette. Flicking the match to the floor, Tu led off sharply, "What is your name?"

"Do van Lanh," answered the prisoner in a strong voice. He was either unintimidated by the setting or he was a good actor.

"Rank?" snapped Colonel Tu.

"Combatant," replied the prisoner.*

"Unit?" queried the colonel.

"Two Hundred Seventy-First Independent Regiment, D8 Battalion, C3 Company," answered the prisoner, looking squarely at his interro-

*In the North Vietnamese Army, a combatant is a private.

137

gator in a glaring display of cheekiness. Prisoners were supposed to be appropriately humble and look at the floor.

"Where is the 271st Regiment now?" pumped Tu, who for the moment was ignoring the prisoner's audacity.

"I don't know. Over in Cambodia, maybe," replied the prisoner evasively. He's pressing his luck, I thought. Captain Nga gave me a glance that said if the prisoner had answered this way to one of his G-2 interrogators, he would have been beaten.

"What were you doing when captured?" asked Tu.

"They just told us to hide there and keep track of the enemy forces that entered the area," replied the North Vietnamese.

"Before you crossed the river, where did your unit hide?" Colonel Tu was maneuvering.

"I don't know. I was in a dispensary with malaria, and I only joined my unit after it had crossed the river. I don't know anything about its other operations." The prisoner was no dummy. He was employing the "I don't know anything so don't waste any more time on me" tactic.

"Do you know what this stands for?" Tu asked, pointing to his own shoulder patch and grinning at his audience.

"Yes, the 25th Division," replied Do van Lanh.

"And what did your comrades say about the 25th Division?" continued the beaming Colonel Tu.

"We heard that the soldiers of the 25th would drop their weapons and run, just like they did when we attacked them in Tay Ninh," shot back the feisty prisoner. I had to choke to keep from laughing. Colonel Tu didn't think it was funny. Redfaced, he didn't like the prisoner's arrogance one bit. For a moment, I thought he was going to hit him. Then, abruptly, Tu's mood and tone of voice changed. Pointing to a chair, he politely invited the prisoner to sit down, then offered him a cigarette. The prisoner accepted, then suddenly spoke up.

"May I ask something?" The room fell silent. Didn't this upstart North Vietnamese understand that prisoners were supposed to answer questions, not ask them?

"Ask!" snapped the surprised Colonel Tu.

The prisoner spoke. "Has President Nixon gone to Moscow yet? Is it true that we are only forty kilometers from Ho Chi Minh City?" He blurted out both questions in one breath, as if afraid that he wouldn't get a second opportunity.

By now, most of the onlookers had begun to pull silently for the underdog prisoner in his battle of wits with the supercilious Colonel Tu. Captain Sang, an ethnic North Vietnamese, jabbed me in the ribs and grinned. Could this prisoner possibly know that his reference to President Nixon's impending Moscow visit would strike South Vietnamese sensitivities over our policy of détente with the Russians? I decided at that moment that I would have to get to know Do van Lanh better.

Colonel Tu was again thrown off balance, both by the prisoner's audacity and by the political tone of his questions. "You were captured by the armed forces of the Republic of Vietnam, forty kilometers from the capital of *Saigon*," growled the colonel. "And President Nixon has not gone to Moscow yet." Motioning to Captain Nga's jailer, Tu indicated that the interrogation was over.

I contacted Colonel Bartlett immediately. With his permission, I wanted to pull Do van Lanh out of normal prisoner of war channels. To do so we would have to get the province chief's approval. Normally, a North Vietnamese prisoner would remain in Hau Nghia a few days at most, enough time to be interrogated by the heavy-handed and incompetent Sergeant Tran. If there was even a remote chance of gaining a prisoner's cooperation, one session with Sergeant Tran would end it. Unless we intervened, Combatant Do van Lanh would soon find himself sitting out the war in a South Vietnamese POW camp.

Colonel Bartlett didn't hesitate, and within the hour, I was sitting in Captain Nga's office waiting for the prisoner. When they brought him in, I sensed immediately that he was not the same person whom I had observed that morning dueling with Colonel Tu. That Do van Lanh had stood erect, eyeballed his interrogator, and spoken out boldly when addressed. The Do van Lanh who stood in front of me was a withdrawn, sullen, and dispirited shadow of the other Lanh. I bristled, certain that he had just been interrogated and abused by Sergeant Tran. But Captain Nga insisted that nothing of the sort had happened. Since the encounter with Colonel Tu, the prisoner had been debriefed by one of his lieutenants—a man whose methods were humane. The prisoner had repeated his story that he had spent the last two months in a dispensary somewhere in Cambodia, recovering from malaria contracted during his walk down the Ho Chi Minh Trail. He had stuck to his story that he had no knowledge of his unit's operations, staging areas, or intentions. Nga insisted that he had been humanely treated.

The North Vietnamese prisoner's change of demeanor puzzled me, but I passed it off to the trauma of captivity and proceeded to implement my game plan. Introducing myself, I extended my hand and told him that he and I were going to "my house" for a few days. Did he understand? Startled at hearing me speak his language, the prisoner hesitated before he limply grasped my hand and nodded that he understood. Captain Nga shot me a confused look, crossing his wrists. Did I want the prisoner bound? I shook my head and headed out the door, motioning Do van Lanh to follow me. As we walked across the courtyard of the headquarters, the officers and sergeants of the staff stared as they realized that my companion was one of Nga's prisoners.

Our first stop was at the home of a Filipino doctor who worked at the province hospital. The doctor obligingly treated the shrapnel wound under the prisoner's eye. That done, we headed across the alley to my quarters, where the guard admitted us without so much as a glance. Our guards had become used to the motley collection of companions I paraded in and out of the villa.

I motioned for Lanh to sit down. Once again, his uncomfortable reaction to what was happening to him was evident. Eyes cast down, he merely nodded his head yes or no when I asked him anything.

"Are you hungry?" A nod. I sent a guard out to pick up a meal.

"Thirsty?" Again a nod.

"Do you drink beer?" An attempt to get a rise out of him. He shook his head—lifeless.

"Tea?" Of course. Another nod. He still hadn't said two words since I picked him up.

The guard arrived with a large plate of steamed rice, a bowl of vegetables, and a small fish on a plate. I beckoned my guest to sit down and eat. He obeyed silently, and the entire meal disappeared in minutes. In the meantime, I asked one of the guards to go to the market and pick up a cheap set of civilian clothes and a pair of sandals. We could get the maid to make any necessary alterations. I was not yet ready to take my new charge to the market.

The next step was to clean him up. He looked and smelled like he hadn't had a bath for weeks—which was probably about right. I led him to the bathroom and instructed him to take a shower. When I heard the water running, I opened the door to retrieve his uniform. Instead of showering standing up, he had hunched down on the floor below the faucet and was splashing the water on himself with his hands. I took his Hanoi-issue outfit and left in its place a pair of black slacks and a white shirt that the guard had just brought me. We would save his uniform for future use.

When he emerged from the bathroom, I told him he looked *dep trai* ("handsome") in his new clothes and showed him to his room. Still no reaction. Just the sullen stare. His room was directly across the hall from mine and furnished with a bed, nightstand, coffee table, and a seventeen-inch portable television set. I turned on the TV and demonstrated the channel selector. The set only received two channels: the American Armed Forces station and Channel 9, the Saigon government station. The television set got me my first reaction. Wide-eyed, he hunched down on the floor and tuned in.

"If you get tired," I told him, "turn it off here and go to sleep. I've got to go back to work."

He nodded without removing his gaze from the television. The Saigon channel was showing newsreel scenes of North Vietnamese tanks that had been knocked out by "the heroic defenders of An Loc." I told Lanh apologetically that I would have to lock his door, but that if he needed to go to the bathroom, he could knock and the guard would let him out. Another nod signaled his understanding. Before departing, I briefed the guards on the need for one of them to sit in the living room outside the prisoner's door. The house was full of weapons of every sort, and for now, at least, we had to assume that our new guest was hostile. I also told the head guard to pass the word that the prisoner was to be treated as much like a member of the family as possible.

Back at the headquarters, I picked up a copy of the report that had resulted from the prisoner's brief interrogation. From it, I learned that Do van Lanh claimed to be nineteen years old and a native of Ha Tinh province in southern North Vietnam. Drafted at the age of eighteen, he had undergone basic training at a camp northwest of Hanoi and been assigned to the 271st Regiment. The 271st was originally a militia unit, and most of the men in it were natives of Ha Tinh and neighboring Nghe An province—Ho Chi Minh's birthplace. Lanh and his comrades had commenced their infiltration into South Vietnam in November, 1971, and the long trek had taken them more than a hundred days. Lanh had told his interrogator that he had contracted malaria on the way down the trail and lain in a Cambodian dispensary until just prior to his capture. He claimed that the skirmish in which he had been captured had been his first combat engagement.

With this report in hand, I dropped by the MSS office to see Captain Sang. Sang glanced over the report and raised an eyebrow when he came to the prisoner's native village. "This will be easy to check," he observed. "He says he is from my native village. If he is telling the truth, we will have common acquaintances. If he is lying, I will know immediately." One of Sang's orderlies brought two tall Cokes as we discussed my plan. Briefly, I proposed to Sang that we convert the young prisoner into a cooperative source, using decent treatment and a bit of psychology. I felt certain that he had been told nothing but the worst about the situation in the south and that he had no doubt been filled with horror stories about Americans. I described to Sang how the frightened prisoner had clammed up the moment he met me. It should be easy to undermine his defenses, and Sang could help by playing the "fellow northerner" role. If the two men turned out to be from the same village, so much the better.

Sang was enthusiastic about the project. A cooperative North Vietnamese prisoner could help us in a myriad of ways. Not only could he tell us about his own unit, but he would be bound to possess much useful information about the situation in North Vietnam and conditions along the Ho Chi Minh Trail. I confessed to Sang that I had a personal interest in our venture. I had long been curious to learn what it was that motivated our North Vietnamese adversaries to fight as hard as they did. Do van Lanh was going to help me heed the ancient admonition, Know your enemy.

I returned to the villa full of enthusiasm for our new venture and confident that we could undermine Do van Lanh's defenses. Lanh was in a deep sleep on the floor, wrapped in a blanket that he had taken off the bed. Later, when I tried to get him to sleep on the bed, he told the guard that the motion caused by the bed's springs made him feel nauseated. He had also told the guard earlier that he was surely going to die of the cold from the room's air conditioner. It appeared that, if we were to make him feel at home, we would have to shut off the air conditioner, string a hammock in his room, and turn a few mosquitos loose to keep him company.

For the next week, the befuddled North Vietnamese lived with us as though he were a member of the family. When he gradually realized that he wasn't going to be tortured or executed, he began to loosen up, although his first conversations were with the maid and the guards. He was still afraid of me. The maid told me that he had plied her with questions about the Americans. Were all Americans rich like the ones he was seeing in Hau Nghia? How much did they pay a Vietnamese who worked for them? How did this convert to North Vietnamese money? By the end of the first week, he began to shed his wounded-animal look, and he took the risk of talking to me. Once the ice was broken, it became my turn to be interrogated. How long had I studied Vietnamese? Was I married? How much money did I earn as a captain? Had I volunteered to come to Vietnam? Why? Did I think that my M-16 rifle was as good as the AK-47? He had a million questions, many of them based on what he was seeing on my electronic assistant—the television set. For that entire first week, I did not ask him a single question, other than to inquire about his personal comfort. Our guards played along perfectly and treated him as if he were an old friend. They guarded him, but they did so discreetly. After a week, we no longer locked his room, though we did secure the weapons in the house. Once, near the end of that first week, I took him to the Bao Trai central market so he could buy a toothbrush and a razor. For about an hour, we plied our way through the market's colorful stalls. Using money I had given him in exchange for his North Vietnamese currency, Lanh bought what he needed. He was astounded by the variety and quantity of the merchandise offered by Bao Trai's commercial class. The Bao Trai market was a far cry from a North Vietnamese cooperative store. Soon we stopped sending out for his meals, and we ventured to the nearby Thu Anh restaurant. At the beginning, I was nervous about taking him out in public, for if he had escaped, I would never have been able to explain my laxity. Finally, I discussed this problem openly with Lanh. He understood that he could easily escape during one of our evening sojourns, but he also knew that it would not have been so easy to link up with a Communist unit. Even if he did manage to evade government ambush patrols and somehow locate a Vietcong or North Vietnamese unit, he could expect to be treated with suspicion, at best. And ultimately, I reminded him, he could expect to once again be sent into combat—only the second time around he was not likely to be as lucky. Lanh understood this and assured me that he had no intention of attempting an escape. I believed him.

Captain Sang invited Lanh to his home for dinner one evening. It was a well-timed gesture that complemented my efforts to disarm Lanh psychologically. Sang understood that we were still at the phase in which no questions were to be posed that might be interpreted as interrogation. The evening had gone well, and Sang had learned that Lanh's family were indeed neighbors of Sang's relatives in Ha Tinh province. The two had spent a relaxing evening reminiscing about life in the north. As he savored the North Vietnamese cuisine prepared by Sang's wife, it never occurred to Lanh that he was under subtle interrogation. Sang reported to me that Lanh had asked him how long he was going to live with the Americans, and that he had expressed concern over what would eventually happen to him. Sang had replied by urging him to trust the American captain, who was trying to help him.

Our experiment was on track. Lanh was confused by our generous reception, and in his confusion, he forgot his lines. Gone were the blank stares, the sullen nods, and the tendency to avoid my glances by casting his eyes down as if he were looking for something on the floor. In their place had appeared an animated, intense, and curious young man— obviously bewildered by his surroundings and by the strange twist that his life had taken. He had even cracked his first smile after I told him one day that I was going out to find him a South Vietnamese wife. "Never!" he had retorted with a smile. "I'm too young to start a family—especially with a southerner."

Lanh cornered me one day as I was donning my pistol belt in preparation for an operation with Lieutenant Tuan's platoon.

"How long will I be living here with you, Dai Uy? When I came, I thought it was going to be for a few days. I don't understand what is going on."

I sat my confused companion down in the living room and explained to him that I had been impressed by his handling of the confrontation with Colonel Tu, and that Sang and I had decided to help him that day. We were certain that a person with his intelligence would quickly come to understand the reality of the situation in South Vietnam if someone merely cared enough to expose him to it. I had waited a week to begin serious discussions because I knew that he needed a rest after the trauma of his capture. I assured him that even though we wanted to help him, I did not want to interrogate him about his unit. He was clearly a good person who would never turn traitor and give information that would result in harm to his former comrades. As a soldier, I respected him for that quality and would never ask him to do anything dishonorable. Our goal, I told him, was to keep him out of a prisoner of war camp, where he would just rot away until the end of the war. But if we were to succeed in this, he would have to help us. Lanh nodded attentively.

My real purpose in coming to Vietnam, I explained, was to help reestablish peace and understanding between the North Vietnamese and their southern brothers. Since my arrival, I had seen the ugliness and bloodshed that the war had produced, and I was horrified at the continued killing of Vietnamese by Vietnamese. If I and other Americans like me were going to succeed in bringing the two Vietnams together in peace, I needed to understand the North Vietnamese view of the war. If he could explain to me the events of his life that had led to his becoming a soldier, I would be better able to continue my efforts to restore peace to Vietnam so that he could return to Ha Tinh province. I promised that if he could provide me with this kind of information, I would keep him out of prison.

Lanh responded eagerly to this appeal. He assured me that he also desired peace for his country and noted that he had seen immediately that I was a good person. He pledged to work with me toward our mutual goal. Whatever I needed to know, he promised, I need only ask him and he would do his best to answer. He was grateful for my understanding of his difficult circumstances and for my pledge not to ask him about the

271st Regiment. I had been good to him, and he wanted to cooperate with me because we both desired peace for his country. With the ground rules for our discussion established, Do van Lanh and I retraced together the events of his life that had led him to the bunker in An Ninh village and ultimately into my hands.

Lanh had grown up in an environment where the virtues of the Marxist-Leninist life were constantly stressed by the government and the party. The successful development of the socialist state in North Vietnam under Chairman Ho Chi Minh was a recurring theme in school, where he and his friends were taught that the communal way of life—the sharing of the state's wealth by all of the people—was the "best, most beautiful" way to live. He and his playmates had revered "Bac Ho" (Uncle Ho) from the time that they were old enough to understand.

In contrast to this idyllic life in the north, Lanh recalled the graphic descriptions that their teachers had provided of the misery that prevailed in South Vietnam. "Our southern brothers," he recalled, "were depicted as living under the brutal heel of the Americans and their puppets. We were even shown films in the village meeting hall that showed the plight of the southerners. These films showed the beggars of Saigon and contained scenes of American military police and Vietnamese police beating the people with clubs. The film's narrator described how the South Vietnamese people were living like prisoners. Many of the older people in the village used to cry when they would see these films. Some of the parents in the village believed that it was their obligation to send their sons into the army to help end the suffering of the poor people in the south. Everyone worshipped Uncle Ho, and the women used to cry when he talked about our enslaved comrades in the south."

Lanh recalled a growing sense of patriotic outrage in his village at the increasing American involvement in Vietnam during the nineteen-sixties. He had not been convinced that the Americans were as bad as the government said until the summer of 1966 when two American F-105 aircraft had bombed the high school in a local village, killing and wounding a large number of students. After this tragedy, he began to believe the reports that Americans were killing and torturing people in the south.

The acceptance of this version of events in Vietnam had led to his next move. When he turned eighteen, Lanh had volunteered for military service. He knew that he would be drafted anyway and hoped that by volunteering he could get into the air force. But as the son of a poor man with no political connections, Lanh soon learned that he didn't stand a chance of getting into the relatively small air force.

During basic training, the several hundred recruits in Lanh's cycle were generally enthusiastic about their common mission. In spite of the stories everyone had heard about the hardships of the infiltration and the dangers of the front, most of the recruits were obsessed with the idea of tackling their "solemn mission." Many of them had even gone to local tattoo parlors and had themselves branded with patriotic slogans. Two of the most popular were "Born in the North to Die in the South" and "Go South and Attack the Americans."

When the thirteen divisions of the People's Army launched the Nguyen Hue Offensive, Lanh's company political officer had informed the men that the offensive would succeed in liberating large parts of South Vietnam. People's Army units would be welcomed as liberators everywhere, they had been told, just as the people of An Loc had welcomed their North Vietnamese brothers. An Loc, the political officer boasted, had been completely liberated by friendly forces. The puppet President Thieu was being kept in power only by American troops, two divisions of whom were permanently stationed in Vung Tau to counter any attempt at a coup. Should Thieu need their protection, the Americans were prepared to surround his palace on request. The political officer had warned Lanh and his comrades that the Americans and their puppets were extremely stubborn and would stop at nothing to maintain their hold over the South Vietnamese people. Brutal and sadistic, the Americans would torture and execute anyone unfortunate enough to fall into their hands.

During that initial session, I made no attempt to challenge any of Lanh's statements. I was more interested in letting him talk at length about what it was that had made him the person he was on the day of his capture. His words confirmed my belief that his upbringing in the north and his training as an NVA soldier had made him an excellent candidate for disillusionment. As I listened to him to describe the hardships he had endured, I became more confident that Sang and I would succeed in turning him around. The picture of life in the south that his Communist political officers had painted for him could simply not withstand the test of reality. Seeing would become believing as we exposed him firsthand to life in South Vietnam. Already he had experienced much that contradicted what he had been led to believe. Do van Lanh was becoming a confused young North Vietnamese, and it was now time to compound that confusion.

Lanh broke into a smile and bounced out of his chair with enthusiasm the day that I told him it was time to take a trip to Saigon. Within minutes, he was ready to go. Grabbing my M-16 and a bandoleer of ammunition, I motioned him to follow me, and we were off, riding in my green police jeep.

The road out of Bao Trai passes a large clay quarry as it nears the intersection with Highway 1. I pulled the jeep off the road at the quarry and grabbed my M-16 as I climbed out. Lanh sat in the jeep with a puzzled expression on his face until I motioned for him to get out. He gave me a quizzical glance and complied. Cradling my M-16, I pulled back the bolt and let it fly forward, chambering a round. "Here," I said, shoving the rifle into his hands. "Go ahead and fire it into the quarry."

My palms were a little sweaty by now. After all, the man I had just armed had been captured a little over a week earlier, and then only after he had been wounded and run out of ammunition. He could easily shoot me now and head for the swamp.

Lanh grasped the rifle hesitantly. "Go ahead," I urged. "It's on automatic. Fire it. We've got to get to Saigon."

Turning in the direction of the pit, he aimed and fired the entire twenty-round magazine in two quick bursts. Laughing, he handed me back the weapon, commenting only that "it's light and doesn't kick like my AK-47."

Later, as we cruised down Highway 1 into Hoc Mon district on the outskirts of Saigon, Lanh started to laugh. "Did you know, Dai Uy, that when you stopped the jeep back there, I thought for a second that you were going to shoot me? I was scared to death when I got out of the jeep."

Hearing this, I couldn't help laughing myself, even though the scare I had given him wasn't my idea of humor. "You were scared!" I retorted. "What about me? I'm the one who gave a POW a loaded M-16. I was so scared that my hands were sweating. You could have easily killed me on the spot."

By now we had entered the city limits of Saigon, passing the sprawling Tan Son Nhut Air Force Base on our left. We drove through the Bay Hien intersection, where a ferocious battle had taken place during the Tet Offensive. I turned down Cach Mang Boulevard, the most direct route to downtown Saigon. We became virtual prisoners of the traffic flow as we sped past the elegant multi-tiered Vinh Nghiem Pagoda, then entered tree-shaded Cong Ly Street which led us by President Thieu's Independence Palace. Lanh's face registered his astonishment at what he was seeing, especially when we turned down Tu Do Street and he caught sight of the heart of the downtown section. I maneuvered the jeep through the crush of traffic to Gia Long Street, a narrow thoroughfare just one block away from the center of the city. Gesturing to a young boy to watch the jeep, I parked on the sidewalk in front of the Ngoc Huong restaurant at 155A. Captain Sang had introduced me to the Ngoc Huong on one of our infrequent forays into the city. It was known for its delicious North Vietnamese cuisine prepared by a kitchenful of black-toothed North Vietnamese women who had fled to the south in 1954. Lunch at the Ngoc Huong, consumed to the sounds of traditional North Vietnamese music, was as good a way as any to commence our tour of "Ho Chi Minh City." Lanh gazed at the menu like a ten-year-old on his first trip to Disneyland.

Do van Lanh was overwhelmed by everything that day, from the delicacies of the Ngoc Huong's kitchen to the bustling Ben Thanh marketplace. He had never imagined that Saigon would be the colorful, fascinating collection of sights, smells, and sounds that unfolded before him during our whirlwind, four-hour visit. I bought him a new shirt and belt at the market, and we walked down Le Loi Boulevard to Nguyen Hue Street, Saigon's famous "Street of Flowers." Everywhere we looked our eyes were treated to the beauty of the girls of Saigon, whose colorful, flowing *ao dai* dresses were easily the most memorable feature of the city's face. Even Lanh, the self-styled bachelor, couldn't help contrasting Saigon's graceful and stylish women with their dark-clad cousins in Hanoi.

Lanh wasn't the only one who left Saigon that afternoon with a positive impression. I, too, had found myself captivated by a city that fifteen months earlier had so offended me that I had been glad to receive orders to the countryside. All of the scars of the sprawling city that had seemed so ugly at the time were still there, but my eyes were focusing elsewhere. As we embarked on the return trip to Bao Trai, I realized that I had actually been showing off Saigon with pride.

The relationship between Lanh and me somehow altered in a fundamental way as a result of that trip to Saigon. It was as if the incident with the M-16 and our day together in the capital had succeeded in removing a lingering barrier to mutual trust—a barrier that had persisted in reminding both of us that we were supposed to be enemies. I no longer found myself glancing nervously at Lanh at every traffic light, fearful that he would leap from the jeep and disappear into the crowd. When we arrived back in Hau Nghia, I met with Captain Sang and we agreed that it was time to move ahead with our plan to convert Do van Lanh.

XI

"THE BEST IN THE REPUBLIC OF VIETNAM"

Do van Lanh was indeed one very troubled young man. One evening shortly after our Saigon expedition, the two of us sat up most of the night while Lanh revealed more of himself than ever before. He admitted that he was confused by the many discrepancies he had seen between what he had been told about South Vietnam and what he had seen in the nine days since his capture. He confessed that he had sincerely believed in his duty to go south and fight the Americans and had been dismayed when he learned that he and his comrades were really fighting other Vietnamese.

The face of Saigon had compounded his confusion. He was too intelligent to absorb what he had seen without a sharp reaction. In Saigon, he had looked in vain for evidence of massive American presence and concluded that either the American troops he had been told about were very well hidden, or they simply didn't exist. I assured him that the latter was true and offered to take him to Vung Tau to see for himself the absurdity of the claim that two American divisions were hidden there.

Lanh smiled as he recalled how absolutely certain he had been that I was going to torture and execute him. He had expected the worst when his South Vietnamese jailers had rousted him out of his cell and told him that the American captain wanted to see him. It had taken him several days before he had dared to hope that the Americans were not the monsters he had been told.

Lanh recalled for me a conversation he had had shortly after his capture with one of the South Vietnamese women who did laundry for Team 43.

"Why did you come all the way down the Ho Chi Minh Trail and attack our province?" the woman had asked.

149

"I came to liberate you from the Americans," Lanh had proudly replied.

"Liberate us?" the woman had scoffed. "We don't need liberation. We are already free to do what we want. If I want to wear a purple blouse, I wear a purple blouse. If I want to go to the market, I go. Thanks so much, but we don't need liberation by the North Vietnamese Army."

Lanh had been disappointed at the reception he and his comrades had experienced when they entered South Vietnam. The southern villagers had been indifferent to them, and most of them had actually fled their homes when they approached, fearful of becoming caught in the impending battles. The assurances of the regiment's political cadre that they would be welcomed as liberators had proven to be hollow. Only a few revolutionary families had welcomed them graciously. The romantic picture of the South Vietnamese peasantry linking arms with their North Vietnamese liberators that had been painted by the cadre in the north had simply not withstood the test of reality. Most South Vietnamese, Lanh had concluded painfully, desired peace, not liberation—and they therefore tended to blame him and his comrades for perpetuating the war. No one seemed to be grateful for their sacrifices in the name of the revolution. Things simply were not adding up.

Lanh had experienced mixed feelings in Saigon. Hanoi, he explained proudly, was serene and beautiful, unmarred by the crush of motor vehicles he had encountered in Saigon. In that sense, he preferred Hanoi. And the sight of amputees begging on the streets of Saigon had shocked him—no such thing would be allowed in the north. Lanh was awestruck by the wealth of consumer goods for sale in Saigon's shops. He had been unprepared for such signs of prosperity and abundance, and the animated and cheerful Saigonese hurrying about their business had made a deep impression on him. Nowhere had he seen any evidence to confirm the horror stories of life in Saigon that had been gospel in the north.

Our conversation revealed Lanh to be as totally disillusioned as a person could be. Closely behind this disillusionment would follow frustration—and then the inevitable anger at those who were responsible for his manipulation. I resolved that I would speed up that process the following day. It was time for our houseguest to pay his rent.

After breakfast the following morning, I again engaged Lanh in conversation about the situation in South Vietnam. The town of An Loc was still surrounded by North Vietnamese troops, but it had not fallen. As South Vietnamese relief forces inched their way up Highway 13 to link up with their beleaguered comrades, fierce American and South Vietnamese air strikes were wiping out entire units of North Vietnamese infantry that had massed in the rubber plantations outside the encircled town. I reminded Lanh that even though he had been told by his unit's political officer that An Loc had been "totally liberated," he had seen with his own eyes the newsreel films that proved the contrary.

Before we began our discussion, I had purposely placed a stack of eight-by-ten glossy black-and-white photos on the table. The pictures were closeups of the corpses of the sixty-five North Vietnamese infantrymen who had been killed on May 11 at the battle of An Ninh village. One of the photos depicted our jubilant militia troops posing with the captured weapons and equipment of the defeated North Vietnamese unit. Lanh picked up the pictures and began to leaf through them. I explained gently.

"Those are the bodies of the men of the C1 company that was wiped out by our forces two weeks ago. You were in the C3 company, but you should recognize many of them since they are almost all from Ha Tinh province. Only the company commander, his political officer, and the mortar crews escaped. The rest were killed while they waited for a withdrawal order that never came because their commander had fled."

As I talked, Lanh thumbed through the pictures, each one of which was grislier than the other. When he had looked at the picture of the last vacant-eyed corpse, he swallowed hard, speechless. Taking a document from my shirt pocket, I handed it to him.

"Now read this report. It is the after-action report on this battle that the North Vietnamese commander sent to his superiors."

The report had fallen into our hands the day before. It described the "great victory" of the C1 company, which had "completely overrun" the An Ninh outpost, "killing twenty-nine puppet troops." The North Vietnamese commander, for understandable reasons, had decided to cover up the debacle that had befallen one of his companies.

When Lanh had finished reading the report, I held up the stack of gruesome photos. "This is what really happened that day in An Ninh village. I've never lied to you, and I won't start now. We have already killed more than five hundred of the men who crossed the river with you two weeks ago. All of them have died fighting for a cause that you know was totally misrepresented to them. During this same period of time, more than one hundred of our own troops have been sacrificed. All of this is a tragic waste of lives, and your comrades have died for a lie. If this is to be stopped, then the leaders in Hanoi will have to be shown that they cannot force a victory at the point of a gun. They almost got you killed with their lies about the poor, oppressed South Vietnamese people. Now you must decide for yourself how you should react to the way in which you were manipulated. If you want to end this senseless killing, then you must work hard to bring about the defeat of the Nguyen Hue Offensive. That is the only language that Hanoi understands. I know this is difficult for you, but you must trust me and Captain Sang. We can only arrange for your freedom if you cooperate. Otherwise, we will be forced to return you to POW channels. That would be a difficult thing for us to have to do, but we might have no other choice. It just depends on you. We are afraid that you could become involved in a prisoner exchange and end up carrying an AK-47 down the Ho Chi Minh Trail for the second time."

Having finally made my long-delayed appeal, I left the shaken and confused Lanh alone for the rest of the day to ponder his decision. At Sang's office, I shared with him the status of our project. Sang volunteered to pay a brief visit on Lanh that afternoon to provide a timely prod in the right direction. It had been almost two weeks since Lanh's capture, and most of the two invading North Vietnamese regiments had already pulled back across the river. If he was to be of any assistance in pinpointing their rear base areas, we needed to secure his complete cooperation now.

That evening, Lanh made his decision. As we sat on the couch in the living room, he abruptly began an emotional outpouring of his feelings toward me and the other Americans and Vietnamese he had met since his capture. He was deeply grateful to Sang and me for taking care of him in his moment of need, and he would never forget the kindnesses that had been extended to him by all of us since his capture. Lanh acknowledged that he had been tricked and used by the Hanoi government. He had considered carefully everything that I had told him and decided that he no longer owed any loyalty to the Communists. That didn't mean, he hastened to add, that he didn't still love his country. The people in the north were mostly decent, industrious workers and peasants to whom he could still relate more easily than he could to the people of the south. For this reason, he wanted to help in reestablishing peace. For only if there was peace, he reasoned, could he ever return to his family in the north.

Lanh admitted that he was ready to work with us, but he had one major reservation. He wanted Sang and me to understand that his freedom would mean nothing to him if he were again forced to carry a rifle. "Dai Uy," he explained, "I never want to carry a weapon again, whether it be an M-16 or an AK-47. I am afraid that when you go back to America, I will be drafted by the Saigon government."

Knowing that his fears were accurate, I evaded promising him any sort of draft exemption. Not only was this not within my power, but I seriously doubted that even the province chief could extend such assurances. Instead, I repeated my conviction to him that if we could deal the North Vietnamese a strong military rebuff, the most likely result would be a cease-fire, after which hopefully no Vietnamese would have to bear arms. To my relief, this reply seemed to satisfy him.

Lanh took a deep breath and began to speak. For the next two hours, I got to know the real Do van Lanh.

To begin with, Combatant Lanh was really Sergeant Lanh, a member of the reconnaissance company of the 271st Independent Regiment. He was twenty-two years old, not nineteen, and he had been in the army for three years. He had been trained in sapper-reconnaissance operations at an elite training center northwest of Hanoi before being assigned to the 271st Regiment. Lanh had infiltrated with his regiment from November, 1971, to February, 1972, but he had not contracted malaria during the trip, nor had he lain in a dispensary in Cambodia. He had been continuously with his unit from the time it left North Vietnam until his capture. As a reconnaissance team leader, Lanh had participated in several battles in Tay Ninh province. His insistence that he had joined his unit only after it had crossed the river had been a convenient fiction he had invented to exempt himself from further interrogation. After crossing the river with his unit on the night of May 10 to 11, Lanh had performed security screening operations for the regimental forward command post. On the day of his capture, he and his two comrades were manning an observation post that protected the southern approach to this command post. They had opened fire on the superior South Vietnamese force in order to alert the command post of the approaching danger and give its personnel time to escape. Lanh was confident that he could identify a number of the places that his unit had passed through from March until his capture if he could see a map. He was willing to do this, but not without misgivings. His memories of the air strikes that he had lived through prior to his capture were still vivid, and he clearly did not enjoy his new role as an informant. Do van Lanh was no Hai Tiet. He had suffered through a traumatic bout with his conscience, and unable to remain uncommitted any longer, he was still repelled at the thought of breaking faith with his comrades. His decision had been the most difficult one of his life. In the name of the greater good of bringing peace to his country, he would cooperate with us.

I assured the troubled Lanh that he had made the right decision and promised him our full support in the procurement of his freedom. Then I hurried across the street to bring the good news to Colonel Bartlett. The colonel would be pleased to learn of Lanh's conversion for more than just tactical reasons. We had learned from Jerry Christiansen, my intelligence sergeant, that some of the men on Team 43 were not at all happy to see me with a North Vietnamese prisoner in tow. To many of our men, Lanh was as guilty in the death of Sergeant Arsenault as if he had been a member of the ambushing unit. They resented his privileged life-style and made no secret of their displeasure at what they considered to be my lax security measures with Lanh, who by now was carrying my radio. Colonel Bartlett had paid them little mind, refusing to retreat from his determination to allow me to pursue my unorthodox methods. When Sergeant Christiansen reported that several disgruntled men were going to protest to the colonel, carrying a "demand" that no POW should be allowed in the team compound, Colonel Bartlett had scoffed, "Let them protest. I know exactly what you are doing, and why. The project's gains far outweigh any imaginary risks they may have conjured up." As it turned out, no one ever dared to approach the colonel, and poor Sergeant Christiansen continued to take the heat from his narrow-minded colleagues.*

The colonel was pleased to learn that Private Lanh had suddenly become Sergeant Lanh. He urged me to waste no time in extracting a target list from our new source so that he could line up air strikes as soon as possible. A helicopter would be available on the following day if I wanted to take Lanh up for a reconnaissance of the An Ninh village area. This established, I hastened back to the villa to debrief Lanh before he could change his mind.

Lanh and I spent countless hours together for the next week as we pinpointed targets that he described from memory. During that week, guided by Lanh, we located and destroyed by air strikes a command post near Loc Giang village and a company-sized bunker complex across the river from An Ninh village. Based upon his recollections of the 271st's river-crossing operation, we called in a B-52 strike on one base area. The bombs from the surprise raid badly mauled an enemy sapper platoon that had the misfortune to be occupying the target area. After Lanh revealed that his unit's bivouac site had been an abandoned rubber plantation on Highway 1 just inside Cambodia, we again summoned the high-flying B-52s to react. Colonel Bartlett and I were pleased at such concrete evidence that our experiment had worked, but Lanh did not

*Staff Sergeant Jerry L. Christiansen. A native of Washington state, Chris was a graduate of the Army's "Instant NCO" program. A former Green Beret medic, he was unquestionably one of the finest men I served with in Vietnam. If he hasn't made E-9 yet—or if he is now a civilian—the Army is the loser.

share our exuberance. Throughout this period, Sang and I had to remain sensitive to his feelings about his new role. To poor Lanh's credit, he took no pride in his box score.

Hanoi's units absorbed a brutal and costly beating in Hau Nghia province during May. When the 271st and the 24th Regiments finally withdrew, they left behind the bodies of more than five hundred men. We later learned that the two units had also been forced to evacuate nearly five hundred wounded soldiers. Since the total strength of the two units had been a little over two thousand, this meant that they had suffered over 50 percent casualties, of whom only a very small number had been captured. In contrast, our casualties had been approximately a hundred killed and some two hundred twenty-five wounded, or less than 5 percent of the forces committed. This lopsided victory of the Hau Nghia territorial forces over units of the North Vietnamese Army prompted General Minh, South Vietnamese Corps Commander, to praise the Hau Nghia province regional forces as "the best in the Republic of Vietnam." Morale among our soldiers skyrocketed as a result of their surprise victory over the Communists. Hau Nghia's officers and men were proud of their performance—and Colonel Thanh would have been proud of them.

The scale of violence in the Nguyen Hue attacks had astonished me. In 1971, a major engagement in Hau Nghia had involved perhaps ten or twenty casualties on a side. Now, entire North Vietnamese regiments were being thrown into the battle with orders to hold onto the rural areas as long as possible. Some North Vietnamese units had even been told that they would be reinforced, when in reality, no reinforcements were available. In Hau Nghia, General Giap sacrificed regiments like companies. Elsewhere in Vietnam, An Loc for example, entire divisions were fed into the battle, suffering horrendous casualties. I saw one interrogation report on a North Vietnamese soldier who was the sole survivor of a three-hundred-man battalion that had been wiped out in an instant by a direct hit from a B-52 strike in a rubber forest near An Loc.

It was almost impossible for me as an American to comprehend the willingness of the North Vietnamese high command to sacrifice its men in so wanton and wholesale a fashion. Even though I felt that I understood the depth of the motivations of the individual Communist soldier, I still had to be in awe of his bravery and selfless willingness to sacrifice. In the streets of An Loc, for example, dead NVA tankers had been found chained to their knocked-out vehicles. Both the media and President Thieu's Ministry of Information had gleefully latched onto this story and cited it as proof that the North Vietnamese tank crews had been forced to fight by their leaders. Actually, Hanoi's tankers were an elite, high-spirited bunch and quite capable of chaining themselves into their tanks as a symbol of their determination to *Danh cho den cuoi cung* ("fight to the end").

Americans and South Vietnamese alike were guilty of wishful thinking about the nature of our North Vietnamese foe. It was common in 1972 to hear the average NVA soldier described as a reluctant draftee, ill trained and motivated primarily by fear of disciplinary action at the hands of his unit's political officer. Not infrequently, reports reached us in the field that a search of North Vietnamese bodies had uncovered various kinds of drugs, or that North Vietnamese troops had fought in a given battle as if they were in some sort of a trance. All of this supposedly proved that Hanoi's commanders were forced to feed drugs to their men in order to extract from them the sacrifices required by their head-quarters. Such reports were common and underscored the unwillingness of Americans and South Vietnamese to accept that Communist soldiers could be true believers in their cause. Since by our standards the North Vietnamese were engaged in unjust aggression, it was somehow unthink-able that their soldiers could sustain their brave performance in the absence of outside stimuli or harsh leaders. But as I was quickly learning, most North Vietnamese soldiers had grown up in a tightly controlled cocoon of information, and they were sold on the justice of their cause. The knowledge that Uncle Ho demanded the ejection of the Americans and the reunification of the country was sufficient tonic to keep the average North Vietnamese soldier motivated on the battlefield.

The month of June brought with it renewed North Vietnamese attacks, forcing us to shuttle our units from one village to another as enemy battalions continued to occupy our populated areas by night in order to force the government to employ air strikes and artillery. More major battles were fought in An Ninh village; then the pressure shifted to the outskirts of Bao Trai (where the villagers had been burying their rice in April). One enemy unit cut Highway 1 for two days, while elements of the North Vietnamese 101st Regiment returned to seize the western edge of Trang Bang city. This time, the stubborn 101st managed to hold on for five days before retreating in the face of dozens of sorties of air strikes. It was during this battle that a South Vietnamese A1-E Skyraider had dropped a napalm canister short of its target and burned a group of children. An alert news photographer had captured one panic-stricken little girl as she fled naked down Highway 1, a picture that became one of the most memorable of the entire war. Hau Nghia was ablaze on all fronts, and our resources were badly strained. Every time our hard-pressed militia troops ejected a Communist unit, destruction was reaped on government-held population centers; new refugees were generated to add to the already heavy burden of the government; and both sides suffered more bloodletting—with the Communists coming out second best by far.

But the North Vietnamese were relentless, and Colonel Bartlett had to face the prospect that Bao Trai was in danger of encirclement. Our militia forces were totally committed in their efforts to contain the offensive at the current level. Some of the citizens of Bao Trai had already quietly gone to Saigon "to visit relatives," and the tension in the air was unmistakable. Even though the Communists had only shelled Bao Trai twice, we learned from one issue of *Stars and Stripes* that we were living in "the oft-shelled capital of Bao Trai."

Our real problem in Bao Trai was simple. Whether or not we could continue to cope successfully with the Nguyen Hue Offensive was essentially up to the North Vietnamese. At the current level—with three North Vietnamese regiments committed—our Hau Nghia militia troops had been able to react to each successive enemy incursion into the province. But if the enemy commander escalated his commitment by throwing in yet another regiment, our militia forces would be dangerously over-extended. Recognizing this precarious situation, Colonel Bartlett was forced to consider what steps might be required in the event of such an escalation. In the worst case, he had reasoned, the North Vietnamese could completely encircle and possibly even overrun Bao Trai. The enemy could decide to attempt this for the prestige of capturing a provincial capital. The colonel also believed that such a defeat could only come about if the North Vietnamese committed additional forces.

Since we could not know the North Vietnamese high command's intentions, Colonel Bartlett advised Colonel Hau to plan for the worst case and commence discreet preparations for the defense of an encircled Bao Trai. Apart from procuring adequate stocks of food and ammunition, Colonel Bartlett suggested that we paint large identification numbers on the roofs of key buildings up and down the town's main street. The numbers would facilitate ground-to-air liaison in the event Bao Trai suffered the same fate as An Loc. Colonel Bartlett had learned that close air support had been hampered in An Loc by the inability of the ground forces to guide the air force pilots to those places in the contested town that had been overrun by the enemy. Colonel Bartlett's suggestion would remedy this problem. In the event of a North Vietnamese penetration of any section of Bao Trai, we could call in air strikes on the attackers by referring to the rooftop numbers. The black numbers were painted on large white rectangles and were easily visible from above. None of us liked to think of the unpleasant prospect of calling in air strikes on our own home, yet this was a contingency that had to be faced. The North Vietnamese had already demonstrated their willingness to sacrifice units in order to force the government to bomb population centers. A logical next move would be to bring the war to Bao Trai in the same manner.

But Colonel Bartlett had to face another, more sensitive problem. If it became clear that our province militia forces could no longer contain the North Vietnamese invaders, at what point should he recommend to his superiors that Team 43 be extracted from Hau Nghia? This was a delicate question, since the withdrawal under pressure of an advisory team was certain to hurt the morale of the South Vietnamese who stayed behind. Already, as more and more of Bao Trai's residents departed for Saigon my counterparts in Captain Nga's G-2 shop had begun to ask me jokingly if I was also going to go to Saigon. Their digs were in good fun, but they also reflected a genuine concern.

To the thirty-odd Americans who made up the shrinking Team 43, the prospect of abandoning our counterparts if the going got tough was distasteful. Almost no one wanted to abandon Bao Trai if the situation deteriorated and we became encircled. Personally, I found the role of the rat leaving the sinking ship repugnant. Professionally, I knew that once we had fled under pressure, we could never regain the respect and confidence of our counterparts. If Team 43 bailed out on the Vietnamese, we could never return. Colonel Bartlett agonized over this dilemma, for he too regarded it as unthinkable to leave Bao Trai under military pressure. But he knew that if our situation deteriorated, he would come under pressure from his superiors either to evacuate his entire team or to reduce its size drastically. As American involvement in the war wound down in an election year, the political pressure to reduce American casualties had become intense.

The colonel announced his decision to me one evening as we were going over the latest intelligence reports, trying to determine which enemy battalion was at that moment occupying a small hamlet several thousand meters west of Bao Trai. He had decided that he would recommend the withdrawal of the advisory team only if the enemy committed additional forces and it appeared imminent that Bao Trai would be encircled. In this event, the colonel had decided to remain behind to assist Colonel Hau in directing the defense of the town. He asked me and Sergeant First Class Jackson, an infantryman, if we would volunteer to remain behind and assist him. If we agreed, the three of us would stay regardless of the situation. The colonel planned to call in air strikes on the attackers until they either retreated or overran the town. In the latter case, the three of us would split up and attempt to escape and evade to friendly held areas.

It was easy to volunteer to remain with Colonel Bartlett, since I harbored no desire to leave Hau Nghia in the first place. I had just extended my tour for the second time in anticipation of the long-awaited cease-fire, and it didn't seem right to leave Bao Trai on the eve of the final jockeying for position that we knew would precede the end of hostilities. I had already invested eighteen months of my life and considerable emotion in the struggle for Hau Nghia province. Six more months was small price to pay for the opportunity to see things through to the end. Besides, if Colonel Bartlett was determined to stick it out, it was unthinkable not to remain with him. He was that kind of a person.

XII

"NVA IN THE MARKETPLACE!"

Sergeant Christiansen brought the long overdue good news. Colonel Hau's troops had just pulled a North Vietnamese prisoner out of a bunker on the outskirts of Bao Trai. We desperately needed information on the stubborn enemy units that were creeping closer and closer to Bao Trai, and prisoners had always been our best source. Chris warned me that the new POW was hostile and uncooperative. The Vietnamese in the G-2 shop had been unable to get him to reveal his name, let alone his unit. We were still in the dark about the identity of a fresh North Vietnamese unit that had crossed the river and dug in within mortar range of Bao Trai. Were our visitors once again from the battered 271st or the 24th Regiment, or had the enemy already upped the ante and committed another unit? We needed to know, and we had a way to find out. If the new prisoner would not talk to an enemy interrogator, perhaps he would feel more comfortable talking to a North Vietnamese comrade. I sent one of the guards to find Lanh.

Lanh donned his old uniform and dirtied his face in preparation for his first test as an interrogator. A cursing South Vietnamese guard shoved him into the small G-2 jail cell. Squatting in the corner was the new POW. Within a few minutes, the two men had begun to compare notes. Lanh told his cellmate that he was from the 271st Regiment's recon company and that he had just been captured. He urged his companion not to talk to the puppet interrogators. The unsuspecting prisoner fell for this ploy, and by the end of their second hour together, he had told Lanh all that we needed to know. The North Vietnamese unit we were pounding with air strikes outside of Bao Trai was our old adversary, the 271st Regiment—back for more punishment. The prisoner told Lanh that his

161

unit's mission had been to liberate and hold the village west of Bao Trai. They had been holding for two days, but at a terrible price. Dozens of the North Vietnamese had already been killed or wounded by the relentless and accurate air strikes of the South Vietnamese. The prisoner himself had been in a bunker that had been engulfed by napalm, and he had been having difficulty breathing ever since.

After two hours, a guard unlocked the cell and roughly escorted Lanh out for "interrogation." In Captain Nga's office, I carefully debriefed him on the results of his mission. Our ruse had provided us with the information that Colonel Bartlett needed. We were not facing a fresh unit, and our militia troops had already demonstrated convincingly their ability to handle the 271st Regiment.

But Lanh did not share my high spirits. He was concerned for the prisoner he had just left.

"Dai Uy," he implored, "we must get him to a doctor at once. He is having trouble breathing, and I think he is hurt inside."

A yell came from the guard. The prisoner had fainted, and his abdomen had begun to swell rapidly. We rushed him to the province hospital, where he died within the hour of internal bleeding. He had apparently suffered his injuries from the bomb concussions earlier in the day, but no one had recognized the symptoms.

Lanh was overcome with depression when he learned that the prisoner had died. He was ashamed of his role in duping a wounded former comrade and blamed himself for the man's death. Nothing I said seemed to help. Like all of us, Lanh handled war's unpleasantness better at a distance than he did up close. It was one thing for him to help call in air strikes on a bunker complex several thousand feet below, but it was something quite different to face a former comrade and lie—particularly when his first subject turned out to be a dying man.

In spite of its tragic outcome, Lanh's performance had played an important role. We had urgently needed what he learned through his charade. Furthermore, the use of a cooperative North Vietnamese to exploit another North Vietnamese had been an idea that had intrigued me from the day I had seen Lanh match wits with Colonel Tu. No one was better equipped to talk to a North Vietnamese soldier than a fellow NVA. Lanh had recently walked down the Ho Chi Minh Trail and fought against the South Vietnamese. His authenticity and his credentials to talk persuasively to another North Vietnamese were thus unimpeachable.

A regular feature of my workweek had become a visit to the base camp of the 83d Rangers. Their numbers depleted by nearly continuous shelling, the plucky rangers had nonetheless continued to take their toll of the attacking North Vietnamese. This was the main reason for my visits. Each time the rangers repelled a Communist assault, they would collect dozens of documents from the enemy bodies, and I had gotten into the habit of examining the personal effects of every enemy who met his end anywhere in Hau Nghia. This relentless and macabre search of enemy dead for clues to the North Vietnamese battle plan is one of my most haunting memories of the 1972 offensive. Try as I might, I was unable to convince my Vietnamese counterparts to perform this distasteful task thoroughly. Some of the G-2 personnel were unwilling to handle enemy dead because of what they claimed was a religious taboo. Others simply couldn't stand to get their hands bloody. On several occasions early in my tour, I had discovered important documents on enemy bodies that the Vietnamese claimed they had already searched.

Many of the troops of the 83d Ranger Battalion were ethnic Cambodians, and they suffered from no such inhibitions. The rangers not only searched the dead North Vietnamese, they stripped them of anything usable, salable, or otherwise of value. Their sergeant major once confided in me that some of his more superstitious men would have gone a step further had he not intervened. Several of the Cambodians had wanted to cut out and eat the livers of the fallen NVA soldiers, in the belief that this would provide them with protection from death on the battlefield.

When I first visited the rangers, they had already been under attack for ten days. As our helicopter descended in a steep spiral, I noticed the signs of a unit under siege. The interior and the perimeter of the star-shaped outpost was pockmarked with craters. In the barbed wire perimeter, dirt trails marked the progress of the North Vietnamese attackers as they tunneled their way closer and closer to the outpost's final defensive barriers. Giap's soldiers were using the same tunneling tactic that had been so effective against the French at Dien Bien Phu eighteen years earlier.

The 83d's commanding officer was a young-looking Vietnamese major. He displayed the unit's booty—an impressive array of North Vietnamese weapons and equipment—and boasted that his men had already buried sixty of their antagonists in the perimeter. He estimated that they could continue to hold off the North Vietnamese as long as the attacks continued to be limited to company-sized probes. Their biggest problem, the major complained, was the failure of his headquarters to provide barbed wire and sandbags to rebuild the outpost's crumbling fortifications. One look at the camp convinced me that he was not exaggerating the need. He was turning to me because it was axiomatic among the Vietnamese that all Americans had mystical powers that enabled them to lay their hands on anything they needed. Sandbags and wire were two of the hottest items in current demand, thanks to thirteen attacking North Vietnamese divisions. We had none of these precious supplies in Bao Trai.

I glanced at the display of war trophies and hit upon an idea. If the major would let me take the North Vietnamese helmets, canteens, and pistol belts, I felt certain that the aviators who flew our helicopters could be induced to "requisition" the badly needed sandbags and wire. The rangers could keep the weapons of the fallen North Vietnamese to show their superiors—if indeed they dared to venture out to see for themselves the 83d's situation. The major looked briefly at his Cambodian sergeant major, who smiled and nodded his concurrence.

With this bargain struck, I collected the booty in a large plastic bag along with a stack of documents and headed to the chopper pad.

The crew of four smiled broadly when they saw what I was carrying. After we took off, the copilot asked me how much I was asking for the pith helmets. I explained the rangers' plight and the bargain that I had struck. The crew responded as I had hoped. "Hell, that's easy," quipped the door gunner. "I know where there's a whole damn conex container full of sandbags, just going to waste. You just keep that stuff coming, and we'll bring all the sandbags and wire you can use."

The aviators were as good as their word. To the delight of the besieged rangers, several times a week for the next two weeks, an American heli-copter spiraled out of the sky at eight-thirty in the morning, hovered momentarily over their base, and disgorged bundles of sandbags and rolls of precious barbed wire. Scrounging and bartering in this manner was frowned upon by our logistics people, who contended that such practices undermined and retarded the development of a properly functioning Vietnamese supply system. They were probably right, but the only meaningful issue at hand to me was that the rangers needed the supplies urgently, and their supply system—for whatever reason—had let them down. Besides, my job was to keep track of the enemy situation on the border adjacent to Hau Nghia—a task that became considerably easier once I had become the 83d Ranger Battalion's favorite American.

It seemed that we were always being asked to brief visitors from Sai-gon. Even though Hau Nghia was in an exposed location, we were still only a brief helicopter ride from Saigon, and we received more than our fair share of visitors—all wanting to be briefed on some phase of the war.

On one occasion, during the most intense week of the Nguyen Hue Offensive, Mr. Walkinshaw, Colonel Bartlett's civilian boss, arrived by helicopter for a briefing on the situation. Colonel Bartlett had no sooner commenced his briefing when shots rang out from the direction of the central market. One of our interpreters poked his head into the room with an alarming announcement—North Vietnamese troops were in the central market, some three hundred meters from our compound. A concerned Colonel Bartlett politely suggested to his boss that it would perhaps be best if the briefing were postponed and he departed immediately. So much for the situation update. As the shaken Walkinshaw boarded his helicopter, Colonel Bartlett and I donned our web gear and helmets and headed for the province headquarters.

In the operations center, Colonel Hau was barking orders to his staff. The 773d RF Company must move immediately to the marketplace and engage the North Vietnamese. Confusion reigned, and no one could tell us how the North Vietnamese had managed to walk into the city during broad daylight without firing a shot. The tension in the room was compounded by the fact that many of the wives and families of the staff lived in the military housing area across the street from the market, and several men had already abandoned their posts and rushed off to rescue their families. As we watched Colonel Hau struggle to bring order to the mounting panic, I thought of Colonel Thanh. This was the kind of situation where he was sorely missed.

The crisis lasted until the return of one of the sergeants who had run home to save his family. The embarrassed man reported that the entire incident was a false alarm. There were no North Vietnamese in Bao Trai. Instead, there had been a marital squabble at the marketplace that had attracted a crowd. The police had arrived to break up the fight, and a revolver had accidentally discharged in the confusion. The wild shot had sparked a panic up and down the street when word was somehow passed that Communist troops had entered the city.

The incident was not without its humorous aspects (for example, the look on Mr. Walkinshaw's face when he left), but it underscored the delicate state of mind of Bao Trai's residents—both civilian and military—as the Nguyen Hue Offensive ground on.*

During this same period, we briefed yet another visitor, this one from

---

*This incident typified one of the major weaknesses of the Vietnamese military—the tendency for the family of a Vietnamese soldier to travel with him, even to a combat zone. What we experienced on a small scale that day in Bao Trai was a prelude to what happened to the ARVN during the final debacle of 1975—the impact of the so-called family syndrome on combat effectiveness.

Washington. Col. Donald Marshall, assistant to the secretary of defense, was on a fact-finding mission to Vietnam. Colonel Marshall was a Harvard Ph.D. who had made a number of trips to Vietnam since the mid-sixties. His *modus operandi* was interesting. On each of his trips, he had made it a point to visit the same places and meet with the same people when possible. This had given him a unique perspective on the course of the war. Colonel Bartlett briefed our visitor while I stood by to participate in a discussion of the enemy situation.

Colonel Marshall nodded his approval when he learned of the performance of our militia forces against the North Vietnamese Army. His questions about our province were informed and perceptive—not the kind of questions we would have expected from someone as far removed from Bao Trai as Washington. The colonel had clearly done his homework. During the discussion, Colonel Bartlett mentioned that we were in possession of a bona fide, cooperative NVA soldier. Colonel Marshall's face lit up with interest. Could he meet the prisoner?

Lanh was lying on the couch listening to Vietnamese music when Colonel Marshall and I walked into the house. I introduced the colonel as a representative of our "Minister of Defense," the term the North Vietnamese used to refer to General Giap's position. Duly impressed, Lanh smiled timidly and shook hands. If Colonel Marshall was someone taken aback by our unorthodox operation (an NVA POW, unguarded, listening to music in an American advisor's quarters), he didn't betray it. Instead, he shook Lanh's hand warmly and asked me to interpret while he posed a few questions. Would Lanh mind answering?

We spent the next half hour or so discussing the rigors of Lanh's hundred-day journey into South Vietnam and his experiences prior to the day he was captured. The colonel was particularly interested in Lanh's reactions to the battlefield in the south. Lanh explained his dismay at what he had found upon entering South Vietnam. His unit's political officer had assured the men before the first battles that the puppet troops were poorly motivated and would flee when attacked by liberation forces. Initially, this had seemed to be the case. His unit's first attacks had been against several isolated outposts in northern Tay Ninh province that were manned by the ARVN 25th Division. These operations had been easy victories. The frightened ARVN troops had done exactly what they were expected to do—*bo chay* (drop their weapons and run). But, after that, the 271st Regiment had suffered a series of costly defeats at the hands of the Tay Ninh and Hau Nghia militia forces. These reverses had caused Lanh and his comrades to wonder. If the puppet troops were so poorly motivated, then why did they fight so well?

Colonel Marshall pressed hard on the question of the motivations of the individual North Vietnamese soldier. Lanh had been poorly paid; he had been forced to serve far from home, virtually out of communication with his family; he had endured B-52 strikes, malarial mosquitos, and poor food—yet he had still managed to fight bravely. Colonel Bartlett had just observed during his briefing that we had taken very few North Vietnamese prisoners during the recent heavy fighting—and those few whom we had captured had been without exception wounded men. To what factors did Lanh attribute this phenomenon?

Lanh replied without hesitation. "The colonel must understand that the average North Vietnamese soldier is convinced that our cause is a just one. This fact is basic to everything else. He must also remember that every unit of the People's Army contains a certain number of men who are either full members of the *Lao Dong* (Labor, or Communist) party or provisional members. These soldiers, though not always of high rank, possess real power, independent of their rank and the military chain of command. It was known in my unit that the party members could and would report poor performance or a bad attitude to the political officer. Since no one wanted his record stained, most of my comrades strove to perform well, lest they be reported by an ambitious party member.

"But you should not make the mistake of assuming that the fear of being reported was the reason why we fought. The major reasons were that we believed in what we were doing and we knew that the only way that we could ever hope to see our homes and families again was by fighting hard to survive. Most of us reasoned that if we survived each battle, then perhaps the war would end and we could go home. Fighting hard to survive was thus the only course of action that we saw as offering any hope of a return to a peaceful life. No one ever considered surrender as a reasonable option. We believed our officers' warnings that the enemy safe conduct passes were a trick."

The colonel was impressed with Lanh's candor, and before he departed for Saigon, he put us on notice that we would be hearing from him soon. With thirteen North Vietnamese divisions continuing their assault on South Vietnam and with the outcome of the offensive still in doubt, he felt that Lanh's message should be heard by someone in Saigon. He would arrange for our visit to MACV Headquarters and notify me when the plans were firm. Sergeant Do van Lanh was about to get a dose of that highly prized military thing known as visibility.

XIII

A PRESIDENTIAL ENVOY

To the great relief of the Vietcong, the heat was finally off in Tan My village. Thanks to the efforts of three North Vietnamese regiments, government forces had all but ceased to operate against the hard-pressed Vietcong, granting them a reprieve just when their backs had been to the ropes. Colonel Hau had been forced by the ferocity of the offensive to commit the Tan My–based forces to the battles with enemy regulars in other areas of the province. As a result, the Tan My Vietcong were able to resume their operations in the village. Nhanh, the teenaged guerrilla who had assassinated Phich, had been promoted to village security chief. As one of his first official acts, he engineered the elimination of a thirty-two-year-old woman whom the Vietcong had long suspected of being a government agent. Nhanh and his men abducted her from her home one night and left her body—stabbed in the heart—lying on the road close to the village office. Pinned to her blouse was the cryptic warning, "Death to Traitors."

Shortly after this incident, several shots and a scream shattered the still night air of Tan My village's Bao Cong hamlet. The sentry at the nearby government outpost reported the incident to his commander—a regular officer with a reputation for seeking out a fight. The officer—a captain—had reacted predictably. Within minutes, he had declared his intention to investigate the strange disturbance. Emboldened by several bottles of "33" beer, the captain had dared several of his men to accompany him. When the men had cautiously demurred, he had announced boldly and with mock contempt that he would go alone. Persuaded by the captain's bravado, or merely determined that he should not go alone, three men joined their commander as his jeep pulled out of the outpost.

169

Not three hundred meters down the road, Nhanh and his man lay in ambush. The target had taken the bait.

The impetuous captain died in the first burst of fire. His three companions, all wounded, managed to crawl to safety in the roadside ditch. By the time a reaction force arrived on the scene, the Tan My guerrillas had fled, leaving the dead officer slumped over the wheel of the bullet-riddled jeep, its headlights still cutting a bright swath through the inky night. The three wounded men lay moaning in the nearby ditch, wondering what sort of devil had induced them to follow their commander into such an obvious trap.

The militia troops had revered their commander. Not only had he been a brave leader—albeit impetuous—but he had spared no effort to take care of his men. He had even pooled his men's meager rice rations and organized a unit dining hall. The head cook of this unique arrangement had been the commander's own wife. The captain's men had eaten better than any soldiers in Hau Nghia and had certainly been the only troops who could boast that their commander's wife cooked their meals and worried over them like a den mother.

The unit's sergeant major vowed to avenge the captain's death, and he sought out Det, the arch-foe of the Tan My Vietcong, for advice. Det told him that the favorite meeting place of the guerrillas was an isolated farmhouse located on the edge of the big swamp. If a team of men could stand the mosquitos, they need only wait patiently in the reeds outside this house until Nhanh and his men made one of their frequent appearances. The sergeant major relayed this tip to the men of the unit's reconnaissance squad—men who had joined him in his vow of revenge. For two nights they had lain on the damp ground, not daring to swat the mosquitos that terrorized them. On both nights, the widow who lived in the house had gone to bed early, and the men had finally given up and returned to the outpost. But on the third night, the woman had lit a lamp and placed it in the window. Within minutes, four figures had slipped out of the shadows and into the house.

Two of the government troops had crawled gingerly across the carefully swept courtyard until they were under the open windows of the house. Inside, the four Vietcong were drinking tea and conversing in hushed tones when the grenades landed in their midst. There was no time to react, and the career of Nguyen van Nhanh ended in the flash of the two explosions. Two other guerrillas also died, while the fourth man and the woman were badly wounded.

I drove to Tan My when word reached Bao Trai of the successful raid. At the gate to the outpost, the body of Phich's assassin lay by the road, waiting for a relative to claim it. There was no mistaking Nhanh—I had

seen his picture in Phich's hamlet. Tall, slim, and handsome, he had a
gentle look about him that belied his record as a Communist hit man.
Now his body lay as if staring skyward, the right side of his head and
body pockmarked by dozens of lethal fragments, dark bloodstains on his
black pajamas. His bare feet were coarse and calloused, and a congenital
birth defect confirmed his identity. Nhanh had been born with only nine
toes.

The intelligence officer of the militia unit proudly described how his
men had stalked their prey and struck without warning. Then he showed
me the notebook that had been found on Nhanh's body. One entire
section of the small green book was devoted to reports of his surveillance
of Phich, Trung, and me. For the several months that we had worked the
Tan My project, Nhanh had carefully tracked our movements in and out
of the village. "18 May, 9:30 A.M.—the green jeep entered Bao Cong
hamlet." "22 May: Green jeep, Phich, Trung, and American in Bao
Cong and Lap Dien [hamlet]." "28 May, Phich and Sergeant in all hamlets; Phich sleeps in outpost."

Nhanh's informants had kept him well informed of our activities—
just as our informants had reported his moves to us. Even though it came
as no surprise that our adversaries operated much as we did in that
strange war, reading Nhanh's entries was a sobering experience. I quietly
resolved once again to be more cautious in my travels anywhere in Hau
Nghia.

The message was a summons. Colonel Marshall, true to his word, had
talked about his encounter with a friendly North Vietnamese prisoner in
Hau Nghia. I was to bring Lanh on the following day to the office of a
Brig. Gen. James Herbert. The office would be easy to locate—it was on
the second floor of MACV Headquarters in Saigon—"Pentagon East."

I made Lanh wear his North Vietnamese uniform for the occasion—it
enhanced his credibility. On the outskirts of Saigon, I bypassed the
American MP checkpoint by driving my green police jeep in the left lane,
holding my breath all the while. I had no papers of any kind for Lanh,
and no travel orders that would have explained satisfactorily to an
American MP what I was doing squiring a North Vietnamese prisoner
around Saigon. We pulled up to the sprawling yellow building that
housed MACV Headquarters, slowing down as we approached the
American MP at the gate. Once again I held my breath, but the MP
spotted my black captain's bars and saluted as he waved us through the
gate with a crisp "Good morning, sir." He didn't even glance twice at
Lanh.

Lanh gaped at the impressive building as we parked the jeep and strolled to the final barrier, a pedestrian gate that was also manned by a tall MP. Our luck held, and he too saluted, admitting us without question. Apparently our Saigon-based personnel wouldn't have known an NVA soldier unless he pointed an AK-47 at them and opened fire.

Once inside the building, it was only a few short steps to General Herbert's office on the second floor. Several of the smartly clad staff officers in the hall stared at us, but no one bothered to issue a challenge. A small sign on the door to General Herbert's office announced that we were about to enter the domain of the Deputy Assistant Chief of Staff for Civil Operations–Rural Development Support (CORDS). Inside, we found ourselves in front of a desk occupied by a real American female secretary. The poor woman looked pale and sickly; her perfume was overpowering; and her nose—her nose was unquestionably her most prominent feature. This was the legacy of eighteen months among the golden-skinned, delicate women of rural Vietnam. The general's secretary was actually not bad looking at all. I had just been in Hau Nghia too long.

Thinking back to that encounter, we probably looked stranger to that woman than she looked to me. I felt a little ridiculous invading her air-conditioned office wearing a steel helmet and carrying an M-16 rifle —with a North Vietnamese prisoner on my arm. But we were expected, and the general's secretary graciously ushered us into the inner office, explaining that the general was out for the moment but had left instructions for us to wait. There was also a note for me from Colonel Marshall.

General Herbert's spacious office was carpeted and furnished with an attractive wooden desk and a brown leather couch. I motioned for Lanh to sit on the couch, and I read Colonel Marshall's note. The colonel instructed me to use the general's desk and prepare a paper summarizing our work in Hau Nghia with prisoners and defectors.

While Lanh relaxed on the general's couch, I hastily composed a summary of our work with Hai Chua, Phich, Hai Tiet, Lanh, and others. I was only interrupted twice—once by the general's secretary, who offered us coffee, and once by a somewhat miffed lieutenant colonel, who poked his head in the door, motioned toward Lanh, and demanded, "Who's he?"

Rising quickly, I replied politely. "Sir, that's Sgt. Do van Lanh, formerly of the reconnaissance company of the North Vietnamese 271st Independent Regiment. He's a POW, here at the general's request for an interview." Glancing at Lanh, I noticed that he had kicked off his Ho Chi Minh sandals and was squatting barefoot on the general's couch. I barked at him in Vietnamese to get his feet off the furniture, then redirected my attention to the colonel—who was by now outraged.

"How did you get *him* in *here?*" the colonel demanded.

"Sir, it was easy," I replied with a chuckle. I was enjoying this now. "I drove into the bus stop parking lot and we just strolled in. The kind lady outside told us to wait here for the general."

The colonel bristled. "You mean that you brought a uniformed North Vietnamese prisoner into this headquarters without anyone challenging you?"

"Yes sir. Several people stared, but you're the first one to say a word. But there's no reason to worry," I tried to make light of the situation. "My friend here is tame." Lanh smiled benevolently.

"Maybe so," replied the colonel, "but you shouldn't have gotten in here so easily. Is that your weapon?" He was pointing to my gear, which was draped on a straight-backed chair next to the couch.

"Yes sir, and it's cleared," I assured him. Shaking his head in disbelief, the colonel turned on his heels and left the room without another word. He'll have quite a story to tell at Happy Hour in the Massachusetts BOQ, I thought, and turned back to my writing.

General Herbert finally arrived, and I sprang to my feet and saluted as he entered the room. Then I introduced Lanh. The general was a big man, and he towered over Lanh as they shook hands. Then he looked to me. "Can he understand any English?"

"No sir," I replied, "but I can interpret for you if you wish."

Motioning for us to sit down, the general launched into a series of questions, covering pretty much the same general areas that had interested Colonel Marshall. Everyone wanted to know about the rigors of the long walk down the infiltration trail, the impact of the B-52 strikes, and above all, why Hanoi's troops were able to fight so well under such adverse conditions. The general also expressed curiosity about Lanh's reactions to South Vietnamese society and his feelings toward Americans. Lanh was nervous and noticeably cowed by the general, but he brightened up when Colonel Marshall entered the room. The colonel asked if we had encountered any difficulties locating the general's office, and I related our run-in with the unidentified lieutenant colonel. Both men laughed heartily at the anecdote, and General Herbert observed wryly that the security people needed something like Lanh's intrusion to keep them on their toes.

Colonel Marshall scanned my hastily penned history of our work in Hau Nghia and nodded his approval, then asked me if Lanh and I had time to pay another visit before returning to Hau Nghia. There was one more person in Saigon who wanted to meet Lanh. A Mr. Juan Trippe, the retired president of Pan American World Airways, was currently in

Saigon on a fact-finding trip for President Nixon. He was staying in the MACV "White House," the command's VIP guest facility in downtown Saigon. Now in his seventies, the former executive was in semiretirement in Hawaii, but he had agreed to make a trip to Vietnam on behalf of the president. Colonel Marshall had arranged for us to meet with him at four o'clock. I explained this all to Lanh, who was overwhelmed at the prospect of meeting a presidential envoy.

Since we still had a couple of hours before our appointment, Lanh and I headed for the Ngoc Huong restaurant for a good meal. The restaurant was packed with its usual early afternoon crowd, which forced us to sit at a small table near the sidewalk. I avoided these exposed tables whenever possible, preferring to dine on the small balcony in the rear of the restaurant. I had once made the mistake of sitting out front and had been forced to fend off assaults by shoeshine boys, blind men playing the guitar (who could somehow spot the only American in the place), and a variety of hustlers from Saigon's seamier side. Today, unfortunately, we had no choice.

We had no sooner sat down when a shoeshine artist attacked my jungle boots, not even bothering to ask for my consent. When I reminded him of his manners, he replied that we should feel sorry for him because he lived on the street.

"Where are your parents?" I probed.

"Both dead since Tet of '68," he replied, his smile revealing badly yellowed teeth.

"Where do you really live?" I continued.

"Here, there, anywhere will do," he answered, making a sweeping gesture in the direction of the street.

"How old are you?" I asked. The closer I looked, the more obvious it was that he was a lot older than the average shoeshine boy.

"I'm nineteen, Dai Uy," he replied, still buffing away at my boots.

"Nineteen," I said, "then why haven't you been drafted?"

"Because I don't have an ID card, and I'm not registered in any district, Dai Uy."

"What's your name?" I asked sharply. Our food had arrived and I was getting impatient.

"Linh," he answered, buffing my left boot rapidly.

"Look, Linh, you should volunteer for the army. In the service, you'll get three good meals, a place to sleep, and some spending money."

"I'd like to, Dai Uy," he replied, "but when I tried, they told me that I needed an ID card from the police, but the police don't like the street dwellers, so I just keep shining shoes."

I was hungry and in no mood for further debate, so I paid him a hundred piasters and told him that if he was ever in Hau Nghia province, he should look me up and I would get him into the military. Colonel Hau's forces needed replacements badly.

At the mention of Hau Nghia, the would-be soldier smiled and disappeared deeper into the restaurant in search of more business. Lanh's North Vietnamese sense of order and discipline was even more easily offended than my American sensibilities, and he gave me a look of stern disapproval. He had been as alienated by the story of the young Linh as I.

We arrived at the White House shortly before the appointed time. The guard at the gate gave Lanh and me a curious stare, but once again we succeeded in getting through. Just inside the front door of the building, we found ourselves in a small foyer, beyond which was a plush living room. At one end of the room was a bar, tended by two young Chinese-Vietnamese girls in turquoise *ao dai* dresses. Dominating the center of the room was a large circular table, whose center was a lazy Susan. The carpet was the thick, cut pile type—the kind that shows footprints. It was the sort of place where it seems natural to whisper. Lanh was overawed at the strange surroundings as he sat down on the couch. I took off my helmet and web gear and joined him, feeling out of place wearing jungle fatigues in dress blues country. I reminded Lanh to keep his feet off the furniture.

Within a few minutes, a white-haired man who proved to be Mr. Trippe strode through the door. Spying us on the couch, he introduced himself warmly. I explained to Lanh that our host was President Nixon's personal representative. Lanh began to stammer something incoherent, and I "translated" that he was honored to meet such a man of high rank. Mr. Trippe laughed and put his arm around Lanh's shoulder.

"Come into my room and I'll show you something," he invited. In his suite, Mr. Trippe produced a letter from Lyndon Johnson, in which the former president invited him to drop by the LBJ ranch when he returned to the States. Lanh wasn't the only one who was affected by Mr. Trippe's connections. Here was a man who was representing President Nixon—to whom he would report upon his return to the States—who was also a confidant of the nation's number one Democrat. Lanh was impressed. Here he was, a lowly former NVA soldier, visiting a presidential envoy in the heart of the city he had come south to liberate, scant weeks after being captured in a collapsed bunker.

The rest of our time with Mr. Trippe flew by, as Lanh responded to a series of questions about his experiences in the North Vietnamese Army.

Our host was particularly interested to know if Lanh and his comrades had been promised that the Nguyen Hue Offensive would lead to a cease-fire. Lanh replied that they had not been told anything about a cease-fire —only that the offensive would enable them to "liberate large parts" of South Vietnam. Mr. Trippe asked Lanh if he had any message to convey to President Nixon. Lanh responded without hesitation.

"Please tell President Nixon that my former comrades are fighting hard because they have been misled about the situation in the south Unlike me, they have no way of knowing this, and so they will continue to fight hard. The Americans must struggle together with the South Vietnamese so that our leaders in Hanoi will understand that negotiations, not bloodshed, will restore peace to my country. I miss my family and native village in the north very badly. If President Nixon can bring peace, I will be able to go home, and all the Vietnamese people will be grateful. Please tell him that for me."

Mr. Trippe was moved by this appeal. He grasped Lanh by the hand with both of his huge paws and assured him that the president would receive his message. Then he thanked us both and politely excused himself to get ready for a dinner engagement.

Lanh was ecstatic and talked all the way back to Bao Trai. He was overwhelmed at the realization that he had actually conversed with a presidential envoy and had the opportunity to make his desires for peace known to the American president. He assured me several times that he would never forget this experience. By now, the impressionable Lanh seemed completely convinced that I could do anything. Had I not told him that if he would cooperate with me, he could help restore peace to Vietnam? Now, only a few weeks later, he had talked with an American general and sent his own form of peace feeler to President Nixon.

XIV

"CHAO, DAI UY"

It had been a near thing, but we knew by July that our hard-pressed militia forces had outlasted Hanoi's exhausted regulars. With the fall of Quang Tri and the encirclement of An Loc, the Nguyen Hue Offensive had peaked just short of what it took to unhinge the South Vietnamese. Now, as the offensive waned, Colonel Bartlett began to push for a resumption of the Phoenix program.

I had begun my tour in Duc Hue with a futile attempt to interest the Vietnamese in Phoenix. Now it was time to try once again. Colonel Bartlett was concerned about what would happen in Hau Nghia province if the Paris peace talks resulted in a cease-fire in late 1972. Most probably, he surmised, Phoenix operations would have to cease. The Vietnamese government shared this concern and promulgated a new official decree directing the national police to assume full responsibility for all Phoenix operations. Until now, the police had played a backseat role to the military in these operations. Apparently the Saigon government sensed that whereas military operations would most certainly be circumscribed under the terms of any cease-fire, police operations might continue. By converting Phoenix into a police program, the government hoped to create an anti-Communist weapon that could survive the terms of the coming settlement. In Hau Nghia, this meant that we had to establish new ties with the notoriously incompetent national police, an unpleasant task that Colonel Bartlett made clear belonged to me.

I was on my way to Police Headquarters when I spotted one of our guards talking to someone at the gate. Spying me, the visitor waved and called out, "Dai Uy, Dai Uy! Do you remember me? I'm Linh. I shined your shoes in Saigon. I need to talk with you for a few minutes."

Nodding to the guard to let him in, I shook the grinning Linh's hand. "Dear God! How did you get here?"

"I came by bus, Dai Uy," he smiled, obviously proud of his achievement. "I had to hide on the floor at the checkpoints because I don't have an ID card, but I did it! I'm here to join the army."

Now I was in a fix. I had invited the pesky shoeshine boy to Bao Trai, but it had never crossed my mind that he would take me seriously. The mere mention of Hau Nghia to the Saigonese evoked the standard shake of the head and the exclamation about the province's "*beaucoup* VC." The three North Vietnamese regiments that had been roaming all over the province for three months had even reinforced this reputation. The notion of one of Saigon's *bui doi* ("dust of life") orphans voluntarily exchanging his shoeshine kit for an M-16 rifle was preposterous. Not only that, but I had no idea whether or not he could enlist in our militia forces. I was over my head on this one.

I invited Linh into the house and sent one of the guards to get Captain Sang. He was the only one who could bail me out of this predicament. Not surprisingly, Linh was hungry, and he was soon wolfing down everything edible in sight. Sang drove up in his jeep within a few minutes.

"Sang," I said with a laugh, "this is all your fault. You're the one who introduced me to the Ngoc Huong restaurant. Now you've got to help me." I explained how my polite brushoff of Linh in Saigon had boomeranged. Now I was stuck with an orphan who would have to be turned into a soldier before he ate me into the poorhouse.

Sang chuckled. "Dai Uy," he quipped, "you are amazing. Hau Nghia teenagers flee to Saigon to avoid the draft, yet you go to Saigon and bring a recruit to Hau Nghia. The province chief will laugh himself to death."

Sang briefly questioned our recruit about his background and then announced, "He'll have to get documentation from the national police. But since he has no relatives, Colonel Hau will have to order the police to issue him an ID card. Then we will draft him and send him for basic training. Once trained, he will return to Hau Nghia for assignment to one of our units. But this is a special case, and I will have to brief Colonel Hau at the morning staff meeting. In the meantime, he can stay at my compound."

This last statement was a relief. Colonel Bartlett had always been understanding of my use of my quarters as a jail, clinic, and interrogation center, but I was certain that he would draw the line if I tried to open a home for wayward shoeshine boys.

That night, Sang invited me to the MSS compound for a traditional beer and dog meat feast to celebrate our victory over the North Vietnamese. Sang himself was an ethnic North Vietnamese; their cuisine was unique and featured the consumption of dog meat. Most South Vietnamese frowned on this custom, insisting that dogs carried leprosy. But Sang had assured me that as long as the dog was carefully selected, there was absolutely no danger of disease. Actually, my educated friend continued, it was a well-known fact that dog meat increased a man's virility and strength. Only dogs with a curled tail or a spotted tongue were to be avoided. But a correctly cooked, short-haired dog was one of the tastiest entrees known to man. Sang continued his buildup, explaining that long-haired dogs had stringy meat and weren't half as succulent as their short-haired cousins. I winced, remembering King, a fawn-colored boxer who had been our family pet for years. Sang concluded his invitation with a boast. His mess sergeant, an old North Vietnamese emigré, had a recipe for Dog Cooked Seven Ways that was incomparable. Sang admonished me with a twinkle in his eye not to miss the evening's festivities.

Before I left the compound that evening, I checked to be certain that our two dogs were safely on duty. In Duc Hue, we had lost at least two advisory team pets to the Vietnamese cooking pot, including Major Eby's own dog. But our Bao Trai canines were too smart to stray into harm's way, and both Bull and Lady were at their posts as I headed out the gate.

The evening turned out to be a pleasant surprise. The dog meat itself wasn't bad, although I had to consciously repress the knowledge that each of the meal's seven courses consisted of man's best friend. As I plowed my way through dog fondue, dog spareribs, and canine cutlets, Sang and his friends observed me gleefully. They were, I knew, engaged in one of the Orient's favorite sports—having fun with a westerner. The inevitable bottles of B-40 beer appeared, followed promptly by dog meatballs, dog sausage, and roast saddle of dog—by far the most delicious course so far. Finally, Sang's white-haired cook produced the *pièce de résistance*, the seventh and final course. It looked like a cranberry gelatin salad to me—but that would have been too easy. The sniggering and leering of my audience told me that there was probably big money riding on whether or not the American could eat this concoction, which turned out to be dog's blood salad—jellied dog's blood laced with chopped up dog giblets. My hosts hastened to point out that the giblets included the sacrificial victim's liver, heart, kidneys, and, of course, his genitals. Naturally, they crowed, this course was the most nutritious, its impact on the male system being one of the major benefits of eating dog meat.

I steeled myself by ordering up another bottle of beer, then attacked the bloody mess on my plate, determined not to betray the slightest hesitancy. The stuff was bland and rubbery. If I could have eaten it with my eyes closed, it would have been completely inoffensive. But I had to look at the gory concoction, and the experience doesn't rank among my fondest culinary memories. Sang's men were full of praise for my performance. I was now the American captain who knew their language, ate their foul-smelling fish sauce called *nuoc mam*, and had consumed a dog meat feast. This was no mean achievement in their eyes, for the Vietnamese had a saying that "Americans love their dogs more than their wives."

The following morning, Colonel Hau's staff greeted me with a chorus of one-liners about my exploit. Did I like dog meat? Had I cried when I ate it? Did I have a stomachache?—and so on. Not to be outdone, I singled out Captain Nga, a southerner who had a houseful of daughters. Nga's wife, I quipped, would have sons instead of daughters if Nga would learn to eat dog meat. Everyone had a good laugh, and our banter reflected the new mood that prevailed in the wake of the offensive. A few weeks earlier, when the military situation had hung in balance, the mood of the morning briefings had been grim, but good training and well-chosen leaders had paid off.

When Sang briefed Colonel Hau on my young protégé from Saigon, everyone laughed at the incongruity of the story. Colonel Hau decreed that since the young Linh was an orphan, Captain Herrington would henceforth be his stepfather. He directed the police and the MSS to do records checks on Linh, and if nothing turned up, he should be issued an ID card and inducted immediately. "If this is OK with the father," Hau grinned.

Then Hau turned on Colonel Ty, the piglike police chief. He would not tolerate continued police incompetence at the checkpoints on the approaches to Bao Trai. The shoeshine boy had managed to enter Bao Trai and obtain directions to the advisory compound in spite of the fact that he carried no documents. The police, Hau demanded, would have to tighten up their checkpoint procedures. The Saigon orphan could just as easily have been a Communist sapper or assassin.

The bumbling Ty, red-faced as usual, put up no defense. He would tend to the matter immediately. I exchanged glances with Sang, who knew what was in store for the unfortunate policemen who had manned the checkpoints when Linh's bus entered Bao Trai. At the same time, I experienced a wave of pessimism as I recalled that Colonel Ty's police were on the verge of assuming total responsibility for the Phoenix program.

The impending transfer of Phoenix to the police boded ill for the future of what had been a marginally effective Vietnamese effort in the first place. The problems of the police were many and had not changed since I had given up on Phoenix in Duc Hue eighteen months earlier. National police personnel assigned to Hau Nghia were usually not the most competent and motivated men available. Hau Nghia was regarded by everyone as a poor assignment—even more so since the Nguyen Hue Offensive. Policemen from Saigon were still being sent to Hau Nghia as punishment for low-level misdeeds or poor performance. Exile to Hau Nghia was one of the worst things that could befall a career officer. Then there was the police chief himself, a notorious buffoon who was respected by no one and under whose "leadership" police morale had sunk to an all-time low. The friction that existed between the police and the military began at the top and extended down to the lowest levels. Military men made no secret of their contempt for the police, whom they saw as a lazy, corrupt bunch whose specialty was the acceptance of petty bribes at province checkpoints. Hence our military counterparts told us openly that its transfer would be the death of the sickly Phoenix bird.

Colonel Bartlett agonized over this problem, for he considered the total demise of the Phoenix effort to be unacceptable. The colonel knew that the success or failure of the new Phoenix effort depended largely on the support of the province chief. Colonel Thanh had understood the threat posed by the Vietcong's growing network of covert agents among the population. We were not confident that Colonel Hau shared this outlook.

Colonel Bartlett communicated his feelings about Phoenix to Colonel Hau by means of a lengthy and carefully worded advisory memorandum in which he traced the history of the program in Hau Nghia and advanced a proposal for advisory support to the new police effort. The content of this letter is revealing for what it shows about our persistent and frustrating efforts in Hau Nghia to find a workable Phoenix combination.

Dear Sir,

As you know I have recently brought Captain Miller to Bao Trai to function as the G-2 advisor and have assigned Captain Herrington the full-time duty of Phoenix advisor. There are several reasons why I made these changes which I would like to explain. Around February, 1971, after reviewing the situation, it was apparent that the Phoenix program was not resulting in the necessary quantity and quality of VCI neutralizations. We therefore decided to try different methods and chose Trang Bang district as the place to begin. After about two months, we conducted an operation into An Tinh village that turned out to be very successful. After that initial operation, we obtained new intelligence that led to new operations. All of our operations met with success. The secret to this success was the excellence of the intelligence which we obtained by first getting the cooperation of a rallier or a prisoner, and then interrogating him in detail about the legal cadre he knew.

After several successful operations we had many prisoners who, because of the limited number of interrogators and case officers at Bien Hoa, had not been exploited. For this reason, I asked if Captain Miller, then the Phoenix Coordinator at Trang Bang, could go to Bien Hoa and assist in developing more intelligence. After a while, Captain Miller's operation at Bien Hoa became a full-time job.

Although these operations have been highly successful, I have been unhappy about one aspect of them. Captain Miller by himself did *all* of the intelligence work to support the Trang Bang operations. The 75 dossiers we brought to you two months ago were prepared entirely by Captain Miller, as were the ones used in *all* of the operations in 1971 and in January and February of this year. Without the work of Captain Miller, there would not have been any operations in Trang Bang. There has been very little Vietnamese participation in developing the intelligence. As Mr. Walkinshaw pointed out to me, the policy of my government is that advisors are not to do anything as a substitute for the Vietnamese, but instead to assist so that they can do it for themselves.

It is in keeping good faith to my government's policy and for the long-range good of the program that I have brought Captain Miller back to Bao Trai.*

The colonel emphasized the dangers posed by the Vietcong's apparatus of covert agents and suggested to Colonel Hau that he direct the national police to designate a number of hand-picked investigators to be trained by Tim and me in Phoenix operations. The key to success was good people, the colonel emphasized:

> As a result of more than one year of experience with the operations in Trang Bang, we know *exactly* the skills that are necessary and the best methods to neutralize legal VCI. Both Captain Miller and

---

*Actually, Mr. Walkinshaw had directed Colonel Bartlett to bring Tim back to Bao Trai. When he learned that Tim was living and working in Bien Hoa, Walkinshaw had reacted angrily. This was the "misuse" of a U.S. Army advisor. Miller was assigned to Team 43 and had no business "playing spook" in Bien Hoa.

Captain Herrington have worked for more than eighteen months against the Vietcong. You know already about the fine work that Captain Miller has done in the Trang Bang operations. What you might not know is that when Captain Herrington was the Phoenix advisor in Duc Hue, working only with his interpreter, he developed his own informant net and neutralized 27 Vietcong cadre and guerrillas in Tan My village. He and Captain Miller know and understand the Vietcong. They have not only advised but they have actually done the work that resulted in VCI neutralizations. I am certain that if the police assign good people, Captain Herrington and Captain Miller can teach them the methods and skills. At this time, Captain Herrington is preparing a training program. When it is complete, I will have him brief you on it and the techniques he will use so that you can give us your guidance and approval.

Stressing the need for 100 percent cooperation from the police if our crash training program was to succeed, Colonel Bartlett concluded his proposal with an appeal. The authority to shape the new Phoenix program must not lie in the hands of the bumbling Colonel Ty. Time was short, and his advisors must have an unusual grant of power if they were to succeed:

Right now Hau Nghia is known everywhere as having the best anti-VCI operation in the whole country. Much of this reputation has resulted from the work done by Captain Miller. Now that I am not permitted to allow Captain Miller to continue in the same manner, there will be many fewer neutralizations because only the G-2 and the MSS have the ability to catch legal VCI. Therefore I think it is absolutely essential that the police develop a strong capability. My advisors know exactly the methods they must use and exactly what training they need. However, if it is left to the police to determine what advice they will accept and what advice they will not accept, then we will not be able to succeed. I do not think we have much time to teach them. If there is a cease-fire, then I believe the advisors will be withdrawn. I am sure that if good people are assigned and Captain Herrington receives 100% cooperation, then in 60 days we will have an effective anti-VCI effort.

There is no more important task than to eliminate the Communist infrastructure. They provide the enemy forces the people, money, food, medicine, and intelligence to conduct operations. They penetrate our military and political organizations, cause our soldiers to defect, kill our administrative cadre, cause demonstrations, and create dissatisfaction among the people. The surest way to bring peace to the countryside is to destroy this organization.

Colonel Hau accepted this unorthodox proposal and directed Colonel Ty to give Tim and me the authority to actually direct the establishment of the police Phoenix effort. Ty was not happy with this infringement of his authority, but Colonel Bartlett was determined to succeed where others had failed, and the news out of Paris seemed to indicate progress toward a cease-fire agreement. The colonel reminded me repeatedly that my final task as a member of Team 43 was of transcendent importance. I was to spare no effort in teaching the national police the *modus operandi* that we had so successfully employed in Tan My and Trang Bang. If we could accomplish this prior to the cease-fire, Team 43 could stand down with a sense of mission accomplishment. Our recent victories over the invading North Vietnamese demonstrated that we had ample reason to be proud of our efforts to upgrade Hau Nghia's militia forces. If, as a parting shot, we could instill in the national police an effective Phoenix capability, we would be leaving our counterparts in Hau Nghia well equipped to cope with whatever 1973 might bring.

But I was to be denied the opportunity to tackle this final task. In early August, I learned that I had been ordered to return to the United States—three months before the end of my twice-extended tour. My first reaction to this news was to dismiss it—since I had a letter from Washington approving an extension of my tour to January, 1973. But when our team personnel officer had told headquarters of this, the decision had stood. Captain Herrington must depart Vietnam on the next available flight.

I called Washington and learned that no one in the officer assignments section understood what we were facing in Hau Nghia. Apologies were in order, but my extension approval had been rescinded. There was a shortage of students for the next "Military Intelligence Officers' Advanced Course," and I had been nominated to help fill the shortfall. Since my extension request was now officially disapproved, I should have left Vietnam several weeks ago.

I argued in vain for a reprieve. But a decision had been made, and I had no choice but to comply. To the personnel specialists in Washington, I was simply an intelligence officer who was long overdue for his next phase of training. I had already "punched my ticket" in Vietnam, and it was time to come home. They could not, in all fairness, be expected to understand the strong desire I had developed to see through to the end our advisory effort in Hau Nghia. Deeply disappointed and even bitter, I began the painful process of terminating my twenty-month tour.

Determined not to leave Hau Nghia without settling the matter of Lanh's future, I drafted a letter to Colonel Hau which detailed Lanh's record of cooperation since his capture. The letter requested Colonel Hau's personal intervention with his superiors to obtain Lanh's freedom. As my final official act, I accompanied Colonel Bartlett to Hau's office, where we received his promise that the prisoner Do van Lanh would be granted his freedom. Colonel Hau also insisted that I could not leave Hau Nghia on the following day, since he was hosting a going-away party for me at his home. This suited me fine. His generous gesture gave me an excuse to remain another day in Hau Nghia, which would give me the time to drive to Tan My and Duc Hue to bid good-bye to my Vietnamese friends.

The party was my final visit to the room where I had first met Colonel Thanh and where we had bid good-bye to him after his tragic death. Colonel Hau had gone to some lengths to say farewell, even managing to find a small band that wasn't intimidated by Hau Nghia's reputation. Young girls in white *ao dai* dresses passed around trays of Vietnamese delicacies while a quartet of black pajama–clad entertainers sang traditional and patriotic songs. The highlight of the entertainment was the debut of the locally composed "Hau Nghia Hero Song," a romanticized recounting of the victories of our militia troops during the Nguyen Hue Offensive. Colonel Hau presented me with the hand-drawn first issue of the music to the new song, and his adjutant read the citations of a pair of awards I was receiving. It was a moving evening for me, and everyone present knew that I felt rotten at the prospect of leaving on the following day.

Captain Sang presented me with an engraved bronze statue of the Emperor Nguyen Hue mounted on his charger, "lest you forget the Nguyen Hue Offensive"—as if I ever could. Sang announced that he would break ground for his new confinement facility soon. The building, he spoofed, would be named after me, since I had donated the funds to purchase the building materials. Sang also promised me that he would insure a timely follow-up on Colonel Hau's pledge to free Lanh. In the meantime, he suggested that Lanh should go to Bien Hoa for a long-overdue debriefing on North Vietnam. Sang was concerned that once I departed Hau Nghia, the privileged Lanh—deprived of his sponsor—might be harrassed by some of the less sophisticated members of the province staff. Like our advisory team, the Vietnamese were split in their reactions to our unusual experiment.

The following day, after the morning briefing, I loaded my single bag into the jeep that was to take me to Saigon. I had already said good-bye to Colonel Bartlett and to my counterparts. Anxious to avoid the need to repeat this ordeal, I clambered into the vehicle. As we pulled out of the compound, I spotted Do van Lanh standing at the gate. *"Chao, Dai Uy,"* he called out as we cleared the driveway. I swallowed hard, recalling the experiences the two of us had shared since his capture in May. I had learned a lot from the Vietnamese of both sides in the strange war that engulfed the rice farmers of Hau Nghia province, and it seemed stupid to be going home just when I had started to feel at home here. I cursed the system as the chickens scattered in front of the wheels of the jeep.

XV

" 'NAM WAS A BUMMER"

As the wheels of our DC-8 "Freedom Bird" left the Tan Son Nhut runway, the spontaneous cheer that erupted from the two hundred GIs on board told it all. I was certainly the only passenger on board who had mixed feelings about leaving Vietnam. When the pilot announced that we would fly via Japan and Alaska to Travis Air Force Base, California, yet another, louder cheer filled the cabin. As for me, I sat numbly in my seat and reflected on what strange forces had been at work on my mind to cause such conflicting emotions about what I had just experienced in Hau Nghia province. Here I sat, the same Captain Herrington who had never wanted to go to Vietnam, feeling sorry for myself and damning the army because I had to go home. But was I really the same person? The intelligence officer who had reluctantly disembarked at Tan Son Nhut twenty months earlier had arrived with a head full of preconceived notions about the Vietnam War—all of them arrived at vicariously. The person who was now reluctantly departing Saigon had just had the opportunity to put these notions to the test of experience—and the results of that test had been both humbling and enlightening.

Just before my abrupt departure from Hau Nghia, I had received a letter from my brother asking for my personal assessment of the chances for South Vietnam's survival in view of the rapid Vietnamization of the war. As my plane winged its way to California, I attempted to collect my thoughts by jotting down a few notes. From these notes, I would attempt to answer my brother's query.

The first thing I noted was that it was extremely difficult to make any objective assessment of the situation because of my intense emotional involvement in the war—an involvement that could not be terminated by merely boarding a plane bound for California. After twenty months of living and fighting with the Vietnamese in Hau Nghia, I quite naturally wanted them to succeed. Reflecting on the loss of Sergeant Arsenault, Phich, Colonel Thanh, and the hundreds of others I had seen suffer death and injury, the very idea that the entire effort might come to naught was repugnant. Still, I reminded myself, "Wishing won't make it so. Don't believe what you feel; just pay attention to what you think, based upon what you saw."

One of the unmistakable realities of the Vietnam I left in 1972 was the unusually high morale of the South Vietnamese military. This sprang directly from their tenacious and impressive performance against Hanoi's fierce Nguyen Hue Offensive. Strictly from a military point of view, what we had seen in Hau Nghia was encouraging. I couldn't erase the image of our militia troops' victories over the NVA, or of the strutting troops of the South Vietnamese 21st Division after their successful battles against the North Vietnamese in Binh Long province, or of the proud soldiers of the 83d Ranger Battalion as they showed off their war trophies. A feeling unquestionably pervaded the South Vietnamese military that they had absorbed the enemy's knockout punch, and then rebounded to dish out more than they had taken. True, American air power had played an important role in some battles, but the South Vietnamese had ample reason to be proud of the performance of their own air force. And it had been South Vietnamese troops, not Americans, who had faced Hanoi's thirteen divisions and bled in the defense of their land. Finally, I could not forget the boost in South Vietnamese morale that resulted from President Nixon's strong response to Hanoi's onslaught. Our Vietnamese allies saw the decision to mine North Vietnam's harbors and waterways as a clear sign that the president was determined to stick by our commitment to them. I had been in the Hau Nghia operations center when the president announced his response to the Hanoi attacks. At the mention of the mining operations, my Vietnamese counterparts had cheered wildly, pumped my hand, and insisted on a trip to the canteen for a cold beer to celebrate. All in all, the morale of our Vietnamese clients upon my departure was heartening.

But I was the victim of mixed feelings about the South Vietnamese military. On one hand, I had the greatest respect for what I had seen of the territorial forces militia troops—but I had to remind myself that I had seen "the best in Vietnam." When it came to the regular South Vietnamese units—the ARVN, I had seen extremes of performance that were plain scary. After a unit of the 25th Division had bombed the North Vietnamese out of one hamlet in Trang Bang district, the ARVN troops had looted the homes that they had just liberated, loading virtually every piece of property that was not nailed down onto their armored personnel carriers. And I remembered the shameful failure of the poorly led 25th Division troops to match the aggressive performance of our militia forces during the critical battles of May, 1972. The 18th Division, which we jokingly referred to as "the ring of steel," had done well on some occasions and miserably on others.* Still, I had to keep in mind that these two divisions were probably the worst regular South Vietnamese units. In contrast, the ARVN ranger units and other regulars that had fought in An Loc and on "Bloody Highway 13" had acquitted themselves heroically. On balance, I had seen some impressive soldiering by many Vietnamese units. In Hau Nghia, we had seen militia units advance into booby-trapped areas that the average American unit would have hesitated to enter.

But to fully appreciate the performance of the Vietnamese soldier, one had to factor an additional variable into the equation—the image of the South Vietnamese government as perceived by the man carrying the M-16 rifle. Americans tend to react with intuitive skepticism to the word "politics"—particularly in the wake of the Watergate revelations. Traditionally, we see politicians as opportunistic figures who divide their time between smoke-filled rooms and the campaign trail, kissing babies in their never-ending quest for reelection. But this is a benevolent stereotype, and on balance, we respect our political leaders.

This was not the case in South Vietnam. One of the most deeply disturbing realities of the Vietnam that I grew to know in 1971 and 1972 was the near universal cynicism of the people toward their government. The average Vietnamese soldier fought remarkably well against the Vietcong and North Vietnamese when one considers that he could not feel the positive things about his government that we Americans tend to feel about our system. Progovernment sentiments were generally limited to the firm conviction that however flawed the central government was, it was nonetheless far preferable to authoritarian communism. The endemic petty corruption of the national police and civil servants in Hau Nghia was a daily fact of life that we advisors encountered and with which the people had to contend. We knew that this was a serious vulnerability and that it lent credence to Vietcong propaganda (or was it propaganda?). We also knew that the corruption would somehow have to cease if the government expected to defeat the Communists. But we simply

*In all fairness to the 18th Division, it was this unit that put up a heroic resistance to three North Vietnamese divisions in Xuan Loc during the final days of the Communist Offensive to take Saigon in 1975.

could not do anything about it as low-level military advisors. When a Vietnamese friend warned me that my persistent inquiries about the reasons for one village's strong Vietcong organization were "going to get you into trouble," I asked if he meant that the Vietcong might mark me for elimination. He replied evasively that it was not the Communists who were upset by my curiosity. What he meant, of course, was that someone in the village office didn't like an American nibbling in his rice bowl. In Hau Nghia, we learned that there was often an inextricable tie between the strength of the revolution in a given village and the quality of the Saigon government's representatives. Where government officials were particularly self-centered and corrupt, the Vietcong would tend to flourish. Everything was tied together. For this reason, killing Communist soldiers or arresting Vietcong legal cadre were not by themselves the panacea for Hau Nghia's security problem. Such things most assuredly bought time, but they could not in any way eliminate what the Communists called the "contradictions" of South Vietnamese society that nourished the revolution. The tragic and dangerous irony of this dilemma was that in spite of the warts on the nose of the South Vietnamese political system, by far the vast majority of the people still preferred it to the Communist alternative. Yet, because of the existence of these "contradictions," a small minority of South Vietnam's population had been driven to accept the Communist insistence that Marxism-Leninism Hanoi-style was the correct medicine for the disease of South Vietnamese society.

These determined insurgents enjoyed the support of the well-connected Hanoi government and the rent-free use of sanctuaries on the territory of two supposedly neutral neighbors. Under these conditions, the Saigon government simply could not afford to expose a weak flank to the opportunistic Communists. By so doing, the result was predictable. A relatively small number of Communist sympathizers in South Vietnam's villages had managed to carry a big stick, and the insurgency had wielded power and influence that was vastly out of proportion to its true base of support. As I flew back to the States that day, I knew that I was now able to answer Colonel Weissinger's question when he had asked me why the Vietcong were not intimidated by the power and strength of South Vietnam. Why couldn't those harried and hunted guerrillas perceive the hopelessness of their cause? The answer that had eluded me at the time was simple—the Vietcong clung to their belief that the power and strength of the Saigon government resided in Washington—and westerners could never outlast a determined Asian foe. To the true believers among the Vietcong, the real test of the Saigon government would take place only after the Americans had gone home.

Yet another dimension of the conflict was the paradoxical role played by the Americans. Simply stated, we were both the redeemers and the curse of the South Vietnamese. To be sure, American military intervention in 1965 and 1966 was required to pull Saigon's chestnuts out of the fire. Yet, time and again I saw clear evidence that our presence was also a liability. One North Vietnamese defector even told me that many of his friends believed firmly in the need for American presence in the south. "Go south and strike the Americans" was too good a rallying cry to lose. Certainly "Go south and kill your fellow Vietnamese" would have never done—as Do van Lanh's testimony so graphically illustrated. Our presence reinforced the Communists' anticolonial propaganda, it enabled Hanoi to exploit the xenophobia of the South Vietnamese, and it lent credence to Vietcong claims that the Saigon government was the illegitimate puppet of the Americans.

The Americanization of the war during the sixties and the subsequent assignment of advisors down to the lower levels of the Vietnamese chain of command probably caused as many problems as it solved. It was almost unavoidable that the widespread presence of American units and advisors would tend to emasculate the South Vietnamese officer corps in the eyes of their soldiers and the Vietnamese people. It required an exceptionally sensitive American officer to forge an effective working relationship with his Vietnamese counterpart in the way that Colonel Bartlett was able to do. Most Americans were simply not equipped to play this delicate role, as my own abortive experience in Duc Hue illustrates. More often than not, American advisors were resented by their counterparts—or merely tolerated as sources of extra gasoline and ammunition. I would be well off if I had a dollar for every time I overheard a Vietnamese speak rudely of an American advisor, but I would do much better if I had a nickel for every time I heard an American advisor speak derogatorily of a Vietnamese counterpart.

Part of the problem was the linguistic and cultural barrier between us —a barrier that was almost impossible for the advisor to breach. Americans and South Vietnamese lived in two different worlds in so many ways that it has always seemed remarkable to me that we were able to accomplish anything together. Many American advisors treated the Vietnamese like so many undereducated and underprivileged children. During my tour in Duc Hue, MACV headquarters actually had to forbid the use of the phrase "little people" that advisors had routinely used over the radio to refer to the Vietnamese. This unintentional practice of relating to them in a condescending manner was sensed—and resented— by the proud Vietnamese. Thousands of Vietnamese learned English, and they were proud of this accomplishment. But only a relative handful of the many thousands of Americans who received language training ever learned to really speak Vietnamese. Ironically, what ultimately emerged was a situation in which the Americans looked down on the Vietnamese, who were at the same time looking down on the Americans. To the Vietnamese, we appeared all too often as arrogant, blundering, clumsy, gullible, and wasteful. Americans loved dogs, had no respect for the elderly or for ancient things, and insulted everything and everyone around them by boisterous, intemperate conduct and by ungracious displays of wealth. The American ability to acquire Vietnamese women was a deep source of resentment to virtually all Vietnamese men. To be seen even talking to an American beyond the requirements of one's job was anathema for any Vietnamese woman who entertained the idea of marrying a Vietnamese man. I monitored thousands of conversations in Vietnam, and it was rare to hear Americans spoken of respectfully. Instead, the Vietnamese used phrases like "that American guy,"* or employed the personal pronoun for "he" or "him" that is reserved in their language for animals and little children (no). The Vietnamese devised elaborate ways to talk about their American advisors so that the American could not detect that he was the subject of conversation. Since many advisors understood the phrase *co van My* (American advisor), the Vietnamese would avoid this phrase, using instead terms like "the blue-eyed guy," or "Mr. Tall Nose," or "the Western guy," to name just a few of the many dodges I overheard.

Victims of the language barrier, most Americans were not fully aware of what was going on around them, and they depended heavily on inter-preters to keep them in touch with events. This in itself was a crippling weakness, since few interpreters could or would render faithfully what they heard. Most Vietnamese interpreters were caught squarely in the middle of the adversary relationship that often existed between the advisor and his Vietnamese opposite number. Failure to interpret accu-rately and completely was the rule rather than the exception. Many inter-preters simply could not understand their American supervisor's English, but they would not dare to compromise their limitations. To do so was to risk reassignment out of their cushy job back to the line units of their own army. The most common result was an incomplete and often inac-curate job of interpreting that was bound to lead to misunderstandings. And sometimes the interpreters' inaccuracies were deliberate. I have sev-eral vivid recollections of situations in which a Vietnamese officer was discussing something in Vietnamese with his staff when he turned to the

---

*"*Cai thang My do,*" a disrespectful usage in Vietnamese.

interpreter and directed him not to share the discussion with the Americans. When a curious advisor asked the interpreter what the discussion was about, the interpreter replied innocuously, "Oh, they just talk about how to get parts to fix jeep."

The inevitable consequence of these limitations was that many Americans were flying blind the entire time they served in Vietnam. These barriers were one of the major reasons why there was too little understanding of both the enemy and the friendly situations—a limitation that renders effective military operations difficult, if not impossible. Many American advisors sensed their own inadequacy early in their tours, but they had no way to penetrate the smokescreen that they sensed was hindering them. The resulting frustration often led to hard feelings and counterproductive conduct.

And if these problems weren't sufficient to make an advisor's tour frustrating, the advisory system itself imposed further barriers to mutual trust and understanding between Vietnamese and Americans. For example, virtually all American advisors were required to report on the unit or area for which they were responsible. A good example of this was the Hamlet Evaluation System (HES) report that was prepared monthly by all district senior advisors. The HES results were published by MACV and accepted by official Saigon as one measure of the progress of the pacification program. Hence, rightly or wrongly, the report quickly took on the character of a report card for the performance of Vietnamese district chiefs. Consequently, in many districts the Vietnamese began to regard their American advisors as spies whose reporting of enemy activity in the district via the HES report could do nothing but reflect adversely on the local Vietnamese hierarchy—and particularly on the district chief himself. The HES report thus had the unintended effect of placing many of our district-level advisors in compromising, adversary relationships with the men whose confidence they had to enjoy if they were to function effectively. In Duc Hue, I can remember Major Nghiem's determined efforts to downplay to Major Eby the level of Communist activity in the district. Nghiem could not afford the kind of accurate reporting that would have caused Duc Hue's HES rating to plummet. One memorable evening, as the three of us filled out the monthly HES forms together, the disparity between our perspectives boiled over. Major Nghiem angrily stalked out of Major Eby's office when Eby insisted on reporting several documented Vietcong penetrations of Tan My village—leaving a befuddled and upset Major Eby to figure out how to repair the damage.

But the facet of the pacification effort that most typified the frustrations and inadequacies we faced as advisors was the Phoenix program.

Phoenix was a classic example of an attempt to graft an American-conceived plan onto a stubbornly resistant Vietnamese situation. The Phoenix concept called for the open sharing of information by all Vietnamese intelligence agencies in order to root out the Vietcong insurgency. It was a forthright, simple, and typically American, direct approach to the problem, and no single endeavor caused more grief and frustration for American advisory personnel.

To begin with, the Phoenix concept envisioned the various Vietnamese intelligence agencies operating together in an open and fraternal manner —something that even our own intelligence community has yet to achieve. In plain language, the Vietnamese intelligence services were disinclined to share their hot intelligence with one another. Some agencies preferred to operate unilaterally in order to receive undiluted credit for any successes; others regarded their sister agencies as security risks. By far the most effective Vietnamese intelligence organization in Hau Nghia was Captain Sang's Military Security Service. Sang and his MSS colleagues made no secret of their conviction that the National Police Special Branch—the police intelligence arm—was penetrated by the enemy and staffed with incompetent, corrupt officers. My counterparts in the province G-2 section accused the black pajama-clad Rural Development Cadre of being shiftless draft-dodgers who wasted their time drinking beer at the village crossroads, and no one trusted the ex-Vietcong of Det's Armed Propaganda Platoon—in spite of their impressive record. The jealousy, rivalry, distrust, and contempt that existed within the Vietnamese intelligence community simply could not be overcome by an enthusiastic, twenty-five-year-old American advisor with a "plan." This problem alone was sufficient to hamstring the Phoenix program, but there were others.

There was an almost universal lack of enthusiasm for Phoenix on the part of most Vietnamese district chiefs. Nothing was more exasperating to Major Eby and me than Major Nghiem's incomprehensibly lukewarm attitude toward Phoenix. To be sure, Nghiem held the expected meetings of the Phoenix staff, and he issued all the appropriate directives as required by the Saigon Phoenix Directorate. But, as the perceptive Sergeant Shelton had told me during my first week in Duc Hue, what we were seeing was the inimitable Vietnamese way of going through the motions to keep the American advisors happy. It was a never-ending battle—the patient, inscrutable Oriental against the enthusiastic, impatient Occidental.

Had Major Nghiem truly desired an effective Phoenix program, he could have brought it about by a show of genuine command interest.

Nghiem would have liked to have somehow made the Vietcong shadow government go away—he knew how dangerous it was—but he simply could not accept Phoenix as the solution to the problem. I sometimes had the impression that he feared Phoenix more than he feared the Vietcong, for a functioning Phoenix program would uncover and centralize information on the extent of enemy strength in Duc Hue, something that he could not accept. Since such an exposure of the enemy's activities would find its way into the HES report, Major Nghiem feared for his job. Sharp declines in a district's HES ratings (which would probably have happened countrywide, had the truth been known) reflected on the district chief. This, of course, is what ultimately happened to Major Nghiem. Since a district chief's job was often a lucrative and prestigious position, small wonder that Phoenix was about as popular as leprosy with most district chiefs.

Finally, Major Nghiem and his fellow district chiefs could hardly be expected to embrace the Phoenix concept enthusiastically in an environment where effective district chiefs often found that the reward for their efficiency was assassination by the Vietcong. It was considerably safer to do an average, status quo job, avoid any heroics, and live to fight another day. Spearheading an aggressive anti-Communist campaign was one sure way to draw fire from the enemy. Stories of hard-core district chiefs who opened their booby-trapped desk drawers abounded. The grim fate of men like Colonel Thanh must have exerted subtle influence over more than one cautious officer.

This was what I confronted when I naively tried to revive the Duc Hue Phoenix program. The apathy, divisiveness, and overall ambivalence of Major Nghiem's support were precisely what most Vietnamese parties desired. In Duc Hue, the sole exception was my S-2 counterpart, Lieutenant Bong. Like me, Bong wanted an effective Phoenix program and, like me, he threw up his arms in defeat and directed his energies toward the pursuit of a unilateral and sometimes successful vendetta.

Did these inadequacies doom the Phoenix program to failure from its inception? Not really. The Phoenix concept, however flawed, was implemented countrywide in as many variations as there were districts. In some districts, the American advisor took over and made it work. In others, it was the S-2, the MSS chief, or even the national police. Rarely have I found a fellow veteran of Phoenix in whose district the concept worked exactly as we were taught at Vung Tau. Yet Phoenix *did* work to varying degrees in many districts. The very existence of the province, district, and village Phoenix offices focused attention on the threat posed by Communist agents. Some districts disseminated "Wanted" posters that displayed pictures of Communist agents. Even rewards and guarantees of anonymity were offered for assistance in apprehending Vietcong functionaries. Even though the program was seldom what its architects had envisioned, Phoenix became a major thorn in the side of the Vietcong, who quickly perceived it as a threat to their organizational and operational security. Vietcong assassinations of Phoenix agents became common as the revolution fought back. Based upon my experiences in Hau Nghia, I have no difficulty in accepting William Colby's estimate that more than sixty thousand Vietcong agents were killed, captured, or otherwise neutralized by the Phoenix program. Phoenix was one of the major reasons why the Vietcong's Provisional Revolutionary Government did not surface to take control of South Vietnam in the wake of the collapse in 1975. The many thousands of Communist village and hamlet cadre needed to run the new government were by then either dead or in prison, thanks to Phoenix.

But I do have difficulty accepting the claims that Phoenix was an indiscriminate counterterror weapon that was ruthlessly employed by us and the South Vietnamese against a defenseless rural peasantry. Or, that of the twenty thousand or so Vietcong agents reported as killed, untold thousands were innocent civilians. During my tour in Hau Nghia, I saw many Vietcong politicians either killed or captured. In virtually every single case, those who were killed in ambushes or in their secret bunkers were armed with Russian, Chinese, or captured American weapons. And in most cases, they were carrying a pouch of incriminating documents as well. The overwhelming majority of those captured on Phoenix operations were picked up based upon tangible and credible evidence, rather than on the mere say-so of one person motivated by some sort of personal grudge. There simply isn't much ambiguity involved when a shakedown of a farmhouse reveals a "liberation radio," a picture of Ho Chi Minh, and enough medicine to take care of a rifle company.

Were mistakes made, and did abuses occur? Yes, if what I witnessed was representative. Some Phoenix cadre did commit excesses against the peasantry in the name of the anti-Communist campaign. The provincial reconnaissance unit in Hau Nghia was infamous for this during the early part of my tour. I once saw four of them decide that a nineteen-year-old girl was lying about something and subject her to repeated near suffocation with a rubber poncho in a cruel and vain attempt to force her to talk. That was the last time we entrusted that unit with such operations. What I saw that day shocked me, though it was the exception rather than the rule.

But as we began to expose and arrest the legal cadre network in Hau

Nghia, the problem of ambiguity did surface to a greater degree. How could we be certain that a Vietcong supply cadre was not purchasing goods for the Communists under duress? The revolution could easily compel a person to cooperate if his house happened to be located in a remote spot, far from the nearest government outpost and close to Vietcong base areas. Usually, however, a legal cadre's arrest would be immediately vindicated by incriminating documents or other evidence that surfaced during a search of his house. In cases where the required three proofs were lacking, the province security council would (and frequently did) order the individual's release. It was not uncommon for the government to release as many as one-third or more of the detainees whose cases came up each month. The rule seemed to be "When in doubt, release them." I can recall my dismay in mid-1972 when the Hau Nghia province security council dismissed more than 40 percent of the cases that were presented. One reason for the high release rate was a martial law decree promulgated by Colonel Hau after the North Vietnamese attacked in May. Hau decreed that Vietcong suspects could be arrested in the absence of the normal required three proofs—simply to take them out of circulation while the North Vietnamese were operating in our hamlets and in need of support. In addition, sloppy staff work in the preparation of the case files accounted for many of the dismissals, as did politics— especially family politics. Everyone seemed to be related to someone, who in turn knew someone else. Tim Miller's dragnet once picked up a pharmacist in Trang Bang district who was wholesaling drugs to the Vietcong. The evidence to convict the man was staggering. But within a day of his arrest, the province chief had received more than twenty outraged phone calls—one of which came from an aide to President Thieu. The enterprising pharmacist walked away to profiteer another day, underscoring dramatically for all of us that the major fault of the Phoenix dragnet was that the holes in the net were too big.

In October of 1972, Tim Miller discovered that Colonel Ty's national police were abusing their new Phoenix responsibility. If the family of a detained Vietcong suspect paid a bribe, the police would "lose" the evidence in the case and the detainee would be released. Tim reported his findings to Colonel Bartlett, who pursued the matter concurrently with the province chief and through American channels. As a result, the careers of the obese Ty and two of his deputies ended in arrest. The new police chief was an ARVN airborne colonel who had been wounded at An Loc. Under his leadership, the Hau Nghia national police began to straighten out at last.

As I winged my way back to the States, my overall impression of the advisory effort was that it had been effective in spite of its many flaws. True, a goodly portion of the program's success had been attributable to the American propensity to take charge rather than to any great skill on the part of our advisory personnel to patiently teach our counterparts. I had personally been guilty of this shortcoming—and regarded it in retrospect as a second-best solution.

But how well we had really done our job as advisors would be revealed in the coming months. The American advisory effort was soon to be closed out, and events thereafter would tell the tale. Hopefully, the creditable performance of the South Vietnamese during the 1972 offensive was more representative than their lackluster showing during the ill-fated 1971 invasion of Laos. The gnawing problem here was that this operation was the only time that the South Vietnamese had waged a major campaign without American advisors. Still, I had seen much during 1971 and 1972 to indicate that, technically and tactically, South Vietnamese commanders no longer needed the crutch of American advisors. Vietnamization was the correct path, even if we did set out on it somewhat late in the game. My experience in Hau Nghia convinced me that the Vietnamese military was well on its way to becoming an effective fighting machine.

But this optimism was tempered by my knowledge of the enemy I had come to know. In taking on the Vietcong and the North Vietnamese together, the South Vietnamese had grabbed a tiger by the tail. True, the dreaded Vietcong were a demoralized, undermanned, and diminishing force. By 1972, the heyday of the Vietcong was over. The war stories I had heard at Fort Benning about the feared *Phu Loi* Battalion and the invincible *Quyet Thang* (Determined to Win) Regiment were now just that—stories about a bygone era. The plain truth was that the South Vietnamese Communist movement—the southern backbone of the revolution—had never recovered from the slaughter of the 1968 Tet Offensive. Since then, the badly wounded southern Vietcong had been attacked relentlessly by the increasingly formidable South Vietnamese military. And the government's anti-Communist crusade was supported more than ever by the population—many of whom had been outraged by the Communists' desecration of the sacred holiday and the widespread destruction that followed. The pacification program had begun to come into its own, while the Phoenix campaign made the role of covert Vietcong too dangerous for the average peasant. The 1970 raids into Cambodia had been destructive—both logistically and psychologically. By mid-1970, it was standing room only at the Hau Nghia Chieu Hoi Center as demoralized Vietcong cadre fell all over one another in the rush to "return to the nation." This phenomenon occurred in province after province all over Vietnam. The Vietcong—the real South Vietnamese Communists—were crippled. So much for the tail, but what about the tiger?

The tiger, of course, was the People's Army of Vietnam—the NVA. The maturation of the South Vietnamese military was encouraging, but one could not avoid a gnawing uneasiness about the situation in 1972. Bluntly stated, I left Vietnam respecting the enemy as much, if not more, than the South Vietnamese. One simply couldn't help admiring the tenacity, aggressiveness, and bravery of both the North Vietnamese soldiers and the relatively few southerners who fought by their side. The men of the three North Vietnamese regiments that assaulted us in Hau Nghia knew that they would be vastly outnumbered, that they would have no close air support, little if any artillery, no armor support, and no chance of speedy medical evacuation if they were wounded. But still they came, absorbing horrendous losses, yet fighting with unflagging determination and discipline. Not that Hanoi's troops had a monopoly on bravery—I had seen too much to ever believe this—but it was awesome that the Do van Lanhs of Giap's army could march for more than a hundred days to the southern front and then fight as well as they did. If I admired the South Vietnamese soldier for his willingness to defend an imperfect system, my heart went out to the North Vietnamese combatant for the hardship and deprivation that I knew he suffered on a daily basis. Like it or not, Hanoi's leaders had done an impressive job of selling the North Vietnamese population on the sacred mission of saving their southern brethren from the clutches of imperialism. As I reflected on the political and military realities I had seen in Hau Nghia, this fact was the most sobering of all.

And if the military hardware I had seen on the battlefield was any indication, the determined Hanoi government was receiving constant and abundant support from its Communist allies. Even though the North Vietnamese Army's first attempt at a combined arms offensive had been somewhat clumsy and costly, the scope of the Nguyen Hue Offensive was a portent of things to come. The next time around—and anyone who understood the Hanoi Communists knew that there *would* be a next time —the next time around was bound to be massive and decisive.

"It is difficult to predict," I wrote to my brother, "how long it will take until the next round, but one thing is clear now. The North Vietnamese badly need a break. It's simply not conceivable that they could commit virtually their entire army, suffer losses in men and equipment as they have, and not require a breather." At that time, Dr. Kissinger and Le Duc Tho were meeting in Paris, and rumors of an imminent cease-fire were rampant. It was an election year, and I had little doubt that the administration would prefer a settlement with Hanoi by the fall. From conversations with my Vietnamese friends, I knew that they viewed the prospect of a cease-fire with mixed feelings. There was no doubt that the vast majority of the South Vietnamese population had long since wearied of the suffering and the bloodletting. The people were tired of this war that wouldn't go away. Peasants and city dwellers alike yearned for an end to the misery that each new round of violence spawned. During my final month in Hau Nghia, hardly a day passed that I didn't have to respond to questions about the likelihood of a cease-fire.

Yet, if the people were war-weary and anxious for an end to it all, there was also a disturbing sense of unrest over the possibility that any cease-fire might bring with it the departure of the Americans. The presence of a handful of American advisors in Hau Nghia carried with it a symbolic importance that was totally out of proportion to any contribution that the few of us could make to the war effort. The repulse of the North Vietnamese by the Hau Nghia territorial forces had been a unilateral South Vietnamese operation. But no matter how hard one tried to convince the South Vietnamese that they no longer needed us—that 1972 was not 1965—they weren't buying. The Vietnamese regarded some form of American presence as an essential precondition for their ability to stave off the Hanoi war machine. When I protested that they had performed admirably during the recent offensive, I was never able to ease their fears of the consequences of another North Vietnamese invasion. The South Vietnamese would admit that they had shown Hanoi that they could defend their soil, then hasten to add that the Communists had two powerful allies—a situation that made American support imperative. And to the Vietnamese people, our support was only credible when Vietnamese and Americans shared hardships together. "You must remember, Dai Uy," one ARVN major told me, "that we are fighting not only for our own freedom, but for yours also. Our people feel strongly that Vietnam is the unlucky pawn in a chess game between the world's two great power blocs. Our sacrifices have been difficult to endure, but we have managed to cope by constantly reminding ourselves that our cause is also America's cause. Every time we see the tall American in jungle fatigues, we are reminded of your country's stake in our success."

By the time my fellow passengers cheered our arrival at Travis Air Force Base, I had composed a reply to my brother's query, "Will South Vietnam make it or not?"

"On balance," I wrote, "whether South Vietnam will or will not survive Hanoi's determined attempts at reunification depends upon two big 'ifs.' First of all, when the cease-fire comes, South Vietnam will have to continue to receive whatever American support the situation requires. Ideally, a residual advisory force of a modest size could constitute an effective, visible sign of this commitment. Should the fighting somehow continue, we must be prepared to give the South Vietnamese the tools to do the job, regardless of how distasteful we might find more bloodletting. Secondly, President Thieu will have to get his house in order if he expects his people to continue to bear the burden of national defense. While it may be true that corruption is endemic in Asian countries, I simply don't believe that South Vietnam can afford the luxury of such a system. Their country suffers from a smoldering insurgency, and there are a couple of hundred thousand North Vietnamese troops camped on or near their territory. In the trials to come, the South Vietnamese soldier will have to perceive that he is fighting as much *for* his government as he is fighting *against* communism. If these two preconditions are met, then I'm confident that our efforts in Vietnam will be vindicated. But if we should fail to provide the Vietnamese with adequate support, or if President Thieu should fail to put his house in order, then the North Vietnamese Army will probably prevail."

This prognosis was a synthesis of my experiences in Hau Nghia, derived from what I had seen on the battlefield during the Nguyen Hue Offensive; from what I had learned of the plight and the perceptions of the rural peasantry; and from the feel I had developed for the attitudes and motivations of the soldiers of all three Vietnamese parties—the Vietcong, the North Vietnamese, and our South Vietnamese allies. These experiences had firmly convinced me that, cease-fire or no cease-fire, the forces of Hanoi and Saigon would ultimately square off for yet another round of fighting. Whether this next episode would result in another North Vietnamese frustration or in the collapse of South Vietnam was difficult to foresee, but I left Bao Trai with a sense of foreboding that the outlook was not good for Hau Nghia province—and that South Vietnam, which was Hau Nghia writ large, was in grave danger.

I had seen nothing during my tour to even remotely suggest that the South Vietnamese government could or would purge itself of the corruption that so hindered its cause and assisted the Communists. I knew all too well from conversations with countless Vietnamese that any attack against corruption would have to be initiated from Saigon. "The roof leaks from the top on down, Dai Uy," was the favorite Vietnamese aphorism my friends were fond of quoting each time we discussed the subject of corruption.

Finally, from what I could glean from the news that reached us in

Vietnam—later confirmed by what I saw during my first weeks back in the States—American disenchantment with Vietnam was extensive and probably irreversible. Shortly after our arrival at Travis Air Force Base, I had entered the rest room in the main terminal. To my surprise, it was standing room only as the GIs from my flight shucked their uniforms in favor of civilian clothes. As I soon learned, the tone of their conversations was representative of prevailing American sentiments. One GI summed it up. " 'Nam was a bummer—a bad trip." Another man, who was shaving at the sink, vowed that when anyone asked him where he had served his active duty, he would tell them Korea or Germany. That way he could put Vietnam out of his mind and not have to answer questions about it. The reactions of the other men present indicated that they approved of his proposed cover story. There was no evidence of pride at having served in Vietnam. This encounter amplified my fears for what lay ahead for my friends in Hau Nghia. For if the American people believed that " 'Nam was a bummer," was it realistic to expect the Congress to continue to underwrite its cost?

For myself, I was fairly certain that, one way or another, the denouement of the long war was at hand. As a shuttle bus whisked me to San Francisco Airport, I wasn't too pleased with the prospect of sitting out the final act of the drama in the Arizona mountains.

EPILOGUE

I returned to Saigon shortly after the cease-fire to spend the final twenty months of South Vietnam's existence as a helpless bystander to the triumph of Hanoi's forces. Like us, Hanoi had failed to win the "hearts and minds" of the South Vietnamese peasantry. Unlike us, Hanoi's leaders were able to compensate for this failure by playing their trump card—they overwhelmed South Vietnam with a twenty-two division force that had been built up during the respite provided by the cease-fire.

Four North Vietnamese divisions overran Hau Nghia province on April 28, 1975. Badly demoralized by the impact of diminishing American aid and increasing corruption, Hau Nghia's vaunted militia troops were easily brushed aside by the mechanized North Vietnamese formations. At Province Headquarters in Bao Trai, a North Vietnamese advance party arrived to assume command, but was forced to fight a sharp battle with a group of die-hard government troops who had barricaded themselves in the command bunker. Captain Nga, my G-2 counterpart, was killed in that final, purposeless battle. I do not know what became of his wife and five children.

Colonel Hau, the province chief, had already been replaced in 1973 under a cloud of suspicion (there was talk of a large sum of money that was missing from the province treasury). His successor, a disciplined marine colonel, was captured by the Communists and sent to a "reeducation camp" in the Mekong Delta, where he remains to this day.

Lieutenant Tuan, the intelligence platoon leader, was trapped by the advancing North Vietnamese in Bien Hoa, after he had sent me a note appealing for assistance in evacuating the country. By the time I received his plea, I could not get to Bien Hoa. In his note, the lieutenant wrote, "Dai Uy, if you cannot help me, I am dead for certain."

Colonel Sinh, the Interrogation Center commander, refused offers of evacuation because he would not leave his family, some of whom could not make it to Saigon. He died in the last hours of combat.

Colonel Thanh, Hau Nghia's fallen province chief, would never have tolerated the performance of duty of the men responsible for his widow's welfare. I met Mrs. Thanh in Bien Hoa during the cease-fire, where she and her ten children were struggling to survive as soaring inflation eroded her meager benefits as the widow of a fallen soldier. In the middle of our conversation, she broke down, wailing that "ten children and not enough rice to eat" was a cruel fate for the wife of a man who had sacrificed himself for the government. Trapped in Saigon by the sudden collapse, Mrs. Thanh and her family eventually joined the throngs of "boat people" and escaped to settle in California.

Captain Sang, Hau Nghia Military Security Service Chief, resides in southern California with his family. I spirited them out of Saigon on an Air Force C-130 several days before the North Vietnamese took the city.

I have been unable to determine the fate of the cheerful Hai Tiet. He remained to fight the advancing North Vietnamese, and I assume that he died doing what he felt was necessary from the day he rallied in 1971.

True to form, Hai Chua (the former Vietcong village chief of Hiep Hoa) recontacted the Communists when it began to appear that he had made a hasty decision by rallying to the government. When we learned of his machinations, we forced him to accompany a government operation during which several Vietcong were arrested. Then we introduced Chua to the villagers and gave him credit for the information that led to the arrests. I do not know what became of the opportunistic Chua after that, but he was *persona non grata* with both the government and the Communists.

Do van Lanh, my North Vietnamese convert, was eventually granted his freedom for his help during the 1972 Easter Offensive. In spite of the cease-fire, the war continued and the hapless Lanh was drafted. He ultimately became a rifleman in the same militia company that had captured him. I visited Lanh several times during the cease-fire, once after he had been wounded in a North Vietnamese ambush. In spite of his misfortune, he believed to the end that carrying an M-16 rifle in a South Vietnamese unit was preferable to his role as a North Vietnamese soldier. We lost track of Lanh during those final, tumultuous days, and he failed to heed my appeals to come to Saigon and flee the country. Since the Communists seized all of the records of the defector program intact, I

am certain that poor Lanh was identified as a traitor. From my debriefings of Vietnamese escapees since the collapse, it would appear that the
Communists forced all defectors to return to their original units to be
dealt with by their former comrades. The reader can draw his own con-
clusions about Lanh's fate.

Shortly after my return to Vietnam in 1973, I revisited the Ngoc
Huong restaurant in Saigon. There, buffing away on a Vietnamese lieutenant's boots, I met my "adopted son," Linh. The irrepressible little
operator confessed sheepishly that he had deserted his Hau Nghia militia
unit after several months of duty. "The platoon leader used me as a cook,
Dai Uy," he explained, "and besides, I can make twice as much money
shining shoes in Saigon."

Finally, Colonel Bartlett proved that the system works and quickly
rose to general officer rank. He is now serving as Chief of the Saudi
Arabian National Guard Modernization Team. The Army knows a good
advisor when it sees one.

PHOTOGRAPHS CAPTURED
FROM THE COMMUNISTS

The photographs on the following pages were captured in Hau Nghia province shortly after the 1968 Tet Offensive. They were taken by Communist progaganda cadre and distributed among the people of Hau Nghia to reinforce Vietcong claims that the entire South Vietnamese population was responding to the Communist call for a "general uprising —general offensive." The captions are direct translations of the Vietnamese text on the original photographs as written by the Communists.

Young in years, old in maturity, young Tran Van Nho, fourteen years old, stole one M-79 grenade launcher from the rich Americans and gave it to the guerrillas. Before that, he had already supplied the guerrillas with eight hundred rounds of ammunition and fifteen hand grenades.

Sawing a cannon tube to help construct a bunker to withstand artillery fire.

Sharpening stakes, thousands of them, to keep the war from coming and burning/destroying the children's school.

Making the porch rail of a house into a pillbox. "With the hated enemy before us, we swear to destroy him." (This was the idea of a guerrilla in Loc Hung village during the encirclement and storming of the wooden bridge, Tet 1968.)

The hull of an American tank becomes a stable public place from which Trang Bang district guerrillas hunt American aircraft.

Captured weapons of the armed pirates, which can supply the guerrillas so that they can continue to strike victoriously against the attacking foe.

One hour after activation, this unit marched over two kilometers and raided a field of the American invaders, knocking out three helicopters.

Families in defense of Loc Hung village resolve to wipe out the outpost at the wooden bridge.

Delegation of the Liberation Women's Association of An Tinh village.

Raising vegetables to resist the Americans.

The voices of song drown out the voice of bombs. Children of An Tinh village. (In Trang Bang district where the N-10 Sapper Headquarters was located.)

GLOSSARY

AWOL: Absent without leave

ARVN: Army of the Republic of Vietnam (the South Vietnamese Army)

G-2: The designator for a unit commander's intelligence officer

G-3: The unit commander's operations and training officer

H & I: Harassment and interdiction artillery fires, usually fired at night at suspected enemy locations or lines of communication

HES: Hamlet Evaluation System—a computerized report that was inputted by District Advisors and purported to show the status of the pacification program

MACV: Military Assistance Command, Vietnam—the major American command headquarters in Saigon

MAT Team: Military Assistance and Training Team—small (3–4 men) teams of American combat arms advisors who usually lived with a Vietnamese unit at its outpost and accompanied it on operations

MP: Military Policeman

MSS: Military Security Service—the South Vietnamese Army's military intelligence organization (primarily a counterintelligence unit)

NCO: Noncommissioned officer—corporals and sergeants

NVA: North Vietnamese Army—official title "Quan Doi Nhan Dan Viet Nam" (People's Army of Vietnam)

PF: Popular Forces—platoon-sized (30–35 men) local militia units that consisted of locally recruited men who performed village security duties for the South Vietnamese Army

POW: Prisoner of War

PSDF: People's Self Defense Force—a South Vietnamese irregular hamlet defense force that consisted of teenagers and older men (members were not members of the South Vietnamese military)

RD Cadre: Rural Development Cadre—specially trained teams of young men and women whose job it was to work with the villagers in improving their lives. RD cadre wore black pajamas, were armed for self-defense, and collected intelligence on Vietcong activities

RF: Regional Forces: company (100–150 men)- and battalion (300-400 men)-sized militia units of the South Vietnamese; usually locally recruited and more lightly armed than the thirteen regular divisions of the ARVN

ROTC: Reserve Officer Training Corps—an on-campus program that leads to a commission as a second lieutenant in the U.S. Army, Navy, or Air Force

S-2, S-3: See G-2, G-3, above

VCI: Vietcong Infrastructure—a military bureaucratic term for the Vietcong's covert, or "shadow," government. The VCI were the targets of the Phoenix Program. "Legal" VCI cadre carried government ID cards and played a covert role in the insurgency. "Illegal" cadre had no ID cards; they were forced to live in bunkers by day and to operate at night.

INDEX

217

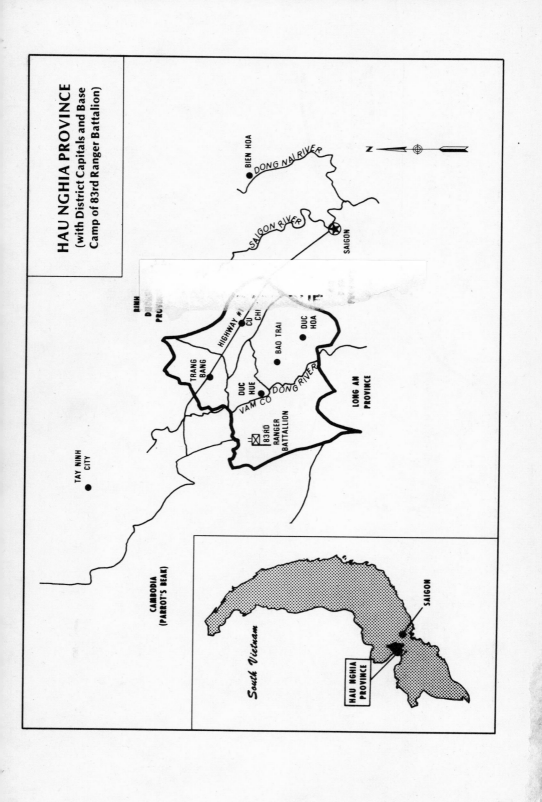

HAU NGHIA PROVINCE
(with District Capitals and Base
Camp of 83rd Ranger Battalion)

BIEN HOA

DONG NAI RIVER

SAIGON RIVER

SAIGON

N

BINH
D
PROV

HIGHWAY #
CU CHI

BAO TRAI

DUC HOA

TRANG BANG

DUC HUE

VAM CO DONG RIVER

LONG AN PROVINCE

83RD
RANGER
BATTALLION

TAY NINH
CITY

CAMBODIA
(PARROT'S BEAK)

South Vietnam

SAIGON

HAU NGHIA
PROVINCE